The Role of the Judiciary in Plural Societies

This book is dedicated to José W. Diokno
(25 February 1923–27 February 1987)

The Role of the Judiciary in Plural Societies

Edited by

Neelan Tiruchelvam and Radhika Coomaraswamy

 Frances Pinter (Publishers), London

1987

© International Centre for Ethnic Studies, 1987

First published in Great Britain in 1987 by
Frances Pinter (Publishers) Limited
25 Floral Stret, London WC2E 9DS

British Library Cataloguing in Publication Data
The role of the judiciary in plural societies.
  1. Judges — Developing countries
  I. Tiruchelvam, Neelan   II. Coomaraswamy, Radhika
  342.7′14′091724   [LAW]

  ISBN 0–86187–664–4

Typeset by Comersgate Art Studios Limited, Oxford
Printed by SRP Ltd, Exeter

CONTENTS

LIST OF CONTRIBUTORS

P.N. Baghwati was Chief Justice of India until 1986 and is the Chairman of the Committee for the Implementation of Legal Aid Schemes, India.

Upendra Baxi is Professor of Law at the University of New Delhi and Research Director of the Indian Law Institute. He is the author *The Crisis of the Indian Legal System*, New Delhi, Vikas (1982) and *The Indian Supreme Court and Politics*, Lucknow, Eastern Books (1980).

Radhika Coomaraswamy is Associate Director of the International Centre for Ethnic Studies and author of *Sri Lanka: A Crisis of the Anglo-American Legal Traditions*, New Delhi, Vikas (1984) and co-editor of *The Ethical Dilemmas of Development in Asia*, Lexington, Lexington Books (1983).

H.L. de Silva is a President's Counsel in Sir Lanka. He was one of the legal advisers to the Political Parties Conference in 1986.

José W. Diokno is a member of the Human Rights Commission of the Philippines. He is a former Senator and Human Rights Activist.

R.H. Kisanga is a Justice of the Court of Appeal, Dar-es-Salaam, Tanzania.

C.M. Peter is Assistant Lecturer in Law at the Faculty of Law, University of Dar-es-Salaam and Advocate of the High Court of Tanzania.

Neelan Tiruchelvam is a Director of the International Centre for Ethnic Studies. In 1986 he was the Edward Smith Visiting Fellow at Harvard Law School. He is the author of *The Ideology of Popular Justice in Sri Lanka: A Socio-Legal Inquiry*, New Delhi, Vikas (1984) and co-editor of *The Ethical Dilemmas of Development in Asia*, Lexington, Lexington Books (1983).

M.K.B. Wambali is Assistant Lecturer in Law at the Faculty of Law, University of Dar-es-Salaam.

Gita Itonwana Welch is Director of Information at the Ministry of Justice of the Republic of Mozambique.

INTRODUCTION

Neelan Tiruchelvam

Most violent conflicts since the Second World War have involved ethnic questions. The fragmentation of the Indian subcontinent into India, Pakistan and later Bangladesh grew out of a traumatic partition and a civil war. The Biafran war in Nigeria and the conflict between Hutu and the Tutsi tribes in Ruanda and Burundi constitute further illustrations of the disintegrative potential of ethnic conflict. In Western Asia, the Kurds in Iran, Iraq and Turkey continue to engage in a struggle for recognition of their distinct identity and for a homeland. Religio-political and ethnic strife have reached tragic proportions in the endless conflict in the Lebanon, which in turn is related to the Israeli-Arab conflict. Successive Spanish governments have had to face agitation for autonomy by the people of the Basque and Catalan regions, while the Flemish and Walloon conflict is at the centre of the linguistic and ethnic politics of Belgium. Albanians in the Kosovo region threatened to revolt in Yugoslavia, while the Catholics and Protestants are locked into bloody confrontation in Northern Ireland.

In the recent history of the Indian subcontinent, ethnic violence has become an increasingly common phenomenon. From the Pathan-Bihari clashes in Pakistan to the anti-Sikh riots in New Delhi, anti-reservation stir in Gujerat and the Sinhala-Tamil conflict in Sri Lanka, racial violence has left a trail of destruction of property and of human life. The emotional and psychological scars that remain after such outbreaks are in fact more destructive than the physical damage. The sense of community within a plural society is often shattered by the cruelty, terror and suffering unleashed by the forces of mob violence.

The competition for scarce resources and economic opportunities has fuelled antagonisms arising out of the sharp cleavages of race, caste, tribe, religion and language. Fragile political institutions have failed to accommodate adequately the demands for power and resource-sharing by marginalised ethnic and religious groups. Policies to advance national cohesion have been pursued at the expense of the linguistic and cultural traditions of minority groups. Ethnic discontent began manifesting itself in secessionist movements resulting in repressive responses by the State posing serious social justice and human rights concerns. The flight of refugees from internal conflicts has strained regional and international peace and stability.

But more recently there has been a growing awareness of the universality and complexities of ethnic problems and the need for concerted action to devise strategies, programmes and structures for the management of ethnic conflicts. Several multi-ethnic polities have incorporated federal forms of devolution into their constitutional and political orders. In the evolution of these constitutional models there has been continuing conflict between unitary and federal efforts, and centralised and decentralised forms. In India, the federal polity is based on division into linguistic states, while in Malaysia there is a Federation of States headed by local rulers and new territories which were given special concessions. The former Nigerian model provides an interesting contrast, with the overlap of certain regional and tribal groupings in the demarcation of states. The diverse ethnic, tribal and regional groupings have varying perceptions of federalism, and these perceptions have tended to shape the conflicts and tensions in the operation of federalism in each of these societies. There is a growing debate within each of these societies on the need for structural rearrangements to strengthen the federal character of these polities. These efforts have been directed towards the need to redefine centre–state relations in educational and cultural policy, police powers, resource mobilisation and redistribution, emergency and residual powers. Such efforts and problems evoke basic issues relating to equitable power sharing between ethnic groups, and the failure to address these issues boldly has accentuated secessionist demands by disaffected ethnic and other sub-national groups. Federal and quasi-federal models of devolution also have a relevance to strife-ridden societies such as the Philippines, Pakistan and Sri Lanka, which have recently enacted new constitutions or are on the threshold of redesigning their present constitutional frameworks.

Another focal point of ethnic conflict has been preference policies directed towards disparities in access to education and employment and in economic opportunities. These policies are often founded on competing perceptions of deprivation which in turn give rise to rival notions of social justice. India, one of the most complex and hierarchically structured societies, has a constitutionally mandated policy of preference towards weak and vulnerable minorities and tribal groups. Policy makers and judges have had to grapple with issues of bewildering complexity in defining the constitutional limits of such policies, balancing the interests of historically depressed caste and tribal groups with those of economically backward classes. Preference policies directed in favour of a politically assertive and dominant majority such as the New Economic Policy in Malaysia pose qualitatively different socio-political issues relating to the legitimate limits of preference policies based on proportionality.

Ethnic conflicts pose fundamental issues relating to human rights, social justice and constitutional and legal reordering. The appellate judiciary in Asian and African plural societies have been called upon to manage such ethnic tensions by upholding the values of legal and political pluralism. The courts have grappled with competing conceptions of equality, distributive justice and secularism, while struggling to maintain their own legitimacy in evolving political and ideological contexts. The hold of the colonial traditions of self-restraint and literal interpretations has been so strong that apex courts in these societies have felt incapable of responding meaningfully to such issues. The crisis of plural societies was often compounded by the impending collapse of judicial administration arising from the explosion of the court docket, and a judicial process which was dilatory and inefficient. The Courts in some socialist societies were increasingly under stress where primacy was being accorded to the political party, and the authority of judicial officials was being undermined by the political and bureacratic process. This volume examines how the judiciary in three Asian and two African societies responded to the demands of strife. Have they been constrained by dominant traditions of legal thought or have the Courts evolved innovative concepts and techniques of overcoming these constraints?

The volume will focus broadly on three problem areas which have called for a more imaginative judicial response: firstly, in defining the legitimate limits of preference policies in education, employment and economic opportunities directed in favour of socially and economically disadvantaged minorities; secondly, protection of civil and political rights of dissident minority groups, where such minorities have been subjected to emergency powers of arbitrary arrest, detention, extra-judicial killings and disappearances; how have the Courts reconciled their primary duty to protect the dignity and integrity of all of the citizens against the perceived needs of national security? Thirdly, this volume examines the plurality of legal systems arising from the continuance of indigenous and customary legal systems with those imposed by the colonial order. To what extent should the continuance of legal pluralism be conceived as the exclusive means of maintaining ethnic diversity? To what extent can a uniform legal system assert gender equality and negate the feudal bias of customary law, procedures and institutions? How do Courts reconcile the need to assert universal legal values and principles relating to the rights of women with the demand of ethnic minorities that their personal legal relations be exclusively governed by religious customary laws?

The three Asian and two African societies that feature in this volume are complex and diverse in character, and the plurality of their societies has been shaped by distinct social and historical processes. Firstly, the Philippines is a society with racial and linguistic units more diverse and numerous than any other in South-East Asian society. Similarly, Mozambique presents a complex mosaic of linguistic cultural and racial groups, with at least twenty different languages and innumerable dialects. The diversity of the Philippines is partly a result of its geography as an archipelago of about seven thousand islands, while the plurality of Mozambique has been attributed to waves of migrations over a thousand years. Both in the Philippines and Mozambique the colonial process resulted in a hardening of ethnic stratifications, and relations between ethnic groups cannot be understood except in relation to colonialism.

Secondly, Tanzania was formed by the merger of Tanganyika and Zanzibar, each of which were subject to diverse European and Arab colonial interventions that had an impact on the political, cultural and social fabric of each of these societies. Most Tanzanians are of Bantu origin and are divided into 102 ethnic groups. In Zanzibar there is a Shirazi minority. In both the mainland and the island of Zanzibar there are small groups of Arabs, Indians and Pakistanis, and some Europeans. The relationship between groups has been evolving within the nation state by a policy of confrontation (as when the transfer of power to an Arab minority was reversed by a revolt by the Afro-Shirazis in Zanzibar) and subsequent effort at accommodation and integration.

Thirdly, in Sri Lanka ethnic conflict between the Sinhalese and Tamils is fuelled by myths and historical memories, despite intermingling and commonalities in the religious and cultural experiences of both groups. However, British rule further altered and distorted the collective perceptions of self and of each other, with the Sinhala consciousness being shaped by the belief that the community was a historically deprived majority.

Fourthly, India throughout the centuries has been one of the most complex and hierarchically structured societies and, despite being further demarcated into linguistic states, it owes its cohesiveness as a nation state to the commitment of a post-Independence elite to a conception of secular and federal polity. We shall now summarise how the judiciary in each of these societies has responded to some of the demands and problems of ethnic pluralism.

Bhagwati's chapter on 'Social Action Litigation: The Indian Experience' provides an insight into the intellectual and social concerns which animated one of the most influential judicial activists in the Indian Supreme Court. The apex Court has been vested historically with the awesome responsibility of judicial review, a responsibility which could not be discharged in a spirit of diffidence or self-restraint. If the judiciary is to play a role in preventing abuse and correcting injustice and discrimination, it should liberate itself from colonial modes of thought that shackle the legal imagination of judges and lawyers. Renewed commitment to the social improvement of the deprived and dispossessed segments of Indian society, who have hitherto been marginalized by the legal system, is required.

This was to be achieved by what Bhagwati calls the democratization of remedies. Towards this end legal pleadings were simplified so that a mere letter could be equated to a fundamental rights' petition to activate the extraordinary powers of the apex court. A complementary development was the status conferred on social action groups to intervene on behalf of those who had suffered a legal injury but were unable, for reasons of poverty or of deprivation, to seek judicial redress. In evolving its new techniques of expanding the access to justice, the Court began to confront some of the basic postulates of constitutional adjudication. One such postulate related to the adversarial nature of judicial processes intended to ensure fairness in such proceedings. To compensate for unequal legal representation of socially disadvantaged litigants, the Court violated the adversarial principle by actively seeking to elicit the factual foundations of their legal claims. This was achieved by appointing socio-legal commissions of inquiry consisting of social activists, former judicial officials, journalists and social scientists. The reports so submitted could, subject to challenge, form part of the record in the adjudication of the facts in dispute. A related innovation was the effort to complement the existing constitutional remedies by providing for interim orders and directions, often requiring the State government to provide interim relief to the petitioners. The court also worked out diverse forms of compensatory arrangements by which activist groups were drawn into the monitoring of Court awards. By such means the Court has been able to secure compliance with its awards without the need to have recourse to its contempt powers. Such arrangements have been effective in improving the conditions of women prisoners in detention and in reviewing the rehabilitation of bonded labour.

Baxi's chapter on 'Taking Suffering Seriously: Social Action Litigation' endeavours to assess social action litigation in the context of the history of constitutional adjudication in India. He argues that it is not merely an incremental movement like public interest litigation in the United States, which emerged in a different political and ideological context. Social action litigation envisaged a more fundamental reappraisal of the role of constitutional adjudication and of the lawyering process, and was specific to the conditions of 'governmental lawlessness' that prevailed in India. It grew out of the trauma of the Emergency in India and of the efforts to provide a new moral basis for the legitimation of judicial power. Unlike its public interest counterpart, the social action litigation movement confronted the fundamental issues of power and of inequality in Indian society. In this regard it was able to forge links with social activists and investigative journalists in arousing the public's conscience on the atrocities against untouchables and tribals, custodial violence in prisons and other detention centres, and extra-judicial killings. The most important challenge that confronted the Court related to the development of legal doctrine that would expand the frontiers of fundamental rights and social justice. Article 21 of the Constitution protecting the right to life and personal liberty under procedures established by law was transformed into a due process clause. This opened up a new normative framework relating to fair trials and rights of prisoners and *détenus*. New concepts of administrative law were evolved to facilitate judicial scrutiny of executive actions on the ground of reasonableness. The court arrogated to itself the awesome 'constituent power' even of reworking and rewriting the provisions of the Constitution.

Although the chapter evocatively refers to the evolving role of the apex Court as a 'third chamber' of Parliament ushering in a new constitutional dawn, it is also sensitive to the complexities and constraints of such a role. Social action litigation has been associated with only a few judges of the Court and, if it is to enjoy a secure place in the constitutional scheme, it could require the collective imprimatur of the Court. The Court has continued to grapple with the complex evidentiary and procedural problems of its epistolary jurisdication and the innovative techniques of fact finding.

Besides, what is described as the 'creeping jurisdiction' of the court, by which the Courts provide interim directions to the executive, has been increasingly resisted by State administrations. The assumption of the administrative tasks and the continuing problems of monitoring the awards has left the ultimate constitutional issues unresolved. The Court may also be faced with the dilemma of devising adequate compensatory arrangements for gross violations of fundamental rights as in the blinding of prisoners. The conservative bar has not been entirely supportive of the high visibility of such litigation and the attention that such cases command from some judges. The serious problems of overload of Court dockets and inevitable judicial delays also constrain the expeditious and effective disposal of such cases.

The Philippines' case study by José W. Diokno deals with the dilemmas of the appellate judiciary in the protection of the civil and political rights of dissident minorities and in defining the contours of preference policies in favour of indigenous tribal groups and historically disadvantaged minorities. Diokno's chapter examines these concerns against the backdrop of the historical, geographical and ethno-linguistic factors which have interacted to define the pluralistic character of Philippine society. On the one hand Philippines society is a 'patchwork of racial, ideological units more diverse and numerous than any other South-East Asian society', on the other hand it has been subjected to continual linguistic and cultural homogenization during its Spanish and American colonial periods. The chapter points out that despite the extraordinary diversity there are discernible ethnic patterns: firstly, the majority group (about 86 per cent) of Westernized low-landers who dominate at least seventy of the nation's seventy-seven provinces; secondly, a Muslim minority of about 5 per cent concentrated in two Provinces in the lowlands of Mindanao; thirdly, tribal Philippines constituting about 9 per cent of the population, concentrated in the hills and the forests of the archipelago; fourthly, a small ethnic Chinese minority of less than 1 per cent of the population, extremely visible in commerce and business. These divisions continued to be hardened during the colonial period. The Spanish pursued a harsh policy of subjugation of 'tribes' and of the 'pagan races' in the south, which was continued during the period of American colonial rule against the Muslim Filipinos. The post-colonial policy of integration through cultural homogenization and disruption of traditional leadership patterns further alienated the tribal Filipinos and the Muslim minority in Mindanao.

Diokno's chapter highlights both the disintegrative impact of colonial policy and the failure of post-independent state policy in forging a multi-ethnic polity. The Philippine judiciary has been reluctant either to correct the imbalances in these policies or to articulate a distinct vision of legal and political pluralism. The judiciary was reluctant to enter the realm of legislation or policy where 'political ideas were the moving force' and thereby showed excessive deferrence to the legislative and executive branches of the government.

Issues relating to political violence by ethnic minorities have only been dealt with obliquely by the judiciary in relation to the declaration of martial law, preventive detention and the suspension of the writ of habeas corpus. The Courts have tended to view these cases as posing political questions beyond judicial review, and thereby upheld the declaration of martial law and the executive orders of preventive detention. The confinement of tribal Filipinos in Reservations and other restrictive orders in respect of these have been challenged as being a denial of equal protection. The Courts have consistently upheld these arrangements as being necessary to protect 'backward' groups. Similar economic measures discriminatory against the Chinese minority and of other 'aliens' have been upheld as valid exercises of state power. These instances further illuminate the reluctance of the Courts to confront declared state policy in respect of ethnic relations.

The third area of concern has been in the reconciliation of indigenous law and tribal customs with the norms and values of modern Philippine law. With regard to the ancestral lands of the tribals and Muslim Filipinos, while seeming to recognise native titles, courts have disregarded customary conceptions of communal ownership of land. Diokno argues that this conception of individual ownership of land could progressively erode the ownership of tribal and communal lands, which is central to the preservation of ethnic identities. A potential source of disquiet amongst the Filipino Muslims relates to codification of Muslim personal laws and the failure to implement the code through a system of Shariat Courts.

Diokno's chapter referred to a judiciary under the shadow of a system of 'developmental authoritarianism'. The political transformations which Diokno helped to bring about have now resulted in a dismantling of the constitutional arrangements associated with this model of development and of political authority. The new constitution founded on the principles of popular sovereignty created a bicameral legislature and clothed the judiciary with the powers of constitutional adjudication and the enforcement of a new bill of rights. It also envisaged new institutional arrangements for power-sharing by providing for the creation of autonomous regions in Muslim Mindanao and in the Cordilleras. The new instrument, transcending the conventional concerns of constitution making, also contained detailed sections on the accountability of public officials and declarations of principles on state policy, human rights and social justice, and on culture. These provisions also envisage an activist role for the judiciary in the articulation and elaboration of the pluralistic values and concepts of Filipino society.

Gita Welch's chapter on Mozambique provides an interesting contrast to the Philippines' case study. Pluralism in the Mozambican context is seen as the existence of two or more legal systems within a nation state. It is thus directly related to Portuguese colonial experience where a policy of indirect rule resulted in a limited tolerance of customary laws and institutions. The relationship between the indigenous legal order and that imposed by Portuguese rule was an unequal one. The chiefs and headmen who administered customary law occupied subordinate and peripheral roles in the colonial administration. Legal pluralism further served colonial interests by maintaining ethnic and social stratifications.

Welch's chapter addresses the ambivalent attitude of some African states towards customary laws and procedures. It refers to feudal class bias and inegalitarian gender relations envisaged by some customary norms. Welch questions the strategy of preserving legal pluralism as the only effective means of sustaining ethnic and cultural diversity of African societies. Mozambique believed that a policy of unification of the legal systems would be more likely to foster gender equality and national integration. This would be achieved by shaping the legal consciousness of the people through their direct involvement in the administration of justice. One of the more important functions of popular courts would be to provide equal access to justice and to inculcate values supportive of 'unity within diversity'. The popular court would thus facilitate the process of unification of various ethnic and cultural groups by forging an inclusive Mozambican national identify.

H.L.de Silva's chapter 'Pluralism and the Judiciary in Sri Lanka' clearly states that the main cause of ethnic rivalry in Sri Lanka has been the conflict between the Sinhalese and the Tamils with regard to issues of political representation, demand for linguistic equality, and protection against discriminatory measures with regard to access to education, employment and allocation of State land. Failure to redress these demands and provide a measure of autonomy to the Tamil speaking areas has resulted in exacerbation of ethnic tensions, political violence and growth of militant secessionist movements. H.L.de Silva points out that the judiciary has been looked upon as a body with a liberal, broad outlook and a capacity to approach issues with a high emotive content objectively. However, he states that given the realities of the power structure and the reluctance of the judiciary to intervene directly in the political arena, it has not been able to fulfil its role effectively in the resolution of Sri Lanka's ethnic conflicts. This failure has aggravated issues that were otherwise capable of rational resolution.

H.L.de Silva has examined carefully the role of the appeal Courts in constitutional adjudication. An early controversy related to loss of citizenship by the estate Tamils of recent Indian origin. Both the Supreme Court and the Privy Council failed to examine the social and political effects of the legislation or the motive for its enactment. They were thus not able to examine section 29, the centrepiece of the Soulbury Constitution on equal protection and non-discrimination, within a broader political concern for its object and purpose. Similarly, when the official language legislation was challenged by a Tamil public servant, the court evaded the constitutional issues and disposed of the case on the ground that a public servant did not have a legally enforceable contract. These judgements tended to reduce section 29 to a 'pathetically inefficient sentinel of ethnic rights'.

Under the Second Republican Constitution the Supreme Court was expressly vested with both a constitutional jurisdiction and also constituted as 'the protector and guarantor of fundamental rights'. The chapter refers to the challenge to an administrative order by which admissions to university were determined by a formula in which only 30 per cent of admissions were based exclusively on merit, while the balance was based on district quotas and a quota for educationally backward areas. The formula was upheld by the Court invoking the principles of State policy relating to the removal of regional disparities. While the Constitution envisaged that incursions into the principle of equality would only be permissible under legislation, the Supreme Court appears to have permitted such incursions even through executive action seeking to implement the principles of state policy.

It is in the realm of political violence and the response of the State to such violence that the Sri Lankan human rights' record has been subjected to the strictest scrutiny. The special powers conferred on the State under the Emergency and the Prevention of Terrorism Act have lead to carefully documented and widespread allegations of extra-judicial killings, arbitrary arrests, tortures and cruel and degrading treatment, and of disappearances. There were very few instances in which allegations of such abuses have been brought to the Court, and the Court has been severely handicapped by its own procedural and evidentiary rules from affording effective redress to the victims of such abuses.

With regard to jurisdictional limits the Court has declined to intervene in respect of the acts of public corporations engaged in commercial business. This was based on an excessively narrow interpretation of the expression 'administrative or executive action'. Similarly narrow interpretation of *locus standi* have further eroded the jurisdiction of the Courts in cases involving the freedom of speech and of publication. The chapter calls for re-examination of the vesting of judicial power itself by arguing that it be directly vested in the Courts as an independent organ of State power. But the future of the judiciary as the custodian of the public conscience in strife-ridden Sri Lanka does not rest in abstract constitutional principles or arrangements. It depends on the quality of those who assume the judicial mantle and their capacity to be morally outraged by injustice and by discriminatory practices, and to draw on the armoury of their legal powers to redress such practices.

Coomaraswamy's chapter, 'Sri Lankan Judiciary and Fundamental Rights: A Realist Critique', examines the type of fundamental rights' cases that have come before the Supreme Court. This chapter also examines the techniques of legal analysis and the principles of constitutional adjudication that have been applied in these cases, the real political constraints and the limitations of judicial administration and fact finding which constrain effective judicial roles in the enforcement of fundamental rights.

This chapter directly addresses some of the subtle pressures and influences to which even the apex judiciary is exposed in an island society where the legal, bureaucratic and political elite is relatively small and exercises disproportionate influence over national decision-making processes. The executive tends in such a context to be extremely sensitive and to view any adverse judicial findings in respect of executive or administrative action as a personalised criticism of the public official responsible for such action. The chapter refers to the instances in which the government and its supporters expressed intolerance of such judicial scrutiny. During the Referendum a leaflet issued by the Secretary of the 'Voice of Clergy', Rev. Ratnasara Thero, was illegally seized by the Police. The Court, in upholding the fundamental rights' petition, ordered the Superintendent of Police, Gampaha, to pay damages and costs. The Government directed that the damages and the costs be paid out of public funds, and that the Police Officer concerned be promoted 'to ensure that public officers do their duty and follow orders without fear of consequence from adverse Court decisions'. Similarly in the case of *Vivienne Gunawardene* the Court upheld the right to peaceful assembly and to procession, but in an extraordinary sequel the justices who constituted the bench were subjected to verbal abuse in an orchestrated protest demonstration.

There are two other instances in which Select Committees of

Parliament were constituted to investigate the conduct of Supreme Court Justices. In March 1983, a Select Committee was appointed to investigate the conduct of a bench of the Supreme Court in respect of a writ petition against the Special Presidential Commission of Inquiry. Similarly, in 1984 a Select Committee inquired into the conduct of the then Chief Justice in respect of a prize-day address in which he was critical of the government's 'inaction' towards political violence in the North. Although many liberals were dismayed by the Chief Justice's rationalisation of the communal violence in July 1983, others contended that he was acting within the limit of free speech. Civil rights groups have, however, consistently criticised such inquiries into the conduct of judges as politically motivated encroachments on the independence of the judiciary.

Coomaraswamy's chapter analyses the different types of cases that were litigated before the Courts and holds that very few cases relating to torture, due process standards, or denial of equality of women or ethnic minorities have been pressed before the Courts. The chapter also argues that in constitutional adjudication the Courts have followed narrow, literal approaches to statutory interpretation. No effort has been made to develop a theory of constitutional interpretation that takes note of the objects and principles of constitutional provisions and the values that they seek to express. Where policy considerations have been invoked, as when reference has been made to the principles of State policy, it has been for the purpose of limiting the scope of fundamental freedoms. Even where the Courts have provided redress to victims of administrative excesses, the intellectual response of the Court has been to root its finding on narrow statutory grounds. The Courts have been reluctant to articulate broad constitutional principles relating to freedom of speech or of assembly. If the Courts are to be an important forum of debate on constitutional values and standards, there must be a more systematic attempt to develop a consistent body of constitutional doctrine.

The chapter further questions the exclusive jurisdiction of the Supreme Court with regard to fundamental rights' litigation and its competence to deal with questions of fact. In the absence of rules relating to oral evidence, the Courts are limited to affidavits and counter-affidavits in judicial fact finding. More innovative approaches, involving the appointment of multi-disciplinary committees of inquiry or seeking the assistance of lower Courts in the determination of the facts in dispute, are called for.

The chapter by M.K.B. Wambali and C.M. Peter on the 'Judiciary in Context: The Case of Tanzania' points to the political and ideological context that defines the role of a judiciary in a socialist society in which primacy is accorded to the political party. The tensions and contradictions of a plural society seek reconciliation within the *ujamaa* ideology, and centrality is accorded to the political party as the custodian of that ideology. The norms and values of the political ideology are considered more important than constitutional safeguards, and consequently there is a decline in the role of the bureaucracy and the associated Court structures.

The Wambali and Peter chapter also refers to a certain ambivalence in attitudes towards the law and judicial processes. The delay and unpredictability of judicial decisions have contributed towards this ambivalence, and the growing trend is towards limiting the jurisdiction of the Courts particularly in the realm of economic crimes and in the implementation of social welfare legislation. On the other hand, Tanzanian Courts have sought to reconcile an independent judicial role with broader political and economic ideologies. Sometimes the judiciary has had to struggle to assert its authority against rival claims of party leaders and officials at the local level. At this level parochial issues sometimes intrude into the institutional conflict and the minor judiciary has not always been successful in resisting political inroads into their sphere of adjudication of disputes. The chapter, however, acknowledges the growing recognition that human freedom is an important component of Tanzanian socialism and that the judiciary cannot abdicate its responsibility to protect the individual against the excesses of the state and its political and bureaucratic instrumentalities. The more recent Fourth Amendment to the Constitution, which entrenched a Bill of Rights, protected not merely social and economic rights but also the right to due process of law and equal treatment under the law. This trend affirms an expanding role for the judiciary in the protection of the rights of the people.

Justice R.H. Kisanga, in his elaboration of the concept of public interest litigation as it evolved in India, sees a new arena for judicial activism within the political and social context of Tanzania. He sees in this concept an opportunity for the much beleagured and even somewhat demoralized judiciary to carve a niche for itself within the political and ideological landscape. By expanding legal access and through a more creative and innovative interpretation of constitutional principles, the courts can provide redress to disadvantaged and marginalised groups.

He emphasises certain areas in which there is a conspicuous denial of the rights of industrial and agricultural workers and of women, and weak enforcement of social welfare legislation and protective policies towards child labour. In the realm of social and economic rights, the judiciary can bring hope to the disadvantaged by expanding the frontiers of justice. Justice Kisanga, while acknowledging the potential of public interest litigation in Tanzanian society, has also identified several factors which constrain the evolution of this concept. Firstly, he has identified the need for organised groups of social activists who are willing to intervene in the public interest on behalf of disadvantaged groups. The perspective of such groups should be animated by a broad vision of society and of the development process. Secondly, the legal profession must play an important role by placing its skills and intellectual resources at the service of groups and interests, which historically lacked effective access to legal resources. The Tanzanian legal profession is a relatively young profession, which has been bedevilled by the crisis within the legal system and demoralised by the widespread disregard of law within the wider society. It has been reluctant to take up even habeas corpus applications in what it regards as a hostile environment, and was losing its cohesiveness and its capacity to serve the wider interests of justice. The decline in the indigenous legal profession would thus prove to be a factor which would impede the growth of this new judicial activism. A third factor emphasised in this chapter is the form of political control that tended to stifle dissent or any challenge to authority. If litigants or social action groups apprehend reprisals by the State, they would be reluctant to confront the State even within a judicial forum. Procedural requirements such as the need to secure the prior consent of the State to institute legal proceedings could effectively discourage social action groups from such litigation.

The eight case studies on five plural societies in Asia and Africa provide a complex and varied picture of the capacity of the judiciary to resolve ethnic conflict in each of these societies. In Tanzania the attitude towards legal and judicial processes remains ambivalent, and the judiciary has been hitherto accorded little importance in constitutional adjudication or in the process of national integration. Both in Sri Lanka and the Philippines under martial law, the Courts have not been an important forum for the articulation of constitutional values and standards and have been reluctant to intervene in the realm of declared State policy on ethnic relations. Mozambique represents a different model of popular participation in the judicial process and the fostering of equality and national unity through the unification of the legal system. In India by the democratisation of remedies the apex Court has expanded the framework for political participation and access to social justice. Although social action litigation in India has been primarily framed on the protection of social and economic rights, its impact on the legal imagination in Sri Lanka, Tanzania and the Philippines under its new

Constitution has been significant. It has renewed faith in the potential of the Court as the custodian of the public conscience, and in the empowerment of ethnic minorities and tribals who are ordinarily excluded from the political arena.

1 TOWARD AN ENGAGED JUDICIARY

Radhika Coomaraswamy

> . . . on the day of reckoning the judges are not exempt from judgement and
> the Beast of Shame cannot be held for long within any one frame of flesh
> and blood, because it grows, it feeds and swells until the vessel bursts.
> Salman Rushdie, *Shame*

Introduction: the judiciary and constitutional law

The timeless issues of the 'role of the judiciary'[1] have recently been the
subject of much discussion in the developing world. The growing
awareness of the need for human rights protection has focused the
limelight squarely on the judiciary. Judges are increasingly finding it
difficult to hide behind the doctrines of judicial 'self-restraint' and
'passive' interpretation. Their judgements in the area of fundamental
rights are scrutinized by a growing international audience interested in
the need to implement social justice. The prestige and legitimacy of the
judiciary is being constantly called into question as an increasing number
of citizens and citizens' groups bring their grievances directly to the
portals of the Supreme Court.

The human rights movement has in many ways made the judiciary a
most dynamic and important government institution. Standing between
individual citizens and the wielders of power, the judiciary has become
the ultimate, and yet unwilling, arbiter in the arena of democratic
politics. This sudden thrust onto the centre stage has made judging a
difficult and complex exercise, especially in the developing world. The
Court often finds that it has moral responsibility without the necessary
safeguards of institutional integrity. Nevertheless, a growing number of
judges are gradually beginning to realise that there is really no escape
from this increasing responsibility[2] and that the time may be ripe to
develop a fresh, innovative, and principled approach to the role that the
judiciary can play in a changing society.

The type of approach to be developed by a given court at a given time must of course differ with the nature of the issues presented before it. This chapter is particularly concerned with the role of the judiciary in plural societies and its possible contribution to the lessening of ethnic[3] tension in third world countries. An increasing number of cases come before the Supreme Court of South and South-East Asia which have some bearing on ethnic rivalry. As a general rule, courts are uneasy with these explosive and controversial issues. Precedents created by Western principles of equal protection appear irrelevant. They were formulated in a different reality and in societies with a different type of ethnic composition. Any new approach must therefore be based on an appreciation of the complex problems as they realistically exist in plural third world societies. To be successful, it must also be augmented by a vision which aims at containing societal conflict while furthering the cause of social justice.

Upendra Baxi writes in his recent book, *The Indian Supreme Court and Politics:*

The Supreme Court is a centre of political power. I believe that the recognition of this fact, howsoever belated, is worth while as it would be conducive to the clarification of the political role of the Court. And such a recognition will impel us to ask more relevant questions as to what kind of political role the Court ought to play in a changing India.[4]

If the Supreme Court is a centre of political power, the process responsible for the exercise of this power is constitutional litigation and the scope of judicial review. Despite its origin in written colonial charters and the need to keep home country legislatures 'within their spheres'[5] judicial review 'is the greatest single source of the Court's prestige'.[6] It has evolved through time from a power used to keep a federal legislature from interfering with the jurisdiction of a state legislature, to a device employed to maintain checks and balances among governmental authorities and to a power used to protect individuals and groups from the 'arbitrary' and 'unreasonable' acts of the state.

Prior to the 1940s, constitutional litigation and judicial review were of minimal concern to judges throughout the world. Even in the United States, the power of judicial review was used sparingly. From 1804–1954, judicial review was exercised to invalidate actions of the State or Federal legislatures in only seventy-eight cases — a rate of one per every two years.[7] Most of the cases involved minor points of interpretation and administration.[8] Only three cases in the one hundred and fifty year period seriously challenged legislative power in the area of civil liberties.[9]

By the 1980s a transformation had taken place not only in the United

States but throughout the Common Law world. Activist forays by a few Supreme Court justices and the increase in public interest activity were the primary reasons for this new approach to constitutional interpretation. The Courts were suddenly presented with numerous cases involving constitutional principles and found that they had to react accordingly. This surge in constitutional activity paralleled a disenchantment with representative legislatures whose preoccupation with 'expediency' and 'majority interests' prevented them from taking special care in protecting the rights of minority groups or individual citizens. It was also augmented by a frustration with an executive bueaucracy which often appeared to be implementing legislation in an 'irrational' and 'unreasonable' manner. Many Supreme Courts throughout the world were increasingly active but not solely in an unilateral attempt to usurp power from other government agencies. They were propelled forward by citizen groups which had become increasingly aware that the fora for the exercise of legislature and executive power were unresponsive to certain types of issues. John Hart Ely's remark that 'Constitutional Law appropriately exists for those situations where representative government cannot be trusted'[10] reflected the attitudes of members of the bar who were committed to social justice through judicial action.

Due to the activities of public interest groups and civil rights movements, questions of judicial review and judicial activism have become the most interesting areas of litigation before the judiciary. Constitutional litigation differs from other 'Appeal Court' issues in that the act of interpretation often involves a statement or exercise of power. While in the former type of case, a court may genuinely attempt to 'interpret' a given situation with regard to the intention of a legislature, constitutional cases involve issues in which the legislature's point of view is only one aspect of the judgement. The Court's interpretation of the fundamental law of the land must prevail over the expectations of any given legislature.[11] This brings to mind Justice Holmes' remarks that 'Whoever hath absolute authority to interpret any written or spoken law, it is *he* who is truly the lawgiver, to all intents and purposes, and not the person who first wrote or spoke them.'[12]

If the act of constitutional interpretation is an act of power, then fear of 'political' action appears to be meaningless. Justice Bhagwati of the Indian Supreme Court recently accepted the fact that the theoretical distinction between law and politics is over-emphasized. In the well-known *Dissolution case* he wrote 'every constitutional question concerns the allocation and exercise of governmental power and no constitutional question can, therefore, fail to be political.'[13] In fact it has long been recognized that judges must be aware of the political and legal ideologies which condition their decisions and responses. As Professor Friedman wrote in his book on *Legal Theory*, 'on the whole those lawyers who are unconscious of their legal ideology are apt to do more harm than their conscious colleagues for their self-delusion makes it psychologically easier for them to mould the law in accordance with their beliefs and prejudices without feeling the weight of responsibility that burdens lawyers with a greater consciousness of the issues at stake.'[14]

Once it is accepted that the Court wields a certain type of political power, then as Upendra Baxi writes, the question is no longer 'whether politics', but 'what kind of politics?'[15] Should it be active or passive? Should it be textual or flexible? Should it be formal or realist? Should it be confrontational or aim at consensus gathering? Should it help in the creation of values? The 'kind of politics' must of course differ with the nature of the issue before the Court. The case of police torture cannot be approached in the same manner as a corporation seeking exemption from corporate taxes. The success of a court must in the final result be judged from the depth and variety of approaches it has adopted to meet the complex problems of a rapidly developing society.

The ethnic factor and pluralism

In this light, the problems caused by ethnic tension and rivalry in South and South-East Asia pose issues of special importance for the Asian judiciary. The problems are so complex that the Western doctrines of equal protection often appear shallow and simple. They appear to call for radical new approaches and innovative formulation of doctrine, which will adequately meet the explosive and controversial aspects of these issues.

Recent outpourings of material on ethnic studies point to the fact that the 'ethnic factor' is fast becoming the primary motivating force in international politics and the major divisive issue in politics for national development and integration.[16] What is unique about the new ethnic revival is that no single nation, rich or poor, capitalist or socialist, has a monopoly of the problem — or of the solution. The issues posed by ethnic rivalry are constantly exacerbated by mass poverty, access to resources, human rights, national integration and issues of international peace and security.[17] The complexity of ethnic rivalry and tension is heightened by the fact that there are many types of ethnic groups pursuing different strategies of political self-assertion. In Asia for example, we have ethnic groups which are marginal in terms of population pursuing a strategy of isolation.[18] We have the problem of large, immigrant, ethnic groups which are attempting to pursue a strategy of cultural and political accomodation.[19] We are also presented with ethnic majorities which are attempting to construct a national vision of a historical polity after years of deprivation.[20] We have the problem of exclusive tribal groupings which are attempting to maintain a degree of cultural autonomy.[21] We are faced with large territorially based ethnic groups which are pursuing a strategy of self- determination.[22] Finally, we have occupationally segregated 'castes' which over time have acquired characteristics of an ethnic group[23] or socially distinctive groupings.

In response to the demand placed by ethnic communities and their advocates, states also have responded with various strategies ranging from confrontation, assimilation or preferential treatment to strategies of co-operation and accommodation. Since the First World War, countries have experimented with a variety of legal and political instruments to contain ethnic tension and to give expression to a societal vision of equality. For example, decentralization and regional development of territorial minorities have characterized constitutional arrangements. Preferential policies and affirmative action have given impetus to legislative approaches to 'backward' groups in society. Though far-reaching in expectations, these policies have not really come to terms with the complex issues surrounding ethnic relations.

State response to ethnic demands since the Second World War has been integrally linked to nationalist revival. The ethnic factor gave specific content to the nationalist movement. Cultural nationalism naturally entailed a measure of exclusivity often directed at other minorities within a nation-state. The defensive posture of twentieth century nationalism in third world societies contains an irrational component which prevents a rational balancing of interests. Instead, it often requires the use of constitutional and legislative instruments to stamp a group identity on national life. This type of nationalist revival, though progressive in its inception, often leads to balkanization and the development of 'reactive' nationalist movements by other minority groups within society.

Thirty-five years after independence, the defensive posture of third world nationalism is gradually giving way to a realization that most societies in the Asian region are plural in composition, and that future ethnic tension can only be resolved by a rational, balanced approach to ethnic harmony. Broad sweeps of policy as adopted in the past appear to have had only a marginal effect on ethnic tension. And yet conflict appears to grow with every year, even in societies committed to an open, plural composition of government. This leads us to consider Urmila Phadnis' remarks at a recent seminar on Ethnicity and Nation-building, 'ethnic conflict in Asia cannot be solved, it can only be managed.'[24]

Pluralism as a guiding legal-political concept has been a controversial principle in third world societies. For many, pluralism is seen as an aspect of 'obscurantism' — a strategy often used by colonialism to maintain outdated laws and customs which prevented the development of modern political, social and economic values. This scepticism has often led to centralisation of power in the hands of the state which then appropriates responsibility for the rapid development of society. This attitude toward pluralism has, however, been questioned by more recent scholars especially in light of the ethnic factor which has become a dominant factor in Asian politics, and also because the centralisation of state power has often led to repression and intolerance.

Pluralism in the 1980s then re-emerges as a democratic principle which fosters devolution of power, equal protection, and democratic forms of dissent. It is today an aspect of human rights which works toward the full participation of all members of a given society. However, it is important to admit at the beginning that pluralism poses a difficulty if it stands alone as a political ideology. In fact, the argument of pluralism is often put forward to justify certain forms of domination within ethnic groups and political parties. Women, smaller minorities, castes and tribals in a given region are often at the receiving end of this type of domination. Therefore, pluralism as an ideology can only further justice if it is seen as an aspect of human rights and not as an end in itself. It is important that the search for a just and plural society should not result in the accentuation of the negative features of a plural ethic.

Judicial doctrine and ethnic relations

If ethnic issues are to become the interminable issues of the contemporary world, what then should be the approach of the judiciary? In many ways, it cannot afford to ignore the question for these issues will appear increasingly before the judicial arm of government, especially in countries with ethnic minorities. It has often been said that the judiciary is the only government body which looks after minority interests whether political, cultural or racial. As Justice Holmes noted, 'fear of mass irrationality has led people who no longer hope to influence the legislature to look to the Courts as expounders of the constitution,'[25] or as Ely concludes, 'the tricky task has been and remains that of devising a way or ways of protecting minorities from majority tyranny that is not a flagrant contradiction of the principle of majority rule.'[26]

Until the 1960s, the Supreme Courts throughout the world have generally followed a 'hands-off' policy to issues of minority rights or individual freedom. This reticence is often explained in the West because of an adherence to the 'pluralist' school of social theory — the prevalent school in political science during the 1950s. The pluralist school urged the Court to intervene only in matters which affect minority franchise. It was based on the belief that any group whose members were not denied the franchise could protect itself by entering into the give and take of the political market place. The notion that minorities could protect themselves by making 'deals' with other interest groups or by entering the arena of coalition politics was widely accepted as being true.[27] However, despite this theoretical insight, legislatures remained impervious to the demands of the minorities. Only with judicial interventions in the 1960s did minorities finally have access to remedies formulted by an activist judiciary. Today this role of the Court as the protector of minority interests is widely accepted. It is inevitable that courts will be called upon to hear more cases which involve ethnic issues. The more organised the ethnic group, the greater will be the constitutional challenge.

If ethnic issues do continue to make an appearance before courts or other judicial tribunals, the question must be asked — at what point and on which issues should the judiciary provide for greater scrutiny and demand a rational and lengthy explanation from state authorities to justify a specific course of action, i.e. when should it adopt an activist posture? The response to such an inquiry must be based on an appreciation of the Court's political role. If the judiciary is seen as a complementing arm of government, active in areas where representative government cannot be trusted;[28] then the following issues must become relevant to whether the Court will scrutinize and overturn state action. Consideration must be given as to whether the ethnic group bringing the case before it is a majority or a minority, the nature of its access to the legislature and the possibility of such groups influencing government policy. If the minority is 'backward' or 'deprived' the level of constitutional scrutiny must naturally increase. On the other hand the greater the access to government decision-making, the less the need for judicial scrutiny.

Any legislation or executive action which hinders the franchise or political participation of any specific ethnic group must of course be scrutinized with special care as it would again lessen the group's impact on other channels of government.

The implementation of policy directives in favour of *deprived* minorities which are explicitly stated in the constitution should enjoy a high level of judicial scrutiny. They must be scrutinised with regard to effectiveness as among other plans or strategies of implementation. The Courts are often the only supervisors of executive action. They have a duty not only to examine challenged action but also to install mechanisms for continual review of government effectiveness in implementing provisions of the constitutions.[29] Without such active scrutiny the reformist element in many developing countries' constitutions, which attempts to bring deprived minorities into the mainstream of political and economic life, would be of no avail.

Most constitutions, however, do not have explicit provisions with regard to ethnic groups. Nevertheless, the general provision requiring 'equal protection' of citizens provides the necessary handle for ethnic group litigation. In many ways the doctrine of equal protection as elucidated in Anglo-American jurisprudence seems extremely simple in the context of an Asian reality. In the context of a scarce distribution of resources, the complexities are such that empirical research must supplant the 'heaven of legal theories'. To ensure that governments are passing legislation based on a rational evaluation of trends and not on past prejudice, convincing empirical evidence must be provided which supports the conclusions drawn by the State.[30] For litigation under the equal protection clause, the Supreme Court could be urged to adopt an activist stance not in using the *equal protection* clause as a sword but in requiring the government to produce substantial evidence to justify special or privileged treatment which has some bearing on ethnic rivalry in a developing society.[31] As a general rule, any classification based on ethnic groups whether it be quotas or schedules should be suspect as it accentuates cleavages in society. Such policies must only be pursued if there is overwhelming empirical evidence to the contrary and the ethnic group concerned has no other recourse. Though this may lead to a battle of social scientists, it would at least require the government to base its judgement on a rational evaluation of existing trends. In addition, the Court may request periodic reporting as to whether these trends continue to exist and whether the legislation considered is having its necessary impact.

The question of equal protection is intricately related to a society's perception of 'equality'. The concept has many institutional and doctrinal manifestations which often counteract each other and which are often in opposition to perceptions of freedom and national growth. If the art of judicial decision-making involves the 'drawing of lines', then the judiciary has a fundamental role to play — not only in defining the content of equality but also in limiting its scope.

Most constitutions contain three major principles of equality — *the numerical* (every individual has an equal share — especially with regard to the franchise); *the meritarian* (every individual according to her ability: the efficiency aspect of modern society); and *the proportional* (equality according to percentage of the population — the setting of quotas).[32] These concepts of equality are often in conflict and the issues concern choices among values, each with a moral content to its argument. In this context, the judiciary plays a most important role as it will be required to deliberate among those competing arguments and conflicting values in the context of a particular case. Its 'political' role, as defined by Baxi and others will thereby have a very specific manifestation. Unless it is creative enough to formulate judicial and remedies which minimise conflict and maximise consensus, the Court may in fact contribute to a deteriorating relationship among ethnic groups in a given society.

The methodology of judging

Once the judiciary has accepted a special level of scrutiny for ethnic issues, questions arise as to the 'methodology of judging'. Until very recently, logical consistency and formal reasoning have been the only methods of legal analysis — especially in South and South East Asia. The Austinian tradition adopted from Great Britain continues to have a strong hold on Asian legal scholars and judges. It remains the major element in law teaching[33] and in the enunciation of legal principles. Despite the stark realities of under-development, law scholars and judges often exist in what Professor Von Jhering called the 'Heaven of legal concepts'. Criticism against this approach, especially in constitutional jurisprudence is not new but as posivist notions of logical consistency are entrenched in juristic thinking, it often has to be reiterated.

Justice Holmes, at the turn of the nineteenth century, recognised that 'the actual life of the law has not been logic, it has been experience.'[34] 'Behind the logical form lies a judgement as to the relative worth and importance of competing legislative grounds, often an inarticulate and unconscious judgement, and yet the very root and nerve of the whole proceeding. You can give any conclusion a logical form.'[35] Especially in the area of constitutional litigation where issues of power and politics play an important role, formal reasoning and logical consistency have no inherent validity. In developing countries they often appear as hypocritical legal constructs aimed at ignoring the stark realities of economic and social development. Such a methodology of judging will eventually discredit the judiciary in the eyes of the citizenry as a 'rational automaton, expounding a barren scholasticism', unconcerned with the larger issues of social justice.[36] As Professor Lawrence Tribe recently concluded, 'there is simply no way for courts to review legislation in terms of the constitution without repeatedly making difficult substantive choices among competing values and indeed among inevitably controverted political, social and moral conceptions.'[37]

If logic and formal reasoning do not suffice, what then is the alternative which will give legitimacy to the judicial process? This too is another time-honoured debate. And yet in the context of plural societies, the methodology of the 'realist' school appears to have special significance. If it is recognised that ethnic issues in Asia are explosive and controversial, then the realist school with its root in empiricism and policy analysis may provide the judiciary with the only possible approach. Firstly the realist school's 'interest in the past is only for the light it throws on the present'.[38] Justice Holmes wrote in his *Path to the Law*, 'I look forward to a time when the part played by history in the explanation of dogma shall be very small, and instead of ingenious research we shall spend our energy on a study of the ends sought to be attained and the reasons for deserving them'.[39] Especially in Asia, the role played by history and historiography in forming perceptions about the nature and legitimacy of ethnic issues is extremely important. As commentators point out this is based more on fiction than on fact, but history has a profound emotional appeal which affects all individuals within a society.[40] This appeal often prevents negotiation and resolution of even minor issues of ethnic rivalry. The judiciary armed with a realist approach can therefore help in this endeavour to sort out fact from fiction and present day realities from past expectations.

The methodology of a 'realist judge' was interestingly analysed by Felix Cohen in his article 'Transcendental Nonsense and The Functional Approach'. He writes, 'The realistic judge, finally, will not fool himself or anyone else by basing his decisions upon circular reasoning. Rather, he frankly assesses the conflicting human values that are opposed in every controversy, appraises the social importance of the precedents to which each claim appeals, opens the Courtroom to all evidence that will bring light to this delicate practical task of social adjustment.'[41] The hallmark of the approach is that judges will focus on the realities of the case before them, rationally evaluate competing values and attempt at a remedy which will meet the concerns in a delicate and a practical manner. The aim is to minimize conflict and maximize practical remedies within a given case and controversy. The social and political nature of the conflict, their implications for social cohesion and power-sharing will be an important element in the Court's analysis.

Adopting the realist method does not necessarily imply an abandonment of general principles. One of the important aspects of this method is that it should lead lawyers to correctly predict the Court's approach and methodology for a given set of issues. Law is the 'prophecies of what the courts will do in fact'.[42] Though the development of principles would depend on case-law, the principles should evolve in a clear and consistent manner, revealing the nature of the policy analysis which is being conducted by the Courts. The 'realist' methodology may be the primary emphasis for a particular case but the evolution of general principles must remain an important aspect of the Court's final deliberation.

Though the 'realist' method may be the 'methodology of judging' in sensitive, delicate issues of ethnic rivalry, it can't stand alone, nor cover all possible cases of ethnic conflict. In certain instances, cases before the court are brutal cases of state repression or private violence directed against individuals or social groups. The brutality of these conflicts would shock the conscience of any civilised society.[43] Such cases do not merit the careful and sensitive deliberations of a realist methodology. They involve the setting of minimum standards and the defence of human dignity. The approach to these issues must parallel that of what may be termed 'natural law' methodology, an attempt to carve out the moral cornerstone of a Constitution. It would only apply in concrete situations and in cases of physical violence which are morally unjustifiable.

As a whole, judges trained in the Austinian tradition will not appreciate the fusion between law and morality. Professor Dworkin attempts a modern synthesis around a theory of rights.[44] His concern for the moral direction of the community's political institutions leads him to the creation of legal principles focused on the right to equal concern and respect — what commentators have called the moral content of welfare capitalism.[45] Despite the scepticism which often attaches to the moral righteousness of a natural law approach, in certain cases, there appears to be no alternative. Even Justice Holmes, the great sceptic, wrote, 'The law is the witness and the external deposit of our moral life. Its history is the history of the moral development of the race. The practice of it, in spite of popular jests, tends to make good citizens and good men'.[46] In certain cases of repression and violence, where state machinery is either the instrument of such violence or negligently avoids to contain such violence, there would be few who would question a strong activist judgement by the Supreme Court even if it were to be cast in moral terms. In such cases it is the duty of the Supreme Court as the protector of individual citizens against the arbitrariness of state action, not only to condemn such action but to set up review mechanisms which will ensure the necessary and appropriate remedies.

Constitutional remedies

One important aspect of 'the methodology of judging' which tests the creativity of Supreme Court judges is in the formulation of constitutional remedies which effectively meet the issues of controversy before the court. It is this aspect in the final result which will determine whether a strong judgement of the court is empty rhetoric. Increasingly constitutional remedies are constructed in terms of on-going judicial review as to whether the state is implementing the decision of the Court. In the United States this has resulted in large-scale judicial intervention in the desegregation policies of state schools.[47] As one of judiciary's special roles is to ensure the effective implementation of government policy in the case of individual citizens, the necessary corollary is that it devises the mechanisms to ensure that such implementation is taking place. And yet, the mechanisms should not result in the judiciary acquiring a coercive, executive role.

The task in these sensitive cases is to devise mechanisms which will aim at a consensus and protect minorities without flagrantly violating majority rule. The Courts should avoid partisanship and attempt to formulate remedies which have the support of all parties. This would of course require them to go beyond the general judicial remedies of damages and punishment. To be creative in this regard is therefore the fundamental challenge.[48]

On the other hand, for flagrant situations of injustice, remedies presented by the Court would of course have to be different. They would not *aim at* a consensus but attempt to ensure effective implementation of constitutional or government policy. In such a context, the judiciary must define effective mechanisms which will ensure government compliance and implementation and which will have some meaningful impact on the lives of those who have brought their grievances before the Courts.

One example of innovation in recent times has been the experimentation in the Indian Supreme Court of 'open letter jurisdiction' where any individual or group with bona fide intention can by open letter activate the fundamental rights jurisdiction of the Court. In addition the Court has made provisions for the setting up of Commissions to inquire into the violations of group rights, especially with regard to social exploitation. These innovations point to the need for creativity on the part of third world legal systems to cope with the actual problems which confront it. Such innovations will in fact turn out to be the most important and effective areas of legal change.

Strategy of 'area demarcation'

In coming to terms with the role of the judiciary in plural societies, it would be unrealistic, and perhaps adventurous, to assume that the judiciary operates in a completely autonomous sphere. Even if the judiciary is a centre of political power, it is a vulnerable centre with no constituency.[49] In a battle with the executive or the legislature, it will eventually have to give way or risk self-destruction. That is why commentators have called it 'the least dangerous branch'.[50] It is interesting to note that despite the halo around the United States Supreme Court, it has a cloudy record with regard to confronting state power on grounds of repression. Jerome Frank concludes his statistical analysis up to the 1960s by claiming that 'no direct action by the court has even had any significant bearing in either stopping or slowing repression'.[51]

It is often felt that the 'vulnerability' of the Supreme Court is a very good thing, especially as judges are unaccountable at public elections. The argument of accountability is the primary rationale given when courts are denied power or are attacked when they challenge actions of the state. This argument of accountability, however, is overstretched and more doctrine than reality. Under all constitutions, the legislature can amend the Constitution or defeat an interpretation of the Supreme Court — if they command a requisite majority. In addition, court rosters are filled with civil rights cases because the legislature and the executive are unaccountable to the public for certain types of questions. The problem is not one of accountability, but of 'area demarcation' and judicial responsibility to the public at large for certain kinds of political issues.

This strategy of 'area demarcation' must be the one through which the Court carves a niche for its own activity. The areas should be defined again in terms of when 'Representative Government cannot be trusted'.[52] Civil liberties and certain ethnic issues will then naturally be an important area for the Court's deliberation.

A deference to imperfection

A major limitation on the Court's response to constitutional litigation is its capacity and workload. Justice Stone once candidly remarked, 'we should still be aware . . . that courts do not conduct their discourse at the highest level of analysis and reasoning of which man is capable. They often miss this goal for reasons having more to do with capacity than desire'.[53] Not all judges have the conceptual rigour of a Holmes or the social conscience of a Bhagwati, or the language of a Denning. Therefore, any principle or approach must be based on a realistic appreciation of facts and line of reasoning which is clear even to laymen. Strictures of legal reasoning have yet to be softened by a general wisdom, if the judiciary is to be responsive to the needs of society. In this regard, training courses for judges at all levels, including instruction in political and economic principles behind certain types of legislation, the expected outcome etc . . . should supplement the types of analysis learned at law school. Unless the judiciary is ready to learn about the nature of current developments in society, it will ensure that judging and judicial decisions will retain a rigid, positivist approach — the type of approach which is increasingly ridiculed by scholars and individuals interested in social justice.

The heavy court calendar is another reason why there is a dearth of principled and consistent reasoning. There is little time to reflect and deliberate on fundamental issues of constitutional interpretation. This problem of 'laws delays' is a common concern throughout the world. Though this is more a question of administration of justice, it has a direct relevance to the quality and style of judicial reasoning. Streamlining arguments and a rational allocation of the Court's time may provide some relief, but many scholars feel that there is a need to completely restructure the judiciary, to allow for specialisation and open procedure so that justice may be dispensed with less formality and more effectiveness.

Any critic of the Court must begin with the truth that the judiciary, like other bodies of government, is subject to imperfections and will not be able to live up to the highest ideals. However, past strategies by civil rights movements and other interested citizens show that the Court can be offered a challenge that it cannot refuse.

The Bar

If it is accepted that the Supreme Court is compelled to choose between contradictory values and competing schools of thought, it is the responsibility of the Bar to articulate these values and offer interpretations, policies and studies which reconcile differences and compel judicial action in a manner conducive to social justice. No Supreme Court is ahead of the Bar which serves it. Unless members of the legal profession take the initiative, it is unlikely that a Supreme Court will make a necessary contribution to the needs of a changing society.

Increasingly it is also becoming obvious that the lawyers cannot work alone and that social scientists, journalists, social activists etc . . . must also play a part, especially in human rights cases. The need to collect and evaluate facts has become one of the most important aspects of modern day litigation. Therefore not only the Bar but other groups interested in social justice are making more effective use of the law and the Courts. Indian social action litigation is a case in point. It is only through the involvement of these various groups that the law will really have a major impact on third world societies.

The problem of access

One major problem with regard to constitutional litigation is the question of 'access' by members of the public to either the Bar or the judiciary. As was mentioned earlier, the Indian Supreme Court has, therefore, adopted a new procedure in fundamental rights cases involving 'an open letter' addressed to the Supreme Court. 'Any public-spirited individual or institution'[54] can bring to the attention of the Supreme Court any injustice being perpetuated so long as he is acting bona fide. The removal of the legal intermediary, especially in societies where intermediaries are power brokers or members of the status quo, will of course throw open 'the portals of the Court to the poor and the downtrodden'.[55] This procedure may still be too new in Asia for any proper evaluation of its success or failure. However, such innovations, if deemed successful, may become the most effective vehicle for constitutional litigation, especially under the chapter of Fundamental Rights.

The problem of social cohesion

Another major limitation on the Court's activity is more subtle to ascertain. It is what David Potter calls the problem of social cohesion and the law.[56] Lord Devlin in the *Heaton's Case* adds, 'if the judges are to do what the law means, if they are also to speak for it, their voice must be the voice of the community. It must never be taken for the voice of the government or the voice of the majority.'[57] However in Asian societies undergoing transformation with complex problems of ethnicity, the question immediately springs to mind — what is 'the community'? As Potter writes, 'what happens to law based upon the norms of the community if there is no prevailing community but only a multiplicity of conflicting communities?'[58] A latter process would naturally lead to a destruction of essential institutions and an increase of adversarial politics. If one of the fundamental aspects of constitutional litigation is that of a recognition of common values,[59] then what is the role of the judiciary in a society which has lost social cohesion and where the judiciary itself is often seen as partisan to certain interests?

Conclusion

Only an imaginative judiciary with an instinctive sense of justice will be able to transcend the forces of social divisiveness and deliver judgements which will be respected by all sections of society. Though the task appears daunting it is rendered even more important because it strikes at the very heart of the Court's legitimacy and prestige. The judiciary is often seen as the pious centre of government power, but 'with this piety must go a taste for courageous experiment, by which alone the law has been built as we have it, organic and living'.[60] The complex issues of our time will not evaporate nor will they find another more conducive forum. The judiciary will be called upon to institute a process of judging which is more open, increasingly sensitive and defiantly honest. The vague justifications 'self-restraint' and evasion are really assertive positions which give a court's negative interpretation of its own role in society and history. Unless the judiciary accepts the modern challenge, it will not only indicate that the Courts in our societies have accepted a redundant role but, more seriously, it would also imply that those very issues such as civil liberties and protection of women and minorities that are the prerogative of the judiciary have been devalued and delegitimized. In the final analysis, the warning that 'a society whose judges have taught it to expect complaisance will exact complaisance'⁶¹ may have a very special meaning for countries of today's developing world.

Notes

The introductory quote is from S. Rushdie, *Shame*, London, Picador, 1983, p.286.

1 In speaking of the judiciary this chapter is primarily interested in the Supreme Court or the highest court of the land concerned with constitutional interpretation.

2 See the judgements of Post-Emergency Indian Supreme Court, e.g. *People's Union for Democratic Rights* v. *Union of India* – court petition No. 8143 of 1981.

3 The term 'ethnic' is defined broadly here to mean any group which has a group identity based on linguistic, cultural, religious or any other social criteria.

4 U. Baxi, *The Indian Supreme Court and Politics*, Lucknow, Eastern Books, 1980, reprinted in Marga documents M/56 – Sem 87 1981, p. 5.

5 J. Thayer, 'The Origin and Scope of the American Doctrine of Constitutional Law' in 7 *Harvard Law* Review 298, 1983, p. 2.

6 John Frank, 'Judicial Review and Civil Liberties' in Friedman, Scheiber (ed.) *American Law and the Constitutional Order*, Cambridge, Harvard University Press, 1978, p. 397–8.

7 Thayer, op cit., p. 299.

8 Frank, op cit., p. 400.

9 Frank, op cit., p. 399.

10 J.H. Ely, *Democracy and Distrust, A Theory of Judicial Review*, Cambridge, Harvard University Press, 1980, p. 179.

11 Unless of course the constitution is amended.

12 Justice Holmes quoted by Professor Gray in 6 *Harvard Law Review*, 30, 1982, p. 33.

13 3SC (Indian Supreme Court), 1977, p. 660.

14 W. Friedman, *Legal Theory*, London, Stevens, 1960, p. 402.

15 Baxi, op cit., pp. 30–1.

16 For a comprehensive survey see Anthony Smith, *The Ethnic Revival in the Modern World*, Cambridge, Cambridge University Press, 1981.

17 See ICES, *Overview paper*, Colombo, unpublished, 1982, p. 1.

18 For example, the Parsee community in India.

19 For example, the Indians and Chinese in Malaysia.

20 For example, the Malays and the Sinhalese in Malaysia and Sri Lanka respectively.

21 For example, tribal groups in India, Veddas in Sri Lanka.

22 For example, the Muslim insurgents in Mindanao and Tamil separatists in Sri Lanka.

23 For example, caste groupings in India.

24 U. Phadnis in her talk on 'Ethnicity & Nation Building' at ICES January 13, 1983.

25 O.W. Holmes, 'The Path of the Law' **10** *Harvard Law Review*, p. 457, reprinted in *Collected Legal papers*, Cambridge, Constable & Co., 1920, p. 184.

26 Ely, op cit., p. 9–10.

27 Ely, op cit., p. 135–81.

28 Ely, op cit., p. 183.

29 For example, *People's Union Case*, op cit., remedies of Ombudsman.

30 To some extent United States cases have opened up such a process, especially in cases involving desegregation, environment, and consumer protection.

31 Levels of scrutiny is a device used by the U.S. Supreme Court to give special attention to certain types of cases—race, aliens' rights, sex, criminal defendants, etc.

32 See Sivaramaya, 'Equality and Inequality: The Legal Framework' in Andre Betaille, *Equality & Inequality, Theory & Practice*, Delhi, Oxford University Press, 1983, p. 33–5.

33 See for example N. Tiruchelvam, 'Legal Education & Development. The Role of the Law Teacher in Sri Lanka', in **4** *Marga Quarterly Journal*, no. 2, Colombo, Marga, 1977, p. 89.

34 Holmes, 'The Common Law' in *The Collected Papers*, op cit., p. 2.

35 Holmes, 'The Path of the Law' in *The Collected Papers*, op cit., p. 181.

36 Learned Hand, *The Spirit of Liberty*, Chicago, Chicago University Press, 1952, p. 17.

37 L. Tribe quoted in Ely, op cit., p. 43.

38 Holmes, op cit., p. 194–5.

39 Ibid., p. 195.

40 See R.A.L.H. Gunawardene, 'The People and the Lion, Sinhala Identity and Ideology in History and Historiography', in *Sri Lanka Journal of the Humanities*, Colombo, 1976, for this type of analysis.

41 F. Cohen, 'Transcendental Nonsense and the Functional Approach', in **35** *Columbia Law Review* 809, p. 829.

42 Holmes, op cit., p. 195.

43 See for example U. Baxi *The Crisis of the Indian Legal System*, New Delhi, Vikas, 1982.

44 See for example R. Dworkin, *Taking Rights Seriously*, London, Duckworth, 1977.

45 Peter Gabel *Book Review* **91** Harvard Law Review 302, 1977.

46 Holmes, op cit., p. 170.

47 N. Glazer, 'Should Judges Administer Social Services' in *The Public Interest*, no. 50, 1978, p. 64.

48 Baxi, *The Indian Supreme Court*, p. 74.

49 Baxi, ibid., p. 10.

50 See Bickel, *The Least Dangerous Branch*, New Haven, 1962.

51 Frank, op cit., p. 399.
52 Thayer, op cit., p. 307.
53 Justice Stone quoted in Baxi, *The Indian Supreme Court*, op cit., p. 9.
54 See *People's Union Case*, op cit.
55 Ibid.
56 David Potter, *Social Cohesion and the crisis of Law*, in Friedman (ed.) op cit., p. 434.
57 Devlin, op cit., p. 24.
58 Potter, op cit., p. 434.
59 Ibid., p. 434.
60 Learned Hand, *The Spirit of Liberty*, Chicago, Chicago University Press, 1952, p. 16.
61 Ibid., p. 163.

2 SOCIAL ACTION LITIGATION: THE INDIAN EXPERIENCE

P.N. Bhagwati

A committed judiciary

Social action litigation is the product of juristic and judicial activism on the part of some of the justices of the Supreme Court of India. Today we find that in third world countries there are a large number of groups which are being subjected to exploitation, injustice, and even violence. In this climate of conflict and injustice, judges have to play a positive role and they cannot content themselves by invoking the doctrines of self-restraint and passive interpretation. The judges in India have fortunately a most potent judicial power in their hands, namely, the power of judicial review. The judicious and sustained use of this power to further the cause of social justice has come to be regarded by many as not only beneficient but imperative in a developing country where there is large-scale poverty and ignorance. The judiciary has to play a vital and important role not only in preventing and remedying abuse and misuse of power but also in eliminating exploitation and injustice. For this purpose it is necessary to make procedural innovations in order to meet the challenges posed by this new role of an active and committed judiciary. The summit judiciary in India, keenly alive to its social responsibility and accountability to the people of the country, has liberated itself from the shackles of Western thought, made innovative use of the power of judicial review, forged new tools, devised new methods and fashioned new strategies for the purpose of bringing justice to socially and economically disadvantaged groups. Through creative interpretation by activist judges it has brought about democratisation of remedies to an extent which could not have been imagined ten or fifteen years ago. The strategy of social action litigation which the Supreme Court has evolved has brought justice within the easy reach of the common man. It has made the judicial process readily accessible to large segments of the population which have so far been priced out of the legal system.

The history of public interest litigation is the history of the last four or five years. It represents a sustained effort on the part of the judiciary in India to provide access to justice for the deprived and vulnerable sections of Indian humanity. With a legal architecture designed for a colonial situation and a jurisprudence structured around a free-market economy, the Indian judiciary has been hard pressed to fulfil the constitutional aspirations of the vast masses of poor and under-privileged segments of Indian society during the first three decades of Independence. As one Indian scholar has stated, the Court appeared to act during this period as the 'conscience keeper of the status quo'. During the last four or five years however, judicial activism has opened up a new dimension for the judicial process and has given new hope to the justice-starved millions of India.

Collective rights

The Supreme Court has evolved the strategy of public interest litigation in response to what Cappelletti calls the 'massification phenomena'. Today in our contemporary society, because of the massification phenomena, human actions and relationships assume a collective rather than a merely individual character; they refer to groups, categories and classes of people rather than to one or a few individuals alone. Even the basic rights and duties are no longer exclusively the individual rights and duties of the eighteenth or nineteenth century declaration of human rights, but rather meta-rights: the collective social rights and duties of groups, classes and communities. This is not to say that individual rights no longer have a vital place in our society; rather it is to suggest that these rights are practically meaningless in today's setting unless accompanied by the social rights necessary to make them effective and more accessible to all. These social rights require active intervention by the State and other public authorities for their realisation, and paramount among them are freedom from indigency, ignorance and discrimination as well as the right to a healthy environment, to social security and to protection from massive financial, commercial and corporate oppression. They include freedom from exploitation by vested interests and from governmental repression and lawlessness. These social rights need protection through effective machinery of implementation devised by the legal process.

This immediately raises the problem, however, as to whether the common law which has developed and grown in an essentially individualistic society to deal with situations involving the private right–duty pattern can face the challenge thrown up by the emergence of these new social rights. How can law based on the rights of individuals dealing with atomistic justice arising out of specific transactions meet the challenge of the collective claims of groups — especially disadvantaged groups? How will this law dispense well-balanced, equitable, distributive justice? Can a twentieth century justice be produced out of a nineteenth century mould? This is the problem which lawyers, judges and social activists have to resolve, particularly in developing countries where there is enormous poverty and ignorance and there are minority groups crying out for social justice. We in India have made interesting and exciting efforts in the past few years and tried to make innovative use of judicial power for resolving these problems. It would not be presumptuous on my part to say that our response to this problem is almost unique in the history of development of the law and the judicial process, and it may well be worth consideration in other jurisdictions. I am not saying for a moment that India's experience must necessarily have equivalence with that of other countries, nor am I suggesting that it should be studied for its own sake. But I do feel that the innovative strategies we have developed may have some relevance to the resolution of other problems in third world societies, which are often not very different from those which we face in India.

Social action litigation

The thrust of social action litigation is naturally directed against the actions of the establishment and vested interests. Despite this, the courts in India have been able to eliminate to a large extent political and bureaucratic opposition to social action litigation by emphasising that public interest litigation is not in the nature of adversary litigation, but that it is a challenge and an opportunity to the Government to make basic human rights meaningful to the disadvantaged sections of the community and to assure them distributive justice. Largely due to the efforts of the highest court in India, social action litigation has been effectively conceptualised and it is now on the way to being institutionalised. It has come to be recognised as an effective weapon in the armoury of the law for securing implementation on the constitutional and legal rights of the under-privileged segments of society and ensuring social justice to them. Though this strategy, evolved by the Supreme Court has come to be known as public interest in western societies, Professor Upendra Baxi, an eminent jurist, prefers to call it 'social action litigation'. The reason for this is that the expression 'public interest litigation' has acquired a certain meaning in the United States of America and it is connected with a particular kind of development which is peculiarly American in its nature. The kind of public interest litigation model which we in India have evolved is different from the public interest litigation model in vogue in the United States. Our model is directed towards finding 'turn around' situations in the political economy for the disadvantaged and vulnerable groups. It also concerns itself with other more diffused and less identified groups. Its focus is the immediate as well as long-term resolution of the problems of the disadvantaged in our quest for distributive justice. Moreover, in our model, the disadvantaged are not regarded just as beneficiaries in a one-to-one relationship with the designated lawyer. They are very much a part of, again to borrow a phrase from Professor Upendra Baxi, 'taking suffering seriously'. That is why, agreeing with Professor Upendra Baxi, I would prefer to call this enterprise in which we are engaged social action litigation rather than public interest litigation. The substance of social action litigation is much wider than that of the public interest litigation of the United States.

In essence, much of social action litigation focuses on the exposé of the exploitation of the disadvantaged and the deprivation of their rights and entitlements by the vested interests of administrative deviance. In addition it also focuses on the repression of vulnerable and under-privileged groups by the agencies of the State and other custodial authorities. Social action litigation seeks to ensure that the authorities of the State fulfil the obligations of law under which they exist and function.

Epistolary jurisdiction

How did this concept of social action litigation emerge in India? One of the main problems which impeded the development of effective use of the law and the judicial system in aid of the disadvantaged was the problem of accessibility to justice. Article 32, which occurs in the Chapter on Fundamental Rights in the Indian Constitution, confers the fundamental right to move the Supreme Court by appropriate proceedings for the enforcement of fundamental rights and confers powers on the Supreme Court to issue any directions, orders or writs for the enforcement of such fundamental rights. Though this Article of the Constitution is couched in the widest terms, and any one can approach the Supreme Court for enforcement of the fundamental rights, the position which obtained during the first three decades of the existence of the Supreme Court was that this provision meant nothing to the large bulk of the population of

India. The Court was for a long time used only by those who were among the affluent and who, to borrow Marc Gallanter's phrase, were 'repeat players' of the litigation game. The poor were priced out of the judicial system, and they had become what I would call 'functional outlaws'. It was impossible for the poor to approach the Court for justice because they lacked awareness and assertiveness. There was no machinery capable of enforcing their constitutional and legal rights. The Supreme Court found that the main obstacle which deprived the poor and the disadvantaged of effective access to justice was the traditional rule of *locus standi*, which insists that only a person who has suffered a specific legal injury by reason of actual or threatened violation of his legal rights or legally protected interest can bring an action for judicial redress. It is only the holder of the right who can sue for actual or threatened violation of such right, and no other person can file an action to vindicate such a right. This rule of standing was obviously evolved to deal with the patterns of law which are relevant to private law litigation. But it effectively barred the doors to the Court to large masses of people who on account of poverty and ignorance were unable to avail themselves of the judicial process. It was felt that even if legal aid offices were established for them, it would be impossible for them to take advantage of the legal aid programme because most of them lacked awareness of their constitutional and legal rights and even if they were made aware of their rights, many of them would lack the capacity to assert those rights. The Supreme Court therefore took the view that it was necessary to depart from the traditional rule of *locus standi* and to broaden access to justice. This has been done by providing that where a legal wrong or a legal injury is caused to a person or to a class of persons by reason of violation of their constitutional or legal rights, and such person or class of persons is by reason of poverty or disability or socially or economically disadvantaged position unable to approach the Court for relief, any member of the public or social action group acting bona fide can maintain an application in the High Court or the Supreme Court seeking judicial redress for the legal wrong or injury caused to such person or class of persons.

The Supreme Court also felt that when any member of the public or any bona fide social organisation espouses the cause of the poor and the down-trodden, he should be able to move the Court by just writing a letter. It would not be right or fair to expect a person acting *pro bono publico* to incur expenses from his own pocket in order to have a lawyer prepare a regular writ petition to be filed in court for enforcement of the fundamental right of the poor and deprived sections of the community. In such a case, a letter addressed by him to the Court can legitimately be regarded as an appropriate proceeding within the meaning of Article 32 of the Constitution. The Supreme Court thus evolved what has come to be known as *epistolary jurisdiction*, where the Court can be moved by just addressing a letter on behalf of the disadvantaged class of persons. This was a major breakthrough achieved by the Supreme Court in bringing justice closer to the large masses of the people.

Socio-legal commissions of inquiry

The Court had for a long time remained the preserve of the rich and the 'well-to-do', the landlord and the gentry, the business magnate and the industrial tycoon and had been used only for the purpose of protecting the rights of the privileged classes. It is only the privileged classes who have been able to approach the Court for protecting their vested interests. But, now for the first time, the portals of the Court were thrown open to the poor and the downtrodden, the ignorant and the illiterate with the result that their cases started coming before the Court through social action litigation. The 'have-nots' and the handicapped began to feel for the first time that there was an institution to which they could turn for redress against exploitation and injustice. They could seek protection against governmental lawlessness and administrative deviance, against denial to them of their rights and entitlements. The Supreme Court became a symbol of hope for the deprived and vulnerable sections of Indian humanity. It acquired a new creditability with the people and began dispensing justice to undertrial prisoners, women in distress, juveniles in jails, landless peasants, bonded labourers and many other disadvantaged groups of people in a manner unprecedented in the annals of judicial history. This new strategy evolved by the Supreme Court was unorthodox and unconventional. It shocked the conscience of conservative lawyers and judges clinging to the worn-out values of Anglo-Saxon jurisprudence. They thought that what the Court was doing was heretical. As far as the large masses of people in the country were concerned, however, they warmly applauded this new initiative taken by the Court. They began to feel for the first time that the highest court in the country was shedding its character as upholder of the status quo, and was assuming a new dynamic role as the protector of the weak through the adoption of a highly goal-oriented and activist approach by some of the judges.

From the very commencement of social action litigation, one difficulty became manifest and it arose on account of the unsuitability of the adversarial procedure for this new kind of litigation. The adversarial procedure is supposed to be a result of the rule of fairness. It has evolved an elaborate code of procedure in order to maintain basic equality between the parties, to ensure that one party does not obtain an unfair advantage over the other. The adversarial procedure can operate fairly and produce just results only if the two contesting parties are evenly matched in strength and resources, and this is quite often not the case. Where one of the parties to a litigation belongs to a poor and deprived section of the community and does not possess adequate social and material resources, he is bound to be at a disadvantage as against a strong and powerful opponent. He will have difficulty in getting competent legal representation, but, more than anything else, he will be unable to produce relevant evidence before the Court. The problem of proof, therefore, presents obvious difficulty in social action litigation brought to vindicate the rights of the poor and the disadvantaged. This problem becomes very acute in many cases because, often enough, the authorities or vested interests, which are the respondents, deny on affidavit the allegations of exploitation, repression and denial of rights made against them; sometimes the respondents contest the bona fides or the degree of reliability of the information of the social activists who come to the Court; sometimes they attribute wild ulterior motives to such social activists; and sometimes they denounce the sources on which the social activists rely, namely media and investigative reports of journalists. How then is evidence going to be produced before the Court on behalf of the poor in support of their case?

It is obvious that the poor and the disadvantaged cannot possibly produce material before the Court in support of their case, and equally it would be impossible for the public-spirited citizen or the social action group which has brought the litigation to gather relevant material and place it before the Court. Of course, there may be well organized social action groups which may be able to carry out research before bringing public interest litigation, and they may be able, on the strength of their own resources to establish the case on behalf of the poor and the disadvantaged groups. But such social action groups are very few and, by and large, it would be difficult for them to collect the necessary material. What is the Court to do in such cases? Would the Court not be failing in discharge of its constitutional duty of enforcing fundamental rights if it refuses to intervene because the relevant material has not been produced before it by the petitioner? If the Court were to adopt a passive approach and decline to intervene in such cases because relevant material has not been produced by the party seeking its intervention, the fundamental rights would remain merely an illusion so far as the poor and disadvantaged groups are concerned. The Supreme Court, therefore, started experimenting with different strategies which involved departure from the adversarial procedure without in any way sacrificing the principle of fair play.

It was found that the problems of the poor and the oppressed which had started coming before the courts were qualitatively different from those which had hitherto occupied the attention of the Court. They needed a different kind of lawyer's skill and a different kind of approach. It was necessary to abandon the *laissez-faire* approach in the judicial process and devise new strategies and procedures for articulating, ascertaining and establishing the claims and demands of the 'have-nots'. The Supreme Court, therefore, initiated the strategy of appointing socio-legal commissions of inquiry. The Supreme Court started appointing social activists, teachers, researchers, journalists, government officers and judicial officers as Court Commissioners to visit particular locations for fact-finding. The Commissioners were required to submit a quick and detailed report setting out their findings and also their suggestions and recommendations. There have been numerous cases where the Supreme Court has adopted this procedure. I will mention only a few below, to illustrate the points.

In one of the early cases in 1981 there was a complaint by a backward community called *chamars*, who had been traditionally carrying on the vocation of flaying the skin of carcasses of dead animals in the rural areas. The *chamars* claimed that their fundamental right to carry on their vocation was being unreasonably taken away through the system of auctioning to the highest bidder the right to flay dead animals and to dispose of the skin, horns and bones. The *chamars* were, by reasons of their poverty, ignorance and backwardness, unable to produce any material in support of their case. The Supreme Court, therefore, appointed a social-legal commission consisting of a professor of law and a journalist to investigate the complaint of the *chamars* and to gather data and material bearing on the correctness or otherwise of the complaint. The commission submitted a detailed report of its socio-legal investigation and put forward an alternative scheme of carcass utilization after exhaustive discussion with the concerned administrators and developmental scientists, which would safeguard the rights of the *chamars*.

In another case concerning the existence of bonded labour in Faridabad stone quarries, the Supreme Court appointed Dr Patwardhan, a Professor of Sociology working in the Indian Institute of Technology, to make a socio-legal investigation into the conditions of the stone-quarry workers, and on the basis of the report made by him, the Supreme Court gave various directions in the well known case of *Bandhua Mukti Morcha* v. *Union of India & Others*, AIR, 1984, Supreme Court 802. Similarly, in the *Agra Protective Home* case, the Supreme Court appointed the District Judge of Agra as Commissioner to visit a Protective Home and to make a detailed report in regard to the conditions in which the girls were living in the Protective Home. In response to the report filed by him, various directions were given by the Court from time to time which resulted in the improvement of the living conditions in the Protective Home.

The practice of appointing socio-legal commissions of inquiry for the purpose of gathering relevant material bearing on the case put forward on behalf of the disadvantaged sections of the community in social action litigation has now been institutionalised as a result of the judgement of the Supreme Court in the *Bandhua Mukti Morcha* case. When the report of the socio-legal investigation is received by the Court, copies of it are supplied to the parties, so that either party wanting to dispute the facts or data stated in the report may do so by filing an affidavit. The court would then consider the report of the commissioner, the affidavits which may be filed, and proceed to adjudicate upon the issues arising in the writ petition. This practice marks a radical departure from the adversarial system of justice which we have inherited from the British.

Relief and remedy

However, even after all these innovations made by the Supreme Court, the question remains: what is the relief that the Court can give to the poor and the downtrodden whose problems are brought before the Court through social action litigation? The Court had to evolve new remedies for giving relief. The existing remedies which were intended to deal with private rights situations were simply inadequate. The suffering of the disadvantaged could not be relieved by mere issue of prerogative writs of *certiorari*, prohibition or *mandamus* or making orders granting damages or injunction, where such suffering was the result of continuous repression and denial of rights. The Supreme Court, therefore, tried to explore new remedies which would ensure distributive justice to the deprived sections of the community. These remedies were unorthodox and unconventional and they were intended to initiate affirmative action on the part of the State and its authorities. To give one example of the utilization of the new remedies, I would take the case of Bandhua Mukti Morcha. In that case, the Supreme Court made an order giving various directions for identifying, releasing and rehabilitating bonded labourers, ensuring minimum wage payments, observance of labour laws, providing wholesome drinking water and setting up dust-sucking machines in the stone quarries. The Supreme Court also set up a monitoring agency which would continuously check the implementation of those directions.

In Bihar pre-trial detention cases, the Supreme Court directed that the State Government should prepare an annual census of the prisoners under trial on 31 October of each year and submit it to the High Court. The High Court should give directions for early disposal of cases where the undertrial prisoners were under detention for unreasonably long periods. The Supreme Court directed in Bihar blinding cases that the undertrials who had been blinded should be given vocational training in an institute for the blind and compensation should be paid to them for setting them up in life. Likewise, in the ASIAD workers' case, the Supreme Court set up a monitoring agency of social activists.

In yet another case brought by a journalist called Sheela Barse, the Supreme Court directed that there should be a separate lock-up for women staffed by women police constables: and that a notice should be put up in each police lock-up informing the arrested person of his rights. The Supreme Court also ordered that a judicial officer should periodically inspect the police lock-ups. The Supreme Court directed in another case that rehabilitation assistance should be provided in consultation with and in the presence of a specified social action group. There are numerous cases where remedy by way of affirmative action has been directed by the Supreme Court, although it is not possible to refer to all these cases or even to the majority of them in a single chapter.

Enforcement of court orders

The question then arises as to how the orders made by the Court in social action litigation can be enforced. The orders made by the Court are obviously not self-executing. They have to be enforced through State agencies, and if the State agencies are not enthusiastic in enforcing the Court orders and do not actively cooperate in that task, the object and purpose of the social action litigation would remain unfulfilled. The consequence of the failure of the State machinery to secure enforcement of Court orders in social action litigation would not only be to deny effective justice to the disadvantaged groups on whose behalf the litigation is brought, but it would also have a demoralising effect and people would lose faith in the capacity of social action litigation to deliver justice. The success or failure of this new strategy would necessarily depend on the extent to which it was able to provide actual relief to the vulnerable sections of the community. If the Court orders passed in social action litigation are to remain merely paper documents, this strategy evolved by the Supreme Court would be robbed of all its meaning and purpose. It is, therefore, absolutely essential to the success of the strategy that a methodology should be found for securing enforcement of Court orders in social action litigation. There are two different methods, listed below, which could be adopted for ensuring that the orders made by the Court in social action litigation are carried out.

1. The public spirited individual or social action group which has initiated the social action litigation and secured the order of the Court providing a wide-ranging remedy to the disadvantaged groups of people should take the necessary follow-up action and maintain constant pressure on the State authorities or agencies to carry out the Court order. If it is found that the Court order is not being implemented effectively, it must immediately bring this fact to the notice of the Court so that the Court can call upon the State authorities or agencies to render an explanation. If there is wilful or contumacious disregard of the Court order, the Court can commit the concerned officers of the State for contempt. The Supreme Court has not so far used the contempt jurisdiction in social action litigation because, by and large, its orders have been obeyed and carried out. If any particular order made in social action litigation is not carried out, however, the obligation of drawing the attention of the Court to such failure should be that of the individual or social action group bringing the social action litigation. The Supreme Court may have to use its jurisdiction in appropriate cases.

2. The Supreme Court has also started appointing monitoring agencies for the purpose of ensuring implementation of the orders made by it in social action litigation. This is again an innovative use of judicial power. The Supreme Court in the Sheela Barse case gave various directions in regard to the police lock-ups for women and directed that a lady judicial officer should visit the police lock-ups periodically and report to the High Court as to whether the directions of the Supreme Court were being carried out or not. This can also be seen in the case of Bandhua Mukti Morcha, which related to the Faridabad stone-quarry workers. The Supreme Court gave twenty-one directions, some of which I have already referred to a little earlier. With a

view to ensuring implementation of these directions, the Supreme Court appointed a socially committed Joint Secretary in the Ministry of Labour to visit the Faridabad stone quarries after about two or three months and ascertain whether the Court's directions had been implemented or not and to make a report to the Supreme Court in regard to the implementation of those directions. The Joint Secretary carried out this assignment entrusted to him as a monitoring agency and submitted a report which is now pending consideration before the Supreme Court. The Supreme Court, in Neera Choudhury's case the other cases coming from the State of Madhya Pradesh, directed that representatives of social action groups operating within the area should be taken up as members of the Vigilance Committee constituted under the Bonded Labour System (Abolition) Act, 1976. They also directed than whenever any case of bonded labour is brought to the notice of the District Administration, by a representative of a social action group, the District Administration must proceed to inquire into it in the presence of the representative of the social action group who is a member of the Vigilance Committee and rehabilitation should be provided to the released bonded labourers in consultation with and in the presence of such a representative. The same strategy was followed in the Asian Construction Workers' case, where the Supreme Court, after clearly enunciating the law on the subject, appointed three social activists as ombudsmen for the purpose of ensuring that labour laws are being observed by the State administration. This new strategy is in the process of evolution. It holds out great promise for the future because, by adopting it, the Court may be able to secure that the orders made by it are indeed obeyed.

These are some of the methodologies which have been evolved for the purpose of securing the implementation of the directions given by the Court in social action litigation. But I may point out that the judiciary in India is still experimenting with new techniques, and in the next few years to come I have no doubt that it will creatively develop new methods and strategies for perfecting this powerful tool of social action litigation.

3 TAKING SUFFERING SERIOUSLY: SOCIAL ACTION LITIGATION IN THE SUPREME COURT OF INDIA

Upendra Baxi

Introduction

The Supreme Court of India is at long last becoming, after thirty-two years of the Republic, the Supreme Court for Indians. For too long, the apex constitutional court had become 'an arena of legal quibbling for men with long purses.'[1] Now, increasingly, the Court is being identified by justices as well as people as the 'last resort for the oppressed and the bewildered.'[2] The transition from a traditional captive agency with a low social visibility into a liberated agency with a high socio-political visibility is a remarkable development in the career of the Indian appellate judiciary.[3] A post-Emergency phenomenon, the transformation is characterized chiefly by judicial populism.[4] The Court is augmenting its support base and moral authority in the nation at a time when other institutions of governance are facing a legitimation crisis.[5] In the process, like all political institutions, the Court promises more than it can deliver and is severely exposed to the dynamics of disenchantment.

For the present and the near future, however, there is little prospect of the Court reverting to its traditional adjudicatory posture, where people's causes appear merely as issues, argued arcanely by lawyers, and decided in the mystery and mystique of the inherited common-law-like judicial process. People now know that the Court has constitutional power of intervention, which can be invoked to ameliorate their miseries arising from repression, governmental lawlessness or administrative deviance. Undertrial as well as convicted prisoners, women in protective custody, children in juvenile institutions, bonded and migrant labourers, unorganized labourers, untouchables and scheduled tribes, landless agricultural labourers who fall prey to faulty mechanization, women who are bought and sold, slumdwellers and pavement dwellers, kin of victims of extrajudicial executions — these and many other groups — now flock to the

Supreme Court seeking justice. They come with unusual problems, never before confronted so directly by the Supreme Court. They seek extraordinary remedies, transcending the received notions of separation of powers and the inherited distinctions between adjudication and legislation on the one hand and administration and adjudication on the other. They bring, too, a new kind of lawyer and a novel kind of judging. They add a poignant twist to the docket explosion[6] which was previously merely a routine product of the Bar committed only to justice according to the fees. They also bring a new kind of dialogue on the judicial role in a traumatically changed society.[7]

The medium through which all this has happened, and is happening, is social action litigation, a distinctive by-product of the catharsis of the 1975-6 Emergency. What emerged as an expiatory syndrome is now a catalytic component of a movement for 'juridical democracy' [8], through innovative uses of judicial power.

Throughout this chapter, I use the term 'social action litigation'(SAL) in preference to the more popular term 'public interest litigation' (PIL). The label PIL has slipped into Indian juridical diction as effortlessly as all Anglo-American conceptual borrowings readily do, but while labels can be borrowed, history cannot. The PIL represents for America a distinctive phase of socio-legal development for which there is no conterpart in India; and the salient characteristics of its birth, growth and, possibly, decay are also distinctive to American history.

The PIL efflorescence in the United States owed much to substantial resource investment from government and private foundations; the PIL work was espoused by specialized public interest law firms.[9] The issues within the sway of PIL in the United States concerned not so much state repression or government lawlessness but rather civic participation in governmental decision-making.[10] Nor did the PIL groups there focus pre-eminently on the rural poor.[11] Typically, PIL sought to represent 'interests without groups' such as consumerism or environment.[12] Given the nature of state and federal politics, PIL marched with public advocacy outside courts through well established mechanisms like lobbying.[13] In brief, the PIL movement in the United States involved innovative uses of the law, lawyers and courts to secure greater fidelity to the parlous notions of legal liberalism and interest group pluralism in an advanced industrial capitalistic society.[14]

No doubt, Indian social action groups should know the essence of the American PIL experience, and particularly the structural reasons for its failures and successes. PIL activism has, instead of generating pressures for structural changes in law and society, ended up servicing the much exposed ideology of interest group pluralism and legal liberalism; indeed, public advocacy programmes have tended to 'enhance the legitimacy of processes that may not really change'.[15] Similarly, PIL activism is, despite the affluent society, unable to overcome problems of resources, both in terms of person-power and finances.[16] Critiques of PIL activism raise doubts concerning its overall impact as regards both the modes of decision-making and the short- and long-term results achieved.[17]

No doubt, there have been fruitful innovations in legal doctrine and technique (for example, liberalization of *locus standi*, growth of techniques of judicial review over administrative action and regulatory agencies, and occasional institutionalization of PIL advocacy). No doubt, too, there are certain items on the *programschrift* of reform of administration, adjudication and legislation of concern and interest to social activists in India.[18] But, at the end of the day, the realization seems to be dawning that while all these technical developments ultimately raise 'basic issues of power and equality in society,' these sorts of developments 'have to do with "justice" in the most impoverished sense of the word' and are 'truly marginal'.[19]

The Indian social action groups should ponder the emerging perceptions of failure of PIL activities in the United States. If these are valid, the challenge before the American socio-legal community is to rethink the basic assumptions behind public advocacy; and this process is now well under way.[20] In India, perhaps, we can learn from the American PIL failures. So great is the hold of colonial legal imagination however, that, in the last analysis, these lessons will be learnt only after the attempts at transferring the success stories (in terms of techniques, doctrines and models of organization of SAL) have demonstrably failed. In the process, the appreciation of the vital political and cultural differences between the two societies will be deferred; and a loose-minded importation of notions apposite to the circumstances of development in the United States will continue to obscure a genuine appreciation of the distinctive social and historical forces shaping, generally, the role of adjudication in India. I propose to use the notion SAL rather than PIL, to avoid these pitfalls.

SAL: some contributory influence

Judicial populism
A striking factor of SAL is that it is primarily judge-led and even judge-induced and it is in turn related to juristic and judicial activism on

active assertion of judicial power to ameliorate the miseries of the masses. Although there was an almost explosive assertion of judicial power in the aftermath of the Emergency, judicial populism had become pronounced even before the Emergency, particularly in the great decisions in *Golak Nath* [22] and *Kesvananda Bharati*.[23] In these decisions, familiar to every student of constitutional politics of India, justices who wished Parliament to have unbridled power to amend the Constitution invariably sought to justify it in the name of, and for the sake of, the 'teeming millions' of impoverished Indians.[24] They sought to mould constitutional interpretation and doctrine in unmistakably and emotionally surcharged people-oriented ways. Populist rhetoric is writ large in many judicial opinions, on both sides, in these landmark decisions. The following excerpts, one from Justice Dwivedi and the other from Justice (now Chief Justice) Chandrachud in *Kesvananda* suffice to offer us a glimpse of the emergent judicial populism in the early 1970s:

The Constitution is not intended to be the arena of legal quibbling for men with long purses. It is made for the common people. It should generally be so construed as that they can understand and appreciate it. The more they understand it the more they love it and the more they prize it.[25]

And further:

The Court is not chosen by the people and is not responsible to them in the sense in which the House of the People is. However, it will win for itself a permanent place in the hearts of the people and augment its moral authority if it can shift the focus of judicial review from the numerical concept of minority protection to the humanitarian concept of the protection of the weaker section of the people.[26]

It is really the poor, starved and mindless millions who need the Court's protection for securing to themselves the enjoyment of human rights. In the absence of an explicit mandate, the Court should abstain from striking down a constitutional amendment which makes an endeavour to 'to wipe out every tear from every eye.'[27]

In much the same vein Justice Chandrachud was moved to say (with reference to constitutional precedents):

But these landmarks in the development of the law cannot be permitted to be transformed into weapons for defeating the hopes and aspirations of our teeming milions, — half-clad, half-starved, half-educated. These hopes and aspirations representing the will of the people can only become articulate through the voice of their elected representatives. If they fail the people, the nation must face death and destruction. Then, neither the Court nor the Constitution will save the country.[28]

The elevation of Justice Krishna Iyer to the High Bench in 1974 reinforced the tendency towards judicial populism. He unremittingly insisted that the law was meant for the people and not the people for the law, and as a neo-Marxist, he meant by 'people' mostly the proletariat and not the propertariat.[29] He used every conceivable occasion, on and off the Bench, to further the cause of the 'toiling masses' and the 'weaker sections of the society'.[30] He also indefatigably demonstrated and criticized the colonial and alienating nature of legal processes and institutions and crusaded for a radical reorientation of the Bench and Bar towards the urgent tasks of development and justice for the Indian masses.[31] Justice Krishna Iyer enhanced the sensitivity of judges and lawyers to exploitation and suffering in a way no other justice of the Supreme Court had ever done.

Emergency populism
During the 1975–6 Emergency, legal aid to the people was one of the key points of the Twenty-Point Programme launched by Indira Gandhi, to which Justices Krishna Iyer and Bhagwati, themselves deeply committed to the spread of the legal aid movement,[32] readily responded. They led a nationwide movement for the promotion of legal services. They organized legal aid camps in distant villages; they mobilized many a high court justice to do *padayatras* (long marches) through villages to solve people's grievances. They, through 'camps' and *lokadalats* (people's courts), sought to provide de-professionalized justice. They also in their extra-curial utterances, called for a total restructuring of the legal system, and in particular of the administration of justice.[33] In a sense, their movement constituted a juridical counterpart of the 1971 *Garibi Hatao* (eliminate poverty) campaign, as well as of the Twenty-Point Programme. Although they stopped short of overtly legitimating the Emergency regime, they remain vulnerable to the charge of acting as legitimators of the regime. Be that as it may, many Supreme Court and High Court justices did systematically become people-prone in a manner conducive to the growth of judicial populism.

In the immediate aftermath of the Emergency, populist rhetoric and stances decided many a vital issue of constitutional policy.[34] Judicial populism was partly an aspect of post-Emergency catharsis. Partly, it was an attempt to refurbish the image of the Court tarnished by a few Emergency decisions and also an attempt to seek new, historical bases of legitimation of judicial power.[35] Partly, too the Court was responding, like all other dominant agencies of governance to the post-Emergency euphoria at the return of liberal democracy.

The SAGS-Press nexus

One such institution was the Press, which for the first time since Independence strove consistently to expose governmental lawlessness and social tyranny through investigative journalism of a high order. Like judges, editors and correspondents realized that some of the 'excesses' of the Emergency were not different in kind, but only in degree, from the everyday excesses of State power on hapless citizens.[36] The Press too felt the need for public atonement; simultaneously, many journalists realized that they owed their freedom of the press ultimately to the people.[37] People's problems began to matter.[38] The Press, for example, highlighted atrocities on untouchables and *adivasis*, the sub-human plight of prisoners, the cruel extra-judicial executions through the so-called 'encounters' involving use of the police as a counter-insurgency force, the excesses of protective custody of women and children, and numerous related instances of violation of fundamental human rights of the people.

This print-media transformation enabled activist social action groups (SAGS) to elevate what were regarded as petty instances of injustices and tyranny at the local level into national issues, calling attention to the pathology of public and dominant group power. SAGS found thus a new ally in their struggle for social development and change. The SAGS-Press nexus provided one fertile setting (as we shall note later) for the birth and growth of the SAL.

At the same time, the Press became a medium of evaluation of how the dominant institutions of the government 'collaborated' against the people.[39] The role of judges and courts was integral to this agonized reappraisal. The Court, and some justices, became exposed to merciless professional critiques of the Court's Emergency performance.[40] In this environment, an Open Letter to the Chief Justice of India written by four anguished law teachers, chastising the Court for its reversal of the conviction of two police officers for raping a tribal girl in the police station, led to a nationwide mobilization of women's organizations and groups. Unexpectedly, it culminated in an unprecedented march by women's organizations to the Supreme Court of India demanding a review of the decision, which it ultimately declined.[41]

All this enhanced the visibility of the Court and generated new types of claims for accountability for wielding of judicial power and this deepened the tendency towards judicial populism. Justices of the Supreme Court, notably Justices Krishna Iyer and Bhagwati, began converting much of constitutional litigation into SAL, through a variety of techniques or juristic activism.[42] The Court began to expand the frontiers of fundamental rights and of natural justice. In the process, they rewrote many parts of the Constitution. The right to life and personal liberty under procedure established by law in Article 21 was now converted *de facto* and *de jure* into a due process clause contrary to the intendment of the makers of the Constitution.[43] This expanding right was soon to encompass within itself the right to bail, the right to speedy trial, the right to dignified treatment in custodial institutions, the right to privacy, and the right to legal services to the poor.[44] Prisons and places of detention, theatres of torture and terror, received high priority attention, especially at the hands of Justice Krishna Iyer who developed, on the whole, a new normative regime of rights and status of prisoners and détenues.[45] The insistence that the states behave in good faith and with utmost reasonableness in dealing with citizens and persons grew apace. Principles of administrative law met with urgent, painstaking and thorough revisions.[46] The doctrinal innovations in their exuberance and normative impact provided further impetus to SAL.

Dramatis Personae of SAL

Some justices of the Supreme Court were thus the prime actors in SAL. Regardless of the argumentative strategies at the Bar, and often regardless of the immediate framework of the writ proceeding, they blazed new trails in constitutional interpretations.[47] By 1979 it was clear to the discerning members of the Bar and to social activists that the Court was indeed in search of a new kind of constitutional litigation.

The first dramatic opportunity was provided by a Supreme Court advocate, Ms. Kapila Hingorani, who filed a writ based on a series of articles in a national daily, the *Indian Express*, exposing the plight of Bihar undertrial prisoners, most of whom had served long pre-trial detention, indeed to a point that they had, as it were, sentences to their credit.[48] In 1980, two professors of law wrote a letter to the editor of the *Indian Express* describing the barbaric conditions of detention in the Agra Protective Home for Women, the basis for a writ petition under Article 21.[49] This was followed by a similar petition for the Delhi Women's Home, by a third year Law Student in the Delhi Law Faculty and a social worker.[50] A law teacher on a social science research fellowship successfully brought to completion the trial of four young tribals, who grew up in a sub-jail awaiting trial.[51] Three journalists, after an exposé of a thriving market in which women were bought and sold as chattels, filed a writ demanding prohibition of this practice and immediate relief for its victims through programmes of compensation and rehabilitation.[52] In the same year, a legal correspondent of *The States-man* brought to the notice of the Court the inhumane conditions of detention of 'Naxalite' prisoners in the Madras Jail, challenging in the process the entire edifice of the Prisons Act, 1892.[53] The special legal correspondent of the *Hindustan Times* also brought to the Court a social activist's report on forced importation of seventy-five young children for homosexual relations in Kanpur Jail.[54] In early 1982, social workers of the Gandhi Peace Foundation, assisted by the author, filed writ proceedings against the state of Madhya Pradesh for allowing bonded labour to be paid wages of disability: that is, wages in kind of Kesari Dal, a toxic substance causing incurable lathyrism among the bonded labourers.[55] A newly formed association of law teachers has brought writ proceedings against the same state for inhuman torture of young prisoners in Chattarpur Jail.[56]

This random listing illustrates the new brand of socio-legal entre-preneurs, who approach the Court *pro bono publico* on their own, without much support from the Bar (and often to its chagrin) and with their social commitment as their only asset. In addition, there are a handful of lawyers and lawyer-led SAGS who have also contributed to SAL.[57] Among the lawyer-led SAGS are three principal groups: the Citizens for Democracy (CFD),[48] the People's Union of Civil Liberties[59] and the People's Union for Democratic Rights.[60]

Of about seventy five SAL writs filed between 1980-2 a preponderant number have been filed by social activists rather than individual lawyers or lawyer groups.[61] This has been made possible by a rather unique development. Much of SAL in this period has arisen out of letters written by individuals to Justice P.N. Bhagwati in his twin capacities as the Justice of the Supreme Court and the Chair-person of the National Committee for the implementation of the Legal Aid Schemes. The letters usually rely on newspaper and periodical investigative reportage. More often than not, the Justice brings them on the board of the Court, converting these letters into writ petitions. Justice Bhagwati has gone so far as to invite members of the public and especially public spirited citizens to bring to his notice violations of basic human rights, as embodied in the Constitution, for suitable judicial action.

In *habeas corpus* petitions, the Court usually acts on letters written by or on behalf of the detenue. But Justice Bhagwati has generalized this technique so radically that it could be justly said that he made a momentous social invention — namely, epistolary jurisdiction. After experimenting with it for some time, he was able, too, to fully legitimate epistolary jurisdiction by imaginatively extending the law of *locus standi* in constitutional litigation in the High Court Judge's case.[62] The judge-led and judge-induced nature of SAL renders it strikingly distinctive.

The social substance of SAL

Not merely in the style and process of generation of the SAL is the contemporary Indian experience unique. The substance of the SAL in India is also distinctive to its contemporary condition. In essence, much of SAL focuses on exposés of repression by the agencies of the state, notably the police, prison and other custodial authorities. Close to this category are the cases which seek to ensure that authorities of the State fulfil the obligations of law under which they exist and function. In other words, much of SAL is concerned with combating repression and governmental lawlessness. Only, so far, in rare instances does the SAL concern assertion of new constitutional rights.[63] The other distinctive feature of SAL proceedings is that all of them are Article 32 petitions; that is, they are writ proceedings for the enforcement of fundamental rights. The Supreme Court is empowered, and some would say rather obligated, to duly consider them.[64]

Both these features lend a special complexity to the SAL in India. On the one hand, they impart high visibility and exalted status to the cause; on the other hand, they present some specific problems for the Court, since all the complaints of governmental repression and lawlessness raise disputed questions of fact which the Court does not as a matter of practice normally handle and which cannot be wholly satisfactorily dealt with by affidavit evidence. We revert to these problems later. For the moment, it would suffice to emphasize this distinct profile of the SAL in India. SAL thus compels judges and lawyers increasingly to take human suffering seriously.[65]

Old structures, new concerns

The Court's handling of SAL is at the present in an experimental phase. Much of the future of the SAL ultimately depends on the organizational learning capacity of the Court in dealing with novel and complex problems. This capacity is affected by existent judicial thought and styles of decision-making.

The most crucial general factor affecting, for weal or woe, the career of SAL is the fluctuating bench-structure. The bench which admits the writ petition is not necessarily the same, unless there is a constitution bench of five justices, as the one hearing it. Even if the presiding judge remains common, his companion justices may differ, often from one hearing to the next. The presiding judge, as well as the SAL petitioner (whether in person or through counsel), thus have to bear additional burdens of persuasion, more so because not all justices are as yet equally attracted by or committed to the SAL.[66] The difficulties are reinforced when the presiding judge is unsympathetic to SAL or, even if moderately sympathetic, he is daunted by the problems of evidence and of shaping new types of reliefs.

Epistolary jurisdiction as developed by Justice Bhagwati was partly addressed to this problem. Once a letter received by him was treated by him as a writ petition, he ensured that it came on his board. His Court No. 2 has, through this process, the largest number of SAL matters. While this result is welcome to many a SAL petitioner, it carries its own costs. First, it indirectly deprives the Chief Justice of India of his undoubtedly important role in docket management and allocation of work to his companion justices. This clearly has its own implications for *inter se* relationships among justices, including perhaps the growth of factionalism in the Court.[67] Second, many justices are deprived by this result of epistolary jurisdiction of the much needed exposure to SAL; in the process, the learning capacity of the Court as an institution is constricted. Third, the existing overload on court No. 2 is accentuated, causing problems of priority in handling. If high priority is accorded to SAL at the cost of other matters, irate leaders of the Bar (as is happening) are bound to seek to discredit SAL.[68] If such priority is not accorded, SAL matters continue to drag on, like others and this (as is already happening) begins to raise serious questions concerning the impact of judicial intervention for such causes.[69]

On the other hand, most SAL matters do require, in their early phases, careful judicial handling. SAL is distinctive in that it does not raise the problems of validity of a law on the ground that it violates fundamental rights. The heart of the SAL proceedings is rather that gross violation of fundamental rights has actually occurred in the exercise of state powers, either by commission (repression) or omission (lawless disregard of statutorily or constitutionally imposed duties). The facts relied upon initially by the SAL petitioner, in most cases, are as stated in the press. Also the SAL petitioner is himself often not the victim of repression or lawlessness, but a public citizen.

Invariably, therefore, the Court has to satisfy itself about the factual foundations of the proceedings; and this requires constancy of the Bench.

Justice Bhagwati's initiative in retaining many SAL matters with himself seems to proceed on the appreciation of this requirement. On the other hand, it imprints the SAL with the insignia of an individual justice, whereas what is needed in days to come is a collective imprimatur of the Court for the new litigation. The future of SAL depends, in great measure, on a satisfactory resolution of this dilemma.

Like the technique of epistolary jurisdiction for its initiation, SAL also requires 'creeping' jurisdiction for its progress. Not a single leading SAL matter has yet resulted in a final verdict; the fundamental issue of how the Court should make the State and its agencies fully liable for deprivations or denials of fundamental rights still remains to be authoritatively answered. It is the task of the SAL entrepreneurs to ensure that these issues are ultimately reached with desired results. In the meantime, the Court rules through interim directions and orders. Bit by bit, it seeks improvement in the administration, making it more responsive than before to the constitutional ethic and law.

This kind of creeping jurisdiction typically consists in taking over the direction of administration in a particular arena from the executive: the blinded undertrials receive medical examination at New Delhi and the expenses of their stay and their relatives are borne by the State under interim orders of the Court; conditions in Agra and Delhi Protective Homes for Women begin to steadily improve, again through a series of interim administrative orders. Fresh directions are issued by the Court to the state of Bihar, from time to time, to ensure that undertrials at least serve less time in pre-trial detention and not in any event more than the time which they would have served had they been tried and convicted! These and many examples show that the Court is undertaking those very administrative decisions which the State should have taken in the first place.[70] In the meantime, the ultimate constitutional issues patiently await their turn.

Doing something about these questions is comparatively far more difficult than compelling the State to do this or that under the creeping jurisdiction because it involves making viable momentous normative innovations in the lawyer's law.[71] Some of these have already been attained: for example, expansion of *locus standi*,[72] whittling down of the range of documents for which government may claim privilege,[73] devising of newer ways of fact-finding in the SAL-type proceeding[74] and devising of prospective inhibitors to potential recurrence of the violations of rights in the same arena.[75] All this is noteworthy only so long as the underlying constitutional issues of citizens' rights against the State for violation of fundamental rights are faced and resolved.

These issues in the final analysis relate to exposing the State to liability for wide-ranging compensatory arrangements for violations of fundamental rights of the people. The Court has, already, rightly rejected the facetious argument of the Attorney General of India in the Bihar blindings case that when police torture prisoners they do so outside the authority of the law and, therefore, the state may not even at the threshold be considered liable for the manifest unlawful actions of its agents.[76] Well begun is indeed half done.

Yet the challenge of devising appropriate compensatory arrangements for such violations is very daunting. How do we compensate young persons manacled for long years in pre-trial detention for their enforced loss of childhood and all deprivation of sociability? How do we compensate the blinded undertrials? Or the ones who have been inhumanly tortured? What does a court do, under fundamental rights jurisdiction, when it finds young persons thrown in jail for no other reason than facilitating homosexual assaults? Or when it finds that inmates of a protective home for women are first allowed to go insane and in the wake of the Court's inquisition are put out on the streets?[77] Or where the woman who was bought and sold vanishes from Delhi even before the hearing of writ petition has to fully commence? What relief may the Court provide in situations of extra-judicial executions? Creeping jurisdiction is an apposite strategy for gradualist institutional renovation; it furnishes no answers to the questions raised by the victims of repression and lawlessness, past, present or future. Inability to forge onerous patterns of liability for the State for gross violations of rights may well deprive the SAL of its future.

Evidentiary problems in SAL

Accomplishing such a jurisprudential feat calls not just for the vision and commitment of a high order on the part of justices; it also requires careful attention to the lowly details of how facts about the violations of rights are proved. Without this, no jurisprudence of liability of the state for constitutional violations can survive for long. We accept the principle of compensation for rights-violation, the State will say then, but it will immediately add: 'prove it'!

The problems of proof are the most severe in cases of State repression and there seems emergent a common pattern of argumentation by State counsel which makes these problems more acute. First, State counsel deny on affidavit any or all allegations of torture or terror. Second, they contest, if not any more the standing, the bona fides or the degree of reliable information of the social activists who come to the Court. Often the wildest ulterior motives are attributed to them.[78] Third, they decry the sources on which the SAL petitioners rely: mostly media and social science investigative reportage. Fourth, they raise all kinds of claims under the law of evidence and procedure to prevent the disclosure of documents relevant to the determination of violation of fundamental rights. Fifth, even when these are disclosed, there is always the possibility of impugning their evidentiary value. This is made possible by the device of multiple investigations; the State sets up many panels, one after another, and often consents, in addition, to investigation by the Central Bureau of Investigation.[79] When despite all this, the State is likely to lose the proceedings in favour of the SAL petitioners, it proceeds to give concessions and undertakings, thereby avoiding a decision on merit.[80]

The Court, too, interested more in the inhibition of future illegalities is ready to develop a jurisprudence of the SAL *ex-concessionis.* The Court, rightly refuses to view the SAL proceedings as adversarial in nature; it likes to foster such collaboration between the SAL litigant and the State as would result in sound institutional arrangements avoiding recurrent injustice and thus avoiding in the long term SAL-type confrontation between the public-spirited citizen and the State. This technique offers a neat way out of the burdens of proof on questions of fact; therein probably lies its appeal to the judges.

At the same time, the Court is experimenting with several different strategies to overcome the problem of disputed facts, without having to take evidence itself. First, Justice Bhagwati has initiated the idea of socio-legal commissions of enquiry. The Court asks social activists, teachers and researchers to visit particular locations for fact-finding and so submit a quick, but complete, report, which may also contain suggestions and proposals. So far the device of commissions has been invoked at least thrice.[81] The commissions are, under the Court's orders, to be financed by the State. Second, the Court has in a number of cases of torture or ill-treatment called upon medical specialists to submit[82] comprehensive reports and suitable therapy at State cost. Third, the Court has used on one or two occasions the services of its own officials[83] or those of the High Court.[84] In some cases, it has asked the district judge not merely to ascertain facts[85] but also to monitor the implementation of the various directions given by the Court.[86]

These modes of fact-finding are somewhat novel and will raise, as the many SAL matters proceed to completion, rather difficult issues of evidence and procedure. But the Court is experimenting with new methods to go beyond the notoriously eclectic affidavit evidence.

SAL as an aspect of judicial statepersonship

The growth of SAL on the Supreme Court bears out amply what I felt concerning the newly emerging role of the Supreme Court in the dying hours of 1979. I said then: 'The politics of the Court — be it the "purest politics" or constitutional adjudication or the hurly burly politics of power-sharing at times, power-grabbing at others, represents the best hope for the millions of Indians for a new constitutional dawn'.[87]

All in all, SAL symbolizes the politics of liberation: the ruled and misruled have added to the might of adult franchise the quiet dignity of constitutionalism in their struggle against the myriad excesses of power. The Supreme Court is thereby slowly marshalling a new kind of social legitimation, which neither the legislature nor the executive nor political parties can contest without appearing to justify injustice and tyranny.

By the same token, the new litigation does not disturb the pattern of institutional comity between the Supreme Court and the supreme executive. Rather, it appears to lend a new kind of intensity to the model of judicial statepersonship which has since Independence steadily enhanced political accommodation and constitutional compromise in certain vital arenas. Even as the new litigation raises great expectations about the Court's role and power, the constitutional compromises in the period from 1980 to 1982 create new sources of anxiety.

The Supreme Court, during 1981, has sustained the powers of the President (i.e. the Prime Minister) to issue ordinances even on the eve of Parliament sessions.[88] They have ruled that the satisfaction of the President as regards declaration or continuance of emergencies cannot be judicially reviewed.[89] The Court has upheld the National Security Act, in spite of the fact that it violates the 1979 amendments to Article 22, which have not yet been brought into force; what is more, it has also ruled that no *mandamus* lies to the President to bring into force such an amendment.[90] The Court has also repelled the challenge to the Bearer Bonds Act which massively legalized black money, crucial, among other things, to the survival of all political parties in India.[91]

These constitutional compromises occur within the framework of retention of legislative, constituent and judicial powers by the Court. Chief Justice Chandrachud and his brethren have now unalterably laid down that judicial review is an aspect of the doctrine of the basic structure and invalidated an Emergency amendment designed to oust judicial review of constitutional amendments.[92] The Court has gone so far as to say that each and every amendment to the Constitution since its inception has to run the gauntlet of the basic structure.[93]

Simultaneously, the Supreme Court has put into cold storage two basic challenges to its supremacy. A year has gone by, without any action at all on the Presidential Reference on the extent of judicial power,[94] and the review petition, moved by the Indira Gandhi government in 1980, calling for reconsideration of the basic structure doctrine has also become a magnificent bit of judicial arrears.[95]

The executive is left with its well-worn conventional weapons system: the power to appoint judges of the Supreme Court and the High Court, and the power to transfer them from one High Court to another.[96] The Supreme Court did not substantially modify these powers in its controversial decision in the High Court *Judges* case.[97] The impact of this decision on the future of the Indian judiciary appears dismal when one speculates on the sources of judicial recruitment.[98] Members of the Bar say that they now see even less reason to be persuaded to judgeship; so that in the future, senior district judges will become High Court and even Supreme Court justices.[99] Regardless of this decision, however, very few members of the Bar were willing to accept a Supreme Court judgeship, and, increasingly, district judges comprise the High Courts. Nothing save persistent preference for obscene levels of conspicuous consumption, in the last analysis, disables senior lawyers from accepting judgeship; and the prospect of maintenance of these levels, and even its augmentation, depend on a high clustering of mediocrity on the Bench.

The *Judges* case furnished considerable political excitement and was designed, in the last analysis, to deprive Indira Gandhi of some of the fruits of her 1980 victory at the hustings. Judges had their own reasons for refusing to play ball: they were worried about the growth of dynastic and incestuous relations between some members of the Bar and the Bench. The Supreme Court was naturally concerned to project an image of incorruptibility of the Indian appellate judiciary. An adverse image in the minds of people would have identified appellate courts as no better than other dominant institutions of the State. By upholding the power of transfer of the High Court justices, with maximum consultative safeguards, the Court has made difficult, if not impossible, hostile political propaganda. This is a probable gain, though I persevere with the view that the power of transfer should never have been thus conceded.[100]

Perhaps, only Supreme Court justices know the dynamics of the will to judicial power. They perhaps think it inconceivable that any amount of Court-packing will produce a situation over-ruling *Kesavananda* because no future group of judges would like to abandon their constituent power.

In this context, the steady growth of the SAL appears to me as a master strategy: give the Executive not even a pretence of complaint on the distribution of political power in the constitutional scheme, treat the power of amendment of the Constitution as coordinate power; having accomplished this much, go Concorde-speed in undoing injustices and unmasking tyrannies. The powers of the President are intact but surely the Police Commissioner must be held fully accountable under the Constitution. The executive may refuse to bring into force laws duly evaded by Parliment; but the district bureaucrat must be brought to book for sins of commission and omission. Leave to politicians their opium-dreams of the omnipotence of their power and influence; but bit by bit prevent them from single-minded excesses of power. The respondents in the SAL matters are always political small fry: so the big ones may not complain. But the results of the SAL irritate the Big Men. No matter how irate (as was Jagannath Mishra, the Chief Minister of Bihar, on the Supreme Court's swift probe in the Bihar blindings), they cannot as easily manipulate public opinion in their favour as the Court. To the print media, the Court is popular (barring the trauma of the *Judges* case) because it is now newsworthy, to say the very least. As regards repression and lawlessness, the Supreme Court since 1980 has become the third chamber of Parliament and is close to acquiring, more effectively, the attributes of the House of the People. The SAL fits in beautifully with the well-conducted orchestration of concord and discord with the Executive.

The Court is now supported by the SAGS and also ORPs (organizations of the rural poor), and PORPs (participatory organizations of the rural poor).[101] The SAL gives to the Court the socio-political space it needs, on the eve of the closure of the post-Emergency era. It adds to the space already available to the SAGs, ORPs and PORPs.

The SAL movement may be viewed as relatively minor exercises in class-transcendence, subject to all the frailties of such struggles. Backslidings are bound to occur, but it is doubtful whether the evolution of the Court as a people-oriented institution can be arrested substantially. Of course, nothing is irreversible, at least in legal history. It would require considerable mobilization of regressive forces, however, to return the Court to its club-house cloisterings. In fact, the SAL movement is well under way to institutionalization. Hopeful signs for the growth of the SAL-type professional competence abound.[102] The national legal aid movement is rapidly acquiring SAL orientation, and more and more High Court justices are becoming SAL-prone.[103]

The surest measure of success of the SAL movement is provided by the changing attitude of the Supreme Court Bar towards it. In 1979, when the Court expressed a hope that the Bar Association would intervene in the

Bihar undertrial cases, there was no stirring of response. When two law professors filed the Agra Women's Home petition, there was a certain amount of amused interest on the part of the senior leaders of the Bar. When the SAL dockets' explosion began, there was anguished protest. A leading State counsel expressed his exasperation in open Court at the day-long proceedings of SAL based on the media investigative reportage; his trenchantly expressed protest was met by Justice Bhagwati with a sharp admonition: 'hold your tongue'. In the course of the Agra proceedings, senior lawyers were openly heard to say that if the Supreme Court thus wants to do social justice, it had better meet at weekends![104]

The Bar's reaction has moved from indifference to indignation at what it regards as freak litigation. At the present moment, two utterly different types of response seem to be emerging. One is a frankly antagonistic and hostile response. A senior advocate and a member of Rajya Sabha moved two motions pertaining to the 'public interest' litigation in the Supreme Court. The first at the end of 1981 urged the Government to prescribe certain guidelines for this kind of litigation; this suggestion was promptly discounted by the then Law Minister, Shiv Shankar. In late April, 1982, the same member made highly derogatory reference to SAL. He saw in it nothing less than a foreign conspiracy to destabilize the Indian government through the activation of the Supreme Court.[105]

On the other hand, some senior lawyers have now begun to say that they have always been pursuing SAL. They cite a number of examples where public interest was involved: the National Security Ordinance and Act, the Bearer Bonds Act, and other such matters.[106] Even Mr. J.M. Seervai could not resist the temptation, despite his contemptuous attitudes towards Justices Krishna Iyer[107] and Bhagwati[108] to assert that the Bombay Bar's initiative in challenging non-appointment of additional High Court justices and their transfers was a shining example of the Bar's deep commitment to the new litigation.

Undoubtedly, an empirical study of the changeful and conflicting attitudes of the Bar to the new litigation is necessary. But available materials suggest a degree of agonizing within the Bar and a slow emergence of a new concern. The SAL movement does pose alternative modes of providing lawyers' services for the Indian people.

The response to the administration of SAL has also been mixed. The top bureaucrats seem to resent the mini-takeover of administration through creeping jurisdiction. Their resentment is shown in indifferent compliance with the Court's interim directions in many proceedings but in some cases over a period of time, the tenacity of SAL petitioners and of the Bench has overborne their resistance.[109]

Conclusion

This impressionistic account of the SAL movement in the last two years does indicate that small, *ad hoc* beginnings have been made. These have received such nation-wide attention as to generate emulation as well as hostility. Many avoidable deficiencies characterize the SAL work.[110] There is considerable introspection among the social activists on the role and limits of the Court's intervention. We still lack an assessment of what is really happening although it is perhaps too early to think of exploring the impact of the SAL.[111] There persists the need also for developing critical thought on the mainsprings and meanderings of SAL.

Projections of the future of the SAL can, at the present moment, be only subjective, but to me the future of SAL looks bright. The future of law in India is partly but vitally linked to the future of social action litigation because through it great and unending injustices and tyranny begin to hurt the national conscience and prod at least one major institution of governance to take people's miseries seriously.

For those who take people's sufferings seriously, there is no rejoicing; but even revolutions provide transietn occasions of celebration. The SAL is at best an 'establishment revolution'.[112] Still, it nourishes hope in an otherwise darkening landscape of Indian law and jurisprudence.

Notes

1. *Kesavananda Bharathi* v. *State of Kerala* (1973) 4 S.C.C. 225 at p. 947 (hereafter cited as *Kesvananda*).
2. *State of Rajasthan* v. *Union of India* (1977) 3 S.C.C. 634 at p. 670 (per Justice Goswami).
3. It is customary to think about administrative and regulatory agencies as 'captive'. See, for example, D.M. Trubek, 'Public Policy Advocacy: Administrative Government and Representation of Diffuse Interests' in 3 *Access to Justice* 445, 1979, and the literature there cited. But, barring small causes and similar other judicical fora, the notion of 'captive agency' has not been explicitly extended to appellate courts. Even these latter can become 'captive' to certain professional interests, backed by societal dominant groups.
4. See U. Baxi, *The Indian Supreme Court and Politics,* Lucknow, Eastern Books, 1980, pp. 121–248 (hereafter cited as 'Baxi, *Politics*').
5. Baxi, *Politics,* at pp. 246–8.
6. See R. Dhavan, *The Supreme Court under Strain : The Challenge of Arrears*, New Delhi, Tripathi, 1977; U. Baxi, *The Crisis of the Indian Legal*

System, New Delhi, Vikas, 1982, pp. 58–83 (hereafter referred to Baxi, *Crisis*).

7. See U. Baxi, 'On How Not to Judge the Judges . . .' (Mimeo: paper presented at a Seminar on Judicial Process and Social Change, Indian Law Institute and Andhra Pradesh University, 1980); Justice O. Chinnappa Reddy, 'Judicial Process and Social Change' 65 *Supreme Court Journal* I, 1981.

8. For an elaboration of the notion of juridical democracy, see T. Lowi *The End of Liberalism : Second Republic of the United States,* New York, W.W. Norton, 1969, pp. 291–303.

9. See L.G. Trubek and D.M. Trubek, 'Civic Justice through Civil Justice: New Approach to Public Interest Advocacy in the United States'in 3 *Access to Justice & The Welfare State* 119, 1981.

10. Ibid.

11. See, generally, J.F. Handler, *Social Movements and the Legal System: Theory of Law Reform and Social Change,* New York, Academic Press, 1979, passim; F.F. Piven and R.A. Cloward, *Poor People's Movements: Why They Succeed, How They Fail,* New York, Random House, 1979.

12. See *supra* note 9. Trubek's analysis of 'interests without groups' needs to be extended to the wider setting of the political economy of advanced capitalist societies. See for example C. Offe, 'Political Authority and Class Structure: An Analysis of the Late Capitalist Societies' 2 *International Journal of Sociology* 73, 1972.

13. J.M. Barry, *Lobbying for the People,* Princeton, Princeton University Press, 1977.

14. See Trubek, *supra* note 9; also see the insightful analysis by Handler, *supra* note 11.

15. Trubek, *supra* note 3 at p. 494.

16. The PIL Movement suffered a grievous setback when the Ford Foundation terminated its grants to the PIL firms in 1979. Until that year the Foundation had provided US$21 million to these firms. See, for a lively account of the resource, 'Viccisitudes of PIL movement', D.S. Broder, *Changing of the Guard: Power and Leadership in America,* New York, Simon and Schuster, 1981, p. 225.

The support from the Bar is miniscule. In 1977 the Carnegie Endowment awarded $250,000 to the Council on Public Interest Law, subject to the condition that the American Bar Association raise a like amount. The award was cancelled because the Association did not raise the corresponding amount! See Trubek & Trubek, *supra* note 9, at pp. 127–8. Specialized public advocacy groups, too, have staggering problems of financial viability. It has been estimated that 'the direct costs to *one* company participating in a *single* regulatory hearing can often exceed $500,000' whereas the 'entire budget for the proposed consumer advocacy agency, including all administrative costs, research programmes and the like was $500,000! In the circumstances PIL activity is unlikely to achieve 'genuine resource equalization'. See Trubek, *supra* note 3, at pp. 477-8.

The resource problems in themselves highlight the need for a thorough-going structural revision of the American legal system; PIL failures may reinforce the need for such changes but cannot provide these.

17. See *supra* notes 3 and 9.
18. For example, the rights of access to information and sources of information; over-delegation of legislative power; quest for refined mechanisms other than court-systems of ensuring accountability. See Lowi, *supra* note 8; T.E. Ely, *Democracy and Distrust*, 1980. For the Indian situation, see Baxi, *Crisis* pp. 41-57.
19. See *supra*, note 9 at p. 119.
20. See *supra*, notes 3, 9, 11.
21. Baxi, *Politics*; K.K. Mathew (ed.), *Democracy, Equality and Freedom*, Lucknow, Eastern Book Company, 1978.
22. *Golak Nath* v. *State of Punjab* AIR (All Indian Reports) 1967 SC 1643.
23. *supra*, note 1.
24. See for examples of populist stances: U. Baxi, 'Politics on the nature of Constituent Power' in R. Dharan and A. Jacob (eds.), *The Indian Constitutions* (1977), pp. 127-51; R. Dhavan, *The Supreme Court and Parliamentary Sovereignty*, 1979. The debate over the reaches of the amending power has pre-eminently been concerned with the 'right' to property (with the conspicuous exception of *Raj Narain* v. *Indira Nehru Gandhi*, 1975 I Suppl. SCC 1). The 'right' now stands deleted. But the socialist content of the Preamble and the Directive Principles of the State Policy have provided, and will continue to do so, fruitful *topoi* for populistic judicial reasoning.
25. *Kesavananda* at p. 947 (para 1947).
26. Ibid. at pp. 948-9 (para 1952).
27. Ibid. at pp. 949 (para 1953).
28. Ibid. at p. 968; See also pp. 991, 1005.
29. Baxi, *Politics*, op cit, pp. 170-2, 233-45; Baxi, *Crisis*, op cit, pp. 209-43. See also K.M. Sharma, 'The Judicial Universe of Mr. Justice Krishna Iyer', **4** SCC (Journal) 38, 1981.
30. For example, V.R. Krishna Iyer, *Law and the People; A Collection of Essays*, New Delhi, People's Publishing House, 1972; id., *Law Freedom and Change*, 1975; id., *Some Half Hidden Aspects of Indian Social Justice*, Lucknow, Eastern Books Co., 1980.
31. Baxi, *Politics*, pp. 121-77.
32. See the Krishna Iyer Committee's report, *Processual Justice to the People*, 1975; and its critique in Baxi, 'Legal Assistance to the Poor . . .' **27** *Economic Political Weekly* 1005, 1975.
33. For example, both Justices Krishna Iyer and Bhagwati called for thorough-going judicial reforms, minimizing reliance on foreign models of adjudication, including the system of *stare deasis*. They advocated return to *swadeshi* jurisprudence including justice by popular tribunals.

34. Baxi, *Politics*, op cit., pp. 121–77.
35. See Baxi, *Politics*, op.cit., pp. 29–120. Also see M. Ghouse, 'Constitutional Law' in XII *Ann. Sur. Ind. L.* pp. 240, 264–74, 1976; H.M. Seervai, *The Emergency, Future Safeguards and the Habeas Corpus Case*, Bombay, Tripathi Pvt. Ltd., 1978.
36. See the balanced account of the vicisitudes of the press during the Emergency in D.R. Mankekar and Kamala Manekekar, *The Decline and Fall of Indira Gandhi: 19 Months of Emergency*, New Delhi, Vision Books, 1982, pp. 88–122.
37. This was, in my opinion, a lasting gain for the free press in India. The Sixth General Elections witnessed the emergence of the consciousness on the part of many a professional, hard-boiled journalist that the so-called 'illiterate', 'dumb' masses of India, and not the decadent leaders and patrons of the 'free press', held the power to ensure continuance of political freedom in India.
38. The exposé of the Emergency excesses, highlighted in the day-to-day proceedings of the Shah Commission and other State level enquiries, created an almost new sensitivity among journalists and correspondents. For the first time, excesses of power against the common people began to be considered newsworthy. People's sufferings did not constitute headline, front-page news in pre-Emergency India. The censorship during the Emergency also prepared ground for this new sensibility. In the absence of newsworthy stories of political goings-on, national newspapers carried on the *front page* stories about bonded labourers and other related aspects of social tyranny. For an overall account of the conditions which fostered the growth of new sensibility in the print media see Arun Shourie, *Institutions Under the Janata Rule*, Bombay, Prakashan Pvt. Ltd., 1980; id. *Symptoms of Fascism*, Bombay, Pakashan Pvt. Ltd., 1978.
39. See David Selbourne, *An Eye to India*, Penguin, 1979; Shourie, *supra*, note 38.
40. The judiciary became, too, an object of the politics of hate in the immediate aftermath of the Six General Elections; see Baxi, *Politics*, pp. 88–98.
41. See, for the text of the Open Letter, I SCC (Journal) 17, 1979. The review bench declined representation by women's organizations, so irked were some justices at what they thought to be the pressure tactics of the protest march. The Bar too was indignant both at the Open Letter and the protest. But Chief Justice Chandrachud not merely publicly welcomed such calls for judicial accountability through the 'Open Letter' but he also received the women's delegation urbanely and even assured them a timely review, which in the event took nearly two years!
42. Juristic activism involves enunciation of new ideas and techniques perhaps not even urged at the Bar, which are in no way necessary to the instant decision but relevant, and in some cases decisively so, for the future growth of the law. See Baxi, Introduction to K.K. Mathew, *Democracy, Equality and Freedom*, op.cit., p. xxviii.
43. Baxi, *Politics*, pp. 151–66.

44. Baxi, *Politics*, at pp. 233–45; Baxi, *Crisis*, pp. 244–95.
45. Ibid.
46. U. Baxi 'Developments in Administrative Law' in A.G. Noorani (ed.) *Public Law in India*, New Delhi, Vikas, 1982; and the literature there cited; U. Baxi, Introduction to I.P. Massey's *Administrative Law*, 1980; id., *Politics* pp.151–66; M.P. Jain, 'Justice Bhagwati and Indian Administrative Law' *The Banaras Law Journal*, 1980.
47. See notes 42 and 46 *supra*.
48. *Hussainara Khatoon* v. *State of Bihar* (six interim decisions so far) discussed in U. Baxi, 'The Supreme Court Under Trial : Undertrials and the Supreme Court' SCC (Journal) 35, 1980.
49. *Dr. Upendra Baxi* v. *State of Uttar Pradesh*, 1981 3 SCALE 1136.
50. *Chinnamma Sivdas* v. *State (Delhi Administration)* W.P. 2526 of 1982; initiated by Ms. Nandita Haksar, who later also assisted the Court by surveying the conditions in the Home as a Member of the Committee headed by the District Judge, Delhi.
51. *Kadra Pahadiva* v. *State of Bihar*, W.P. 5943 of 1980; see also V. Dhagmwar, 'The Pahadiya File: A Cry in Wilderness' *Mainstream* (Annual Number), 1981.
52. *Ms. Comi Caopor, Aswini Sarin and Arun Shourie* v. *State of M.P.*, W.P. 2229 of 1981.
53. *Ghanashyam Pardesi* v. *State of Tamil Nadu*, W.P. 2261/80; 3947/81 & 4252/81/.
54. *Khrishnan Mahajan* v. *State of Uttar Pradesh*, W.P., 1981 (initiated by Krishnan Mahajan).
55. *Jyoti Prakash* v. *State of Madhya Pradesh*, May, 1982.
56. *Association for Social Action & Legal Thought (ASSALT)* v. *The State of Madhya Pradesh*, W.P. 8332 of 1981.
57. Among the lawyers who have individually initiated SAL at the Supreme Court are: Ms. Kapila Hingorani, who brought the undertrial as well as the Bhagalapur blindings cases; Ms. Indira Jaising, who is steadfastly insisting on the fundamental right of people in Bombay to live on pavements; and Mr. Vimal Dave of the Supreme Court Legal Aid Association. Younger members of the Bar seem to have responded more enthusiastically to SAL. Mr. Kapil Sibal, notably, helps court No. 2 almost as an institutionalized *amicus*.
58. The CFD is led by Tarkunde, a Senior Advocate, Supreme Court, and a retired High Court Judge of the Bombay High Court. A veteran fighter for public causes, Tarkunde's ideology is shaped by the radical humanism of M.N. Roy (whose message he is struggling to make relevant to contemporary India) and the latter day thought of Jayprakash Narayan. Tarkunde was in the forefront of the exposé of the torture of Naxalites in Andhra Pradesh and Punjab and in the crusade against the constitutional changes during the Emergency. The CFD has intervened in many cases, including notably the Bihar undertrial cases.

59. The PUCL is a body having wide enrolment from a cross-section of intelligentsia throughout the country. Its members are intellectual activists, most of whom have been shocked into social action by the trauma of the Emergency. Its leadership includes many leading lawyers, journalists and opposition leaders. The PUCL has investigated many cases of atrocities and corruption. It has chapters throughout India and has potential for emerging as a significant shaper of public opinion and as a pressure group.

60. The PUDR is a breakway group of the PUCL, attracting a more radical social activist membership. It is led by Gobinda Mukhoty, a senior advocate of the Supreme Court. A small group of dedicated workers, it is noticably more active than the PUCL or the CFD. It has produced a large number of reports investigating the conditions of landless and bonded labourers, police and jail atrocities and treatment of political dissenters, including Naxalites. Among the notable SAL brought by the PUDR are : bonded labour cases from Punjab and Haryana and treatment of migrant and contract labourers in the construction of the prestigious Asian Games stand in New Delhi.

61. The number of 75 SAL cases is based on a rough count; a more detailed census is on the way with the help of an enthusiastic group of final year law students at Delhi (Ms. Nandita Haksar, Messrs Arun Tyagi, Ananta Barua and Shashibhusan Upadhayaya). The category SAL needs careful operationalization. Some senior leaders of the Supreme Court Bar, when approached, maintained that they too have been initiators of 'public interest litigation'. They have mentioned, among others, the following important cases; *Azad Hickshaw* v. *Punjab* (1981) 1 SCR 366; *Fertilizer Corp. Kamqar Union, Sindri* v. *Union of India* (1981) 2 SCR 52; *Municipal Council Ratlam* v. *Vardichand* (1981) 1 SCR 47; *R.K. Garq* v. *Union of India* A.I.R. 1981 S.C. 2138; *A.K. Roy* v. *Union of India* 1981 (3) SCALE 1601; and *I.M. Chagala* v. *Union of India* 1981 SCALE 1959. Each one of these cases raised very basic questions; and in most, the justices resorted to both judicial and juristic activism strategies. Also, public-spirited lawyers either *initiated* these matters or participated substantially in these. The present count includes some of these matters, as well as some cases conducted by the Supreme Court Legal Aid Committee, headed by Justice D.A. Desai. The magnitude of the SAL will be high on a liberal operationalization of that notion; all the more so, if we were to further include all cases involving corruption in high places in our listing as well. If one simply went by the criteria of weighty social interests at stake, almost every fifth matter on the board of the Court would have to qualify as SAL. My preference at this stage of investigation is to confine SAL to mean; (*i*) Court-recourse against repression, terror and torture; (*ii*) activation of judicial power against dominant group exploitation of the specially vulnerable strata of society and (*iii*) assertion of new rights, either *sui generis* or in aid of (*i*) and (*ii*) above.

62. Among the many justifications provided by Justice Bhagwati, the following are important from the present perspectives. First, the rules of law will be 'substantially impaired' if 'no one can have standing to maintain an action

for judicial redress in case of public wrong or public injury'. It is 'absolutely essential that the rule of law must wean people away from the lawless street and *win them for court of law*'. If breach of public duties was 'allowed' to go unredressed by Courts on the ground of standing, it would 'promote disrespect for rule of law'. It will also lead to corruption and encourage inefficiency. It might also create possibilities of the 'political machinery' itself becoming 'a participant in the misuse or abuse of power'. Finally, the newly emergent social and economic rights require new kind of enforcement. *I.M. Chaqla* v. *P. Shiv Shankar* (1981) 4 SCALE 1975 at 1991–2.

63. The petition moved by Ms. Indira Jaising asserts the existence of constitutional fundamental right under Article 21 previously uncontemplated by anyone — namely, the right of pavement dwellers in the city of Greater Bombay to dwell on pavements so long as they do not constitute obstruction to pedestrian and vehicular traffic *on the roads*. It also argues that the State is under a corresponding duty to provide them with appropriate house-sites as close as possible to their workplaces. Incidentally, the argument that the State does not have vacant land and therefore cannot perform this duty is not to be taken seriously in this case since in early 1982 the deposed Chief Minister of Maharastra (A.R. Antulay, who is also a Bar-at-Law) invited four justices of the High Court, and in the full glare of television cameras at his residence was seen to hand over to judges scrolls of agreement conveying housing sites. The many applicants for the housing scheme include aside from High Court justices, Chief Justice Chandrachud, Justice P.N. Bhagwati, Justice V.D. Tulzapurkur and Justice D.A. Desai. So the State has enough land as of date to give away for good causes. Pavement dwellers have an equal, if not greater, moral right to housing (while they manage to exist) as justices upon their superannuation. That is in any case what Justice Chandrachud has said, in general terms, in *Kesavananda* (see text accompanying note 28; the 'teeming millions' passage).

64. See U. Baxi 'Laches and the Right to Constitutional Remedies: *Quis Custodiet Ipsos Custodes?*' in *Constitutional Developments since Independence*, p. 559 Indian Law Institute 1975.

65. We here modify Professor Dworkin's felicitious title *Taking Rights Seriously*, 1977. Perhaps in a context like India's one may not take rights seriously if one is unable to take suffering seriously.

66. See *infra*, note 77. Also, U. Baxi, article cited *supra* note 48, at pp. 49–51.

67. The erosion of the Court as an institution did not begin with the 1973 'supersession of judges', but it did accelerate thereafter. During the tenure of Chief Justices Ray and Beg the Court virtually ceased to be an institution and became instead an assembly of individual justices (see Baxi, *supra*, note 42 at x–xi). The intense post-Emergency political criticism of Justices Chandrachud and Bhagwati created in the Court a perception that justices who did not participate in the Emergency decisions had a 'clean' record as against the Emergency *wallahs*; and some justices began to act and react as such. This created considerable pressure on the 'Emergency *wallahs*'

(improperly so called) to recant and reform; and to demonstrate that they were as good, and even better, libertarians than their colleagues. The conscious policy of the Janata Government to elevate those High Court justices to the Supreme Court who had demonstrated 'political courage' during the Emergency reinforced the stereotypes. Now, people, including justices, have began talking about 'Janata Judges' as distinct from the Emergency *wallahs*. For a general account, see Baxi, *Politics, passim*. The tensions were getting resolved to tolerable proportions by 1980. But the public disclosure in March 1980 of a letter written by Justice Bhagwati to Mrs. Indira Gandhi marked the beginnings of an overt conflict between Chief Justice Chandrachud and Justice P.N. Bhagwati. The letter, apart from its deferential tone, contained references to the management of the judicial administration which were readily construed by all and sundry as pointed criticism of the Chief Justice. The Bar was quick to exploit this tension and make it grow. A full account of the processes outlined here must await later analysis. It is necessary to note, however, that to some extent the birth and growth of the social action litigation on the high bench has been somewhat affected by the malevolent forces seeking to pit against each other two of India's most talented and gifted justices.

68. See the section of this chapter entitled 'SAL as an aspect of judicial statespersonship'.

69. *Ibid.*

70. Of course, even these directions are also not readily obeyed. Often, they require reiteration by the Court and a veiled threat of contempt proceedings by the SAL petitioner. Contempt jurisdiction is, more or less, in disuse in the Supreme Court; also, as full scale strategy to implement judicial directions, it may well, if resorted to, prove diversionary and overstrain the already severely strained resources of the SAL petitioner. The Court also prefers in SAL matters to nudge the executive, gently now, sternly on other occasions, into postures of compliance. See, *Dr. Upendra Baxi* v. *State of Uttar Pradesh* (1981) 3 SCALE 1136 *Khatri* v. *State of Bihar* (1981) SCALE 26.

71. The types of innovations required in combating governmental lawlessness and repression require a high degree of collective and sustained judicial activism. The task confronts justices with monumental demands on their judicial craft and creativity. It also makes similar demands on the SAL Bar, both in terms of strategies of argumentation and of deft manipulation of indigenous and comparative law materials.

72. See *supra* note 62.

73. See the notable analysis of executive privilege in the opinions of Justice Bhagwati, Desai and Tulzapurkur in the High Court Judges Case, cited *supra* note 62.

74. See the section of this chapter entitled 'Evidentiary problems in SAL'.

75. See note 70 *supra*.

76. *Khatri* v. *State of Uttar Pradesh* (1981) 2 SCALE 536. Justice Bhagwati held that to accept this argument would be to 'make a mockery of Article 21 and

reduce it to nullity, a mere rope of sand . . .'
77. *Baxi* v. *State of Uttar Pradesh,* cited *supra* note 70.
78. In *Baxi* v. *State of Uttar Pradesh, supra* note 70. Despite strong strictures, the allegations have not ceased. They still continue to be made on affidavit drawn by state counsel; Professor Lotikar and I, as petitioners, were irritated and thought of doing something about this. But on mature reflection, we decided that it was no more than a cheap tactic by state counsel to worry us and divert our limited energies to a knowingly false statement on oath. We instead stated in our reply that in India SAL petitioners are under a duty to face character-assasination in the public interest.
79. In *Associaiton of Social Action and Legal Thought (ASSALT)* v. *State of Madhya Pradesh* the counter affidavit of the State showed that there were three enquiries containing the allegation by undertrials that they were rendered impotent by continuous appliction of electric shocks to the penis. These were young persons, some of them just married, arrested under anti-dacoity operations. We had affidavits made by some of them in our hands. When we asked for disclosure of these documents, and the State furnished a massive 300 page affidavit, the sheer bulk of it moved the presiding judge to ask us to apologize to the police for proceeding on a report in the national weekly! The analysis submitted by us on these reports shows that no real enquiry was made, even once, into the matter! We now await the Court's verdict on this. In *Khatri, supra* note 76, just after the Court ordered the disclosure of various enquiries made by the State into the blindings episode, the state announced that it has now given consent for a Central Bureau of Investigation enquiry.
80. For example, in *Baxi* v. *State of Uttar Pradesh supra* note 70, after a year's protracted litigation, the State has itself shown willingness to amend its rules and prescribe new schemes for rehabilitation, thus, in effect, avoiding a decision on merits of the writ petition. In the Bhagalpur blindings case, too, a similar strategy has been followed.
81. In *Hira Lal* v. *Zilla Parishad* (W.P.1869/80–81) the Court asked Kishen Mahajan and myself to conduct a socio-legal investigation on a complaint by *chamars* that their fundamental right to trade, profession and business was unreasonably being taken away from them (through the system of auctioning to the highest bidder the right in carcass utilization). We submitted a report, based on seven days' intensive fieldwork in some sampled villages in Sarsaul block in Kanput District. We also devised alternate schemes of carcass utilization, after exhaustive discussions with many concerned scientists and developmental administrators. See Upendra Baxi and Kishen Mahajan, *The Chamars and the Supreme Court,* mimeo, 1981. This first experiment seems to have encouraged courts and SAL parties, as well as the State, in further efforts of a similar nature. There is a commission looking into the conditions of migrant bonded labourers in Faridabad brick-kiln industries; and a team of officials appointed by the Court to investigate the alleged violations of labour welfare laws for migrant

and contract labour in the construction of the Asiad stadia and related facilities like the multitude of flyovers now 'beautifying' New Delhi.
82. In *Baxi* v. *U.P., supra* note 70, the Court appointed a panel of physicians and psychiatrists for the inmates of the Home. In *Khatri* extensive investigations by the top-ranking eye specialists in India were ordered to ascertain the precise agent and scope of blindings.
83. In *Khatri* v. *Bihar* two batches of separate petitions reached two different benches. The first presided over by the Chief Justice asked the Registrar of the Supreme Court to conduct the investigations in Bhagalpur jail: in the second, Justice Bhagwati expanded the registrar's mandate somewhat further, while stating that a socio-legal commission would have been a more preferable device.
84. For example, Justice O. Chinnappa Reddy directed the Bombay High Court in *Olga Tellis* v. *State of Maharashtra* to appoint an official to hear and investigate the finding of the Municipal Commissioner that pavement dwellers were constituting an obstruction to traffic on the road. No demolition order can be made without this procedure being fulfilled.
85. Kanput undertrial 'rape' case at *supra* note 54. The Court here asked the District Judge (also an ex-officio chairperson of the legal aid board) to investigate and report.
86. The District Judge, Agra, has been performing this role for about a year in *Baxi* v. *Uttar Pradesh, supra* note 70. Further proceedings embodying the Court's appreciation of the several reports made by him are yet to be reported.
87. Baxi, *Politics*, p. 248-A.
88. See *A.K. Roy* v. *Union, supra* note 61.
89. *Minerva Mills* v. *Union of India* A.I.R. (1980) S.C. 1789; *Waman Rao* v. *Union of India* (1980) 3 SCC 587.
90. See *supra*, note 61.
91. *R.K. Garg* v. *Union of India, supra* note 61.
92. See *supra*, note 89.
93. Ibid.
94. Arising out of a remarkable assertion of judicial power in the Insurance Corporation bonus case.
95. No one seems seriously interested in pressing it just yet. Also, a proper consideration would require a full court; and the Court is always working with many vacancies. Technically, there is no reason why thirteeen justices cannot sit and review a decision given by a similar bench. But then this is not at all a 'technical' matter.
96. These powers it had always had. And short of an elective judiciary, there is really no alternative to executive pre-eminence in judicial appointments in a society like India.
97. The scope of modification consists in the assertion that the opinion of the Chief Justice of India has no 'primacy' over the Chief Justice of High Courts or Governors when their opinions differ on a particular proposal.

98. See U. Baxi, 'Appointment of the Chief Justice and Justices of the Supreme Court of India: How Long Shall We Evade Real Questions?' mimeo, 1981.
99. Ibid.
100. See U. Baxi, *Politics*, pp. 198–209.
101. See U. Baxi, 'Legal Mobilization of the Rural Poor' (paper presented March 1982 to ESCAP Seminar on Law & Participation, mimeo) for detailed elaboration of this typology.
102. The National Committee on the Implementation of Legal Aid Schemes is shortly establishing an autonomous public interest litigation cell. Several groups of lawyers, mostly young, have started small centres of PIL in some High Courts. The Consumer Education Research Centre, at Ahmedabad, is now moving into concerns wider than consumerism and is heavily using court process in all its campaigns. Equally active are organizations like the Free Legal Aid Scheme, Rajpipla; Legal Support for the Poor Programmes organized all over India by Harivallabh Parekh; the Free Legal Aid Clinic at Jamshedpur; the Public Interest Litigation Services, Cochin.
103. Of course, the activism in SAL historically arose first in some High Courts, although the caste-view of judiciary in India has so far forbidden explicit recognition of this fact. The Gujarat High Court, notably through Justice (now Chief Justice) M.P. Thakkar, has been a pioneer in this direction.
104. This kind of attitude arose as senior lawyers found that the docket of Court No. 2 had decreasing scope for priority to their matters.
105. The matter was thus raised by Shri Murli Bhandari, a Senior Advocate and a sometime office-bearer of the Supreme Court Bar Association.
106. They also point out that they have undertaken such litigation at their own initiative and cost (of professional time).
107. See Seervai, *Constitutional Law of India*, pp. 2026–9 (second edition), 1979; U. Baxi, 'On How Not to Judge the Judges', a paper presented to a seminar on *Judicial Process and Social Change*, Delhi, Andhra University, Waltair and the Indian Law Institute, mimeo, 1980.
108. Mr. Seervai's public denouncements after Mr. Justice P.N. Bhagwati's opinion in the Judges case reveal his deep-seated hostility to Justice Bhagwati. He asserts now that one could not have expected any *other* pronouncement from the Justice, since he was the author of the letter to Mrs. Indira Gandhi. Mr. Seervai overlooks the fact that Justice Bhagwati has refused, consistently with his earlier opinion, to allow the transfer of High Court Justices. Mr. Seervai does not also realize that the best course for him would have been to file a protest at the nomination of Justice Bhagwati as a presiding Judge, had Mr. Seervai *honestly* held doubts concerning the judge's integrity. To attack a judge, after arguing a case for over two months, because he failed to hold in favour of counsel, gives the appearance of something just short of professional pique.
109. See *supra*, notes 70 and 80.
110. These include multiple petitions in relation to the same subject matter by different persons, inadequate prior research, variable levels of commitment

and competence and inability to deal with hardened lawyers, mostly state counsel.

111. The National Legal Aid Committee had the services of Dr. Rajeev Dhavan for a report on 'public interest law' in India. Despite my close association with the SAL movement, and despite every research effort, this report (like all government reports) is not available to ordinary mortals. One also fears for its availability upon publication, since most government reports are unpriced and therefore not on sale. See Baxi, *Crisis*, pp. 41–57 on the 'colonial' profile of administration through secrecy.

112. I borrow here my friend Rajeev Dhavan's favourite phrase.

4 'THE FILIPINO IS WHAT HE CHOOSES TO BE'

José W. Diokno

> The Filipino is Muslim; the Filipino is Christian; the Filipino is what he chooses to be.
>
> Eric S. Casino

Introduction

The popular picture of Philippine society is that of 'a patchwork of racial, ideological and linguistic units more diverse and numerous that any other South-East Asian Society'.[1] This picture is somewhat exaggerated, but not basically distorted. The Philippines today is a plural society. One could almost call it a fragmented society: its people are divided by extremes of poverty and wealth; split by conflicts between Christianity and Islam, and within Christianity, by rivalries among different sects; and torn apart by clashes between the creeds of democracy and totalitarianism, self-determination and dependence.

Those divisions are grist for another paper. This chapter focuses on the judicial approach to ethnic differences. Ethno-linguistically, Philippine society is made up of about a hundred different groups.[2] For convenience, however, this chapter subsumes these groups under four broad classifications:

— The majority group, who number about 86 per cent of the total population, and dominates at least 70 of the nation's 77 provinces. They belong to eight major ethno-linguistic groups of westernized lowlanders — westernized in the sense of having not merely adopted but adapted aspects of western culture and integrated them into indigenous culture.

— An Islamic minority who number about 5 per cent of the population of the archipelago. They belong to three major and about ten smaller ethno-linguistic groups, and are concentrated in the lowlands of Mindanao, the second largest Philippine island, which is located at the southern end of the archipelago. They constitute the majority of the population of two provinces.

— A highland minority, composed of six major ethno-linguistic groups comprising about 50 tribes, who number about 9 per cent of the national population. They are spread throughout the country, inhabiting the hills, mountains and forests of the archipelago. They constitute the majority of the population of three provinces. Originally, they were called 'pagan' or 'uncivilized' or 'pagan non-Christian' tribes to distinguish them from Muslim Filipinos, later, 'national' or 'cultural' minorities. Today, they are generally called 'tribal Filipinos'.

— An ethnic Chinese minority, ethnic in the sense that, whether Chinese or Filipino citizens, they retain their language and culture, and in many ways behave as a separate community. They number less than 1 per cent of the population but possess much economic power and control important sectors of Philippine commerce, industry and finance.

The diversity implied in this classification should not blind us to the basic homogeneity of Philippine society. Racially, more than 99 per cent of Filipinos are indistinguishable one from the other: all trace their roots to the same Malayo-Indonesian stock. The more than 80 languages they speak all belong to the same Malayo-Polynesian family. The only exceptions are the tribal Filipinos collectively referred to as Negritos, probably the earliest settlers in the Philippines, who belong to the Negroid race, and the ethnic Chinese. These two groups together are less than 1 per cent of the population. All Filipinos, including Negritos and ethnic Chinese, share a common tradition of resistance to foreign tyranny and a common pool of values: the values of the extended family, particularly the role of mother and children; a fierce defence of personal dignity; a view of land as more than mere property; hospitality; and a longing for freedom, justice and peace.[3]

The evolution of plurality

It is my purpose in this section to ask what transformed so homogenous a people into such a plural society?

The reason lies partly in the country's location. It lies at the rim of mainland Asia, a barrier preventing the Pacific Ocean from swallowing the China Sea. So it has been and is exposed to influences from Asia, the Pacific and the West, which have varied in intensity in different parts of the country.

Partly responsible also is the country's geography. It is made up of a string of 7,100 islands, 2,800 of them inhabited, stretching 1,850 kilometres from North to South, and at its broadest point, 1,062 kilometres from East to West. Its major islands are divided by mountain ranges and broad rivers. Climate and soil differ within and among islands. Geographic differences, of course, lead to differences in language, dress, manners and customs.

However, it was colonialism that chiefly created the plurality of Philippine society. Before the Spanish came to the Philippines, Philippine society had three broad types of population: lowland inhabitants, who resided in settled coastal and river bank communities and lived from fishing, farming and handicrafts; highland and forest inhabitants, including Negritos, who lived mainly from hunting, forest product gathering and swidden farming; and boat people or sea nomads.

An extensive network of trade connected these populations: upland and lowland inhabitants, upstream and downstream communities, and sea nomads. All communities, except sea nomads of whose history little is known even today, were organized in basically the same way, under a *datu* or chief or a counsel of elders, who led the community in war, apportioned farming lands and settled disputes; *maharlikas*, or the well-born 'equals of the *datu* in all respects except authority'; *timawas* or freemen; and *alipin* or bonded servants. Land was, for the most part, communal, although rights of individual possession and use were respected. The people were, as the first Spanish Jesuit mission to the Philippines noted, 'of a happy disposition, candid, loyal and sociable . . . . They have a lively wit and most of them read and write in their own [language].' The *maharlikas* were 'highly cultured and urbane. The men work at various trades in Manila or hold public office in their own and neighboring towns; the women are so skilled in embroidery as in no repect to yield to those of Flanders . . .'.[4]

Coastal villages were also overseas trade centres: there is evidence of yearly trading missions from Manila to Brunei and Malacca, and of Arab, Persian and Chinese traders coming to various Philippine islands. These pre-Hispanic contacts introduced new technologies into the islands. Most important, they introduced the Islamic faith, and led to more centralized forms of political administration. Trading centres like Manila, Cotabato and Jolo flourished into cities. Sultanates were established in Sulu and Cotabato with jurisdiction over several communities. Increasingly, conversion to Islam spread across the archipelago — until Spain came to conquer.[5]

Spain's interest in the Philippines was more than merely to occupy, Hispanize and Christianize the archipelago. It saw the archipelago as desirable less for itself than as a gateway for its merchants to gain a share of the profitable spice trade and for its missionaries to Christianize China and Japan.

But to attain these objectives, it had first to establish a safe base in the archipelago. This was urgent because, when its colonists came, they found themselves confronting Islam here as they had in Spain; Islam was, as noted above, firmly entrenched in the Southern islands and spreading north. But Spain did not then have — and was never able to settle — enough peninsulars to consolidate control over the entire archipelago. So it adopted the following strategy:

First: to concentrate on the coastal villages and their dependencies of central and northern Philippines. This would stop the spread of Islam, provide Spain with the base it needed and, above all, be relatively easy to accomplish, since the villages were not united under a central authority.

Second: to leave the highland villages and the Muslim South for later. The former presented formidable physical barriers, and in any case were not needed immediately as a base. The latter were too well organized, and the Islamic faith gave them reason to fight fiercely and tenaciously, so that to conquer them would require more men and better arms than the colonizing force could count on.

Third: to win over some villages and use their warriors to support Spanish forces in subjugating other coastal and lowland villages.

Fourth: to use whatever methods were expedient to accomplish the task quickly, even if they violated the Royal instruction to win over the natives peacefully, refraining from aggressive acts and using force only in self-defence.

Using this strategy, Spain required less than two decades of bloody, vicious battles to conquer and consolidate control over the coastal regions of Central and Northern Philippines, now known as the Visayas and Luzon. The strategy proved to be an admirable success for Spain, a disaster for the unity of Philippine society. It disrupted the hitherto generally peaceful relations of trade and interdependence among the Muslims of the South, the lowlanders, the highlanders, and the boat people. It separated each of them from the others because, to safeguard its lowland base, Spain had to resettle lowland inhabitants into compact communities 'under the bells of the church towers', isolate them from the unconquered Muslims and highlanders, and control their inter-village and external trade. For some years, in fact, natives were forbidden to leave their villages; and by using warriors from one village to conduct punitive raids or to conquer other villages, Spain created enmities or at least distrust between them which were fuelled by the slave raids that Muslims levelled against central and northern islands in retaliation for punitive raids by Spaniards on Muslim strongholds.

Thus did Spanish colonization divide Philippine society. Since, in addition, Spain was never able to bring either the highland villages or the Muslim lands under its control nor integrate them into one archipelagic society, the divisions persisted to the end of the Spanish era.

Spanish colonial policy — particularly the galleon trade that for two centuries was the base of prosperity for the Spanish community in the Philippines — led to the creation of the last classification in present day Philippine society: the ethnic Chinese minority. To supply the two galleons a year which came to Manila from Acapulco with Chinese silk and other products in exchange for Mexican pesos, Chinese traders brought their goods in junks to Manila. They stayed, at first, to watch over their goods and to collect payment for them. As the trade stabilized, many took up permanent residence and engaged also in other trades or crafts. By the 1580s, they had become so numerous, they were assigned a separate quarter, the Parian, outside the city walls. The Parian became the centre of commerce, and soon the Chinese acquired a virtual monopoly of the retail trade, and expanded into crafts, agriculture, shipping and other industries.

Their success, their distinctiveness and their clannishness created strong racial tensions between them and Spaniards and Filipinos. The tension exploded in several anti-Chinese riots and massacres. The Spaniards, however, could not get along without the Chinese, nor the Chinese without the Spaniards, so that, despite restrictive regulations, Spanish officials tended to favour the Chinese. Near the end of Spanish rule, Rizal, the national hero, complained that to free his countrymen from the clutches of the Chinese traders in Dapitan, Zamboanga, where he had been exiled, he had helped them organize a cooperative, 'but I have to talk long with the local governor who, despite being a good man, is nevertheless partial to the Chinese, and favours them over the inhabitants of Mindanao'.[6]

By the time the United States supplanted Spain in the Philippines, the division of Philippine society into Christianized lowlanders, Muslims, highlanders and Chinese had hardened.

Colonial law and policy

The Spanish Law of the Indies required that Philippine customary laws be respected as far as they were 'not incompatible with our holy religion or with the laws of this book, as well as those they [the natives] have recently made or declared'.[7] At the outset of Spanish colonization, this decree was substantially complied with. In 1589, a Franciscan friar, Juan de Placencia, upon instructions of the Governor General, compiled two reports, one on the 'Customs of the Tagalogs'[8] and another on the 'Customs of the Pampangos in their Lawsuits'.[9] Magistrates used these reports until at least the middle of the eighteenth century to guide them in deciding litigation among natives.[10] Incidentally, the similarity between the customs of lowland Tagalog and Pampango villages reported by Placencia in the sixteenth century and those of highland tribes in Luzon and Mindanao reported by anthropologists like Barton,[11] Dozier, [12] Schiegel[13] and others, in the twentieth century, attests to the common roots of Philippine ethno-linguistic groups, or at least to their common level of development at the start of Spanish colonization.

By the 1880s, however, the Spanish government felt that the lowland villages had been sufficiently Hispanized and Christianized to apply one law to them all. On January 14, 1881, the Spanish Governor General issued a decree that summarized Spanish policy towards the different divisions of Philippine society. The decree provided that settled Christianized communities (lowlanders) would be governed 'by common law', meaning Spanish codal law. It divided 'pagan races' into three classes: 'one, which comprises those which live isolated and roaming about without forming a town nor a home; another, made up of those subdued pagans who have not as yet entered completely the social life; and the third, of these mountain and rebellious pagans . . .' and required that 'the limits of the territory of the rebellious *indios* [natives] shall be fixed and whoever should go beyond the said limits shall be detained and assigned governmentally wherever convenient'. It offered 'rebellious pagans' inducements if they agreed to settle in new towns, and threatened those who did not agree that: 'The armed forces shall proceed to the prosecution and punishment of the tribes, that, disregarding the peace, protection, and advantage offered them, continue in their rebellious attitude on the first of next April, committing from now on the crimes and vexations against the Christian towns'. And with respect to Muslim Filipinos, it stipulated that: 'With respect to the *reduccion* [resettlement] of the pagan races found in some of the provinces in the southern part of the Archipelago, which I intend to visit, the preceding provisions shall be conveniently applied to them'.[14]

In short, Spanish colonial policy towards ethnic minorities was a policy of conform or die. The United States' colonial policy did not differ much from Spanish policy.[15] It was not as punitive of highland villages as Spanish policy had been, but it equalled, if not surpassed, Spanish ferocity toward Muslim Filipinos. It recognized the differences of socio-economic development between the westernized, Hispanized majority, on the one hand, and the Muslim and highland villages, on the other. The former it treated as full-fledged Philippine citizens; the latter as second class citizens, in much the same way as it had dealt with American Indians. When it created the first Philippine legislature, it allowed westernized lowlanders to elect the lower house; but Muslim and highland Filipinos had no representation; authority over them was vested exclusively in the Philippine Commission which was appointed by the United States' President. When the Commission was abolished and an elective Senate became the upper house of the legislature, Muslim and highland Filipinos were allotted seats in the House of Representatives and the Senate, but these were filled by appointment by the American Governor General. A Bureau of Non-Christian Tribes was created to exercise general supervision over the public affairs of Muslim and highland Filipinos. Local governments for westernized lowland Filipinos consisted of regularly organized municipalities and provinces. 'Non-Christian' Filipinos living within the territory of these provinces could be forced to settle in reservations and imprisoned if they refused.

These differences reflected the basic United States policy which viewed Muslim and highland Filipinos as having 'a low grade of civilization' and so insisted on 'civilizing' them, even against their will, in order to achieve a 'complete fusion of the Christian and non-Christian elements populating the provinces of the Archipelago'.[16] The policy had an economic justification: 'the encouragement of immigration into, and of the investment of private capital in, the fertile regions' occupied by Muslim and highland Filipinos.[17]

Philippine law and policy

In 1935, the Philippines became a commonwealth in transition to independence. Among the first steps the Commonwealth took was to abolish most distinctions between the majority and Muslim and highland Filipinos. Representatives of provinces where the latter predominated were elected in the same way as those of other provinces. The same textbooks were used and the same educational, administrative and political systems were applied across the land. Religious and traditional and tribal leadership were not to be permitted to interfere in, or influence the discharge of, the duties and functions of public office.[18] Integration became uniformity.

The basic defect of this policy was that, by failing to respect real religious and cultural differences, it doomed both uniformity and integration to failure. Textbooks, for example, used predominantly westernized examples that tended unconsciously to offend Muslim and highland Filipinos' sensibilities, and denigrate the Islamic faith of the former and the ways of life of the latter. The attempt to do away with religious and traditional leadership was seen by minority groups as an attempt to change the character of their societies. Uniformity, for them, meant psychological, if not physical, death.

Moreover, the policy of uniformity did nothing to change the poor view of the minorities which was held by the majority group and vice versa. 'Moro' (Muslim) or 'Igorot' (highlander) were — and still are — used by westernized Filipinos as derogatory words; on the other hand, the Muslim term for slave is 'Bisaya', the generic name of the people of central Philippines. Muslims believe

'they have a longer history in the struggle for freedom than other inhabitants of the Philippines . . . they resent what appears to them as an attitide of . . . superiority on the part of some non-Muslims . . . neglect, if not outright discrimination, in the distribution of . . . social benefits . . . what they resent most of all is the questioning of their patriotism and loyalty.[19]

On the other hand, the majority cannot erase the memory of Muslim raids during the Spanish era, and of the petitions sent by groups of Muslim leaders in 1920 and repeated on the eve of the Commonwealth in 1935 and of independence in 1946 asking that the Muslim islands of Mindanao and Sulu be retained as American colonies or given independence as a separate state.[20] Much of this mutual rejection still remains. However, as violence continued to erupt in Muslim lands, government policies have undergone changes — at least on the surface.

Today, Muslim Filipinos are no longer lumped with highland Filipinos into one category. The affairs of the former are handled by two 'autonomous' regions comprising ten provinces, and by a Ministry of Muslim Affairs. The affairs of the highland Filipinos are handled by PANAMIN, the office of the Presidential Assistant on National Minorities.

The policy on highland minorities is 'to integrate into the mainstream of Philippine society certain ethnic groups who seek full integration . . . and . . . protect the rights of those who wish to preserve their original lifeways'. To this end, PANAMIN has authority to initiate eminent domain proceedings to acquire property for 'reservations', and its policy in general has been to herd highland tribes into reservations, on land owned by PANAMIN. It has, however, also helped a few tribal Filipinos to acquire title to small plots of land. Among other duties, PANAMIN is required to inspect areas covered by applications for forest concessions to make sure that land occupied by tribal Filipinos is excluded from the grant.[21]

Muslim personal laws were codified on February 4, 1977[22] and a system of Shariat district and circuit Courts established to enforce them. However, no judges have been appointed and the Code remains unenforced six years after its enactment. A 1979 study concludes that the Code was adopted as 'a new means of preserving the old goal of integration/assimilation'; that 'the test of Sharita courts has not even begun and already the prognosis is not good;' and that its major result has been 'immense foreign relations benefit to the Philippine government'.[23]

Exemptions from statutory requirements are granted Muslim and highland Filipinos in the matter of appointments[24] and marriages,[25] special rights to title land have been granted them, and protective requirements on their transactions affecting land have been imposed.[26] Unfortunately, the special rights to title land have never been implemented.

Judicial approaches

Equal protection
The Constitution of the United States never operated in the Philippines.[27] Philippine constitutional law, however, is derived from it; and the Philippine constitutional guarantee of equal protection of the laws has the same scope and effect as the similar provision in the United States' Constitution.[28]

Briefly, the guarantee of equal protection requires that persons or classes in the same situation be treated alike.[29] It does not prohibit reasonable classification provided the latter is based on substantial distinctions that make real differences; is germane to the purposes of the law; is not limited to existing conditions only; and applies equally to each member of the class.[30]

The cases involving ethnic minorities in which this guarantee has been invoked dealt with measures purporting to protect tribal Filipinos by imposing restrictive measures on them, and measures denying aliens the right to acquire lands or engage in certain occupations. Both during the United States' colonial period and after independence, such measures were generally upheld. The following are some examples of such cases.

Rubi v. *The Provincial Board of Mindoro*, 39 Phil. 660 (1919) was a petition for habeas corpus, filed on behalf of a highland tribe who were held on a reservation against their will, under a law that authorized a provincial governor 'in the interest of law and order' to create such reservations and penalized those who disobeyed with imprisonment of up to 60 days. The Court ruled that the law was valid exercise of the police power and did not violate the equal protection clause because the tribe in question were 'citizens of a low degree of intelligence . . . who are a drag upon the progress of the State' and that 'they are restrained for their own good and the general good of the Philippines'. This is, to say the least, hardly an edifying rule. Fortunately, the law is no longer in force.

De Palad v. *Saito*, 55 Phil. 832 (1931), was an action to recover a parcel of land sold by a tribal Filipino without the approval of the Director of the Bureau of Non-Christian Tribes required by statute. The Court upheld the statute as a reasonable protection of people who belong to 'a class . . . easily duped by designing individuals,' and declared the sale void. To the same effect, see the cases *Parkan* v. *Yatco*, 70 Phil. 161 (1940); *Parkan* v. *Navarro*, 73 Phil. 698 (1942); *Madale* v. *Sa Raya*, 92 Phil. 556 (1953); and *Manggayao* v. *Lasud*, 11 SCRA 158 (1964).

U.S. v. *Tubban*, 29 Phil. 434 (1915) involved the question of whether the benefits extended by the Philippine Penal Code to a husband who, having surprised his wife in the act of adultery, kills her or her paramour, could be extended to a highland Filipino who was married under tribal law but not under the Philippine marriage law. The Court answered in the negative. Instead, it considered that circumstance and the fact that he was 'a member of an uncivilized tribe' as attenuating circumstances and reduced the penalty imposed upon him from seventeen years and one day to six years and one day. In a one-paragraph dissent, one justice pointed out that the decision would 'completely wipe out the marriage relations among the wild tribes as an institution and make the relations between those who have married according to their tribal custom adulterous, and their children illegitimate'. Fortunately, as pointed out above, the new Civil Code now explicitly recognizes tribal marriages.

So much for 'legislation enacted to benefit "backward minorities".' What about legislation 'to contain "achievement minorities"'? The Supreme Court has consistently upheld such legislation, though it has never justified it on that ground alone, and, instead, has relied on the police power of the State. The following are some examples.

Prior to the 1935 Constitution, aliens could acquire private land, but not public agricultural land. In *Li Seng Giap* v. *Director of Lands*, 59 Phil. 687 (1934), this prohibition was assailed as an unfair discrimination. The Court rejected the contention because the State has the right 'to the integrity of its territory and the exclusive and peaceful possession of its dominions'.

The 1935 Constitution barred aliens from acquiring both public and private agricultural lands. The question arose whether the term 'private agricultural land' included land used for residential, commercial or industrial purposes. In *Krivenko* v. *Register of Deeds*, 79 Phil. 461 (1947), the Court ruled that it did because, as used in the Constitution, 'agricultural land' refers to all lands other than timber and mineral lands. In *Philippine Banking Corporation* v. *Luis She*, 21 SCRA 52 (1967), revoking earlier decisions, the Court ruled that a Filipino could recover lands sold to aliens if to do so would implement the declared public policy of preserving lands for Filipinos. The Court further ruled that, while aliens could lease private lands (*Smith Bell* v. *Register of Deeds*, 96 Phil. 53 (1954)), they could not combine the lease with an option to buy the land, since that would prevent the owner from disposing of his land and would be a virtual transfer of ownership. So stringently has this disqualification been applied that a Chinese religious organization was held disqualified to acquire lands (*Register of Deeds* v. *Ung Siu Si Temple*, 97 Phil. 58 (1955)). However, the Court held in *Roman Catholic Adm. of Davao, Inc.* v. *Land Registration Commission*, 102 Phil. 596 (1957) that a Roman Catholic Bishop though a foreigner, could have land titled in his name for the church because, as a corporation sole, the Church has no nationality.

In other cases, the Supreme Court has upheld an ordinance that required all commercial receipts to be in Spanish and English (*Kwong Seng* v. *City of Manila*, 41 Phil. 103 (1920)), and laws that limited the operation of public utilities and inter-island shipping (*Smith Bell* v. *Natividad*, 40 Phil. 136) and market stalls (*Co Cheong* v. *Cuarderno*, 83 Phil. 242 (1949) to citizens of the Philippines. In *Yu Cong Eng* v. *Trinidad*, 47. 385 (1925), the Court upheld a law that required all merchants to keep their books of account in English, Spanish or a local dialect. On appeal to the United States Supreme Court, however, the law was struck down (*Yu Cong Eng* v. *Trinidad*, 291 US 500 (1926)) for unfairly discriminating against alien merchants.

The attempt to wrest economic control from Chinese businessmen resulted in a series of laws nationalizing the retail trade (Republic Act No. 3018) and barring aliens from employment in such industries (Anti-Dummy law, Commonwealth Act No. 103). The Court has sustained these laws as valid exercises of the police power, rejecting claims that they violated the guarantee of equal protection. The Court justified the nationalization of the retail trade as 'absolutely necessary to bring about the desired legislative objective, i.e., to free the national economy from alien control and dominance' (*Ichong* v. *Hernandez*, 101 Phil. 1155 (1957)). It sustained the ban on alien employees in *King* v. *Hernaez*, 40 SCRA 792 (1962) and *Universal Corn Products* v. *Rice and Corn Board*, 20 SCRA 1048 (1967) and on alien directors in *Luzon Stevedoring* v. *Anti-Dummy Board*, 46 SCRA 479 (1972). And in *Go Ka Toc* v. *Rice and Corn Board*, 20 SCRA 147 (May 23, 1967), it interpreted the Rice and Corn Law to bar aliens from buying the by-products of rice and corn to manufacture or convert them into another product for purpose of commerce.

If any general rule is to be gathered from these cases it is that, in applying the equal protection clause, the Court will follow declared public policy. The Court explicitly said so in the *Rubi* case:

'Most cautiously should the power of this court to overrule the judgment of the Philippine Legislation, a coordinate branch, be exercised. The whole tendency of the best considered cases is toward non-interference on the part of the courts whenever political ideas are the moving consideration. Justice Holmes, in one of the aphorisms for which he is justly famous, said that 'constitutional law, like other mortal contrivances, has to take some chances,' (*Blinn* v. *Nelson* (1911), 222 U.S., 1). If in the final decision of the many grave questions which this case presents, the court must take 'a chance', it should be, with a view to upholding the law, with a view to the effectuation of the general government policy, and with a view to the court's performing its duty in no narrow and bigoted sense, but with that broad conception which will make the courts as progressive and effective a force as are the other departments of the Government.
Rubi v. *Provincial Board of Mindoro*, 39 Phil. 666. 719.

Political violence

No case of political violence related to ethnic tension has reached the Supreme Court. It is safe to say, however, that precedents laid down in cases of general political violence would be followed. To deal with political violence, the Philippine Constitution authorizes the President to call out the armed forces, to suspend the privilege of the writ of habeas corpus or to declare martial law; the last two only in cases of actual or imminent invasion or rebellion when the public safety requires it, and the first in those same cases and also to meet lawless violence. No constitutional provision spells out the effects of such steps.

During the United States' colonial era, the Supreme Court ruled that the suspension of the privilege of the writ of habeas corpus raised a political question that the Court could not review (*Barcelon* v. *Baker*, 5 Phil. 87 (1905)). This doctrine was adhered to after independence (*Montenegro* v. *Castanaeda*, 91 Phil. 882 (1952)). However, the later case of *Lansang* v. *Garcia*, 42 SCRA 488 (1972) revoked it and ruled that the Court could determine if the Executive, in suspending the privilege of the writ of habeas corpus, had gone beyond the constitutional limits of his jurisdiction and had acted with patent arbitrariness. This rule was followed in *Aquino Jr.* v. *Ponce Enrile*, 59 SCRA 183 (1974) and *Aquino* v. *Military Commission No. 2*, 63 SCRA 546 (1975). But in two recent decisions, *Garcia-Padilla* v. *Enrile*, G. R. No. 63188, April 20, 1983 and *Morales* v. *Enrile*, G. R. No. 61016, April 26, 1983, the Court revoked *Lansang* and returned to the *Barcelon* ruling.

A simplified but substantially accurate summary of current case law on the extent of Presidential power in situations of grave emergency is that:

1. The Court may not inquire into the validity of a Presidential declaration of material law or suspension of the privilege of habeas corpus, or even of orders issued by the President under authority of these emergency measures such as orders of arrest or orders to kill resisters (*Garcia-Pailla* v. *Enrile*, G.R. No. 63188, April 20, 1983).

2. Upon the declaration of martial law, the President acquires the power to try civilians by military courts (*Aquino Jr.* v. *Military Commission No. 2*, 63 SCRA 546 (1975)); to order the detention of persons without bail (*Buscayno* v. *Military Commission*, 109 SCRA 273 (1982)), and to legislate not only on matters to repel invasion or quell insurrection and to remove their causes, but also to meet an economic crisis brought about by world recession (*Aquino Jr.* v. *Commission on Election*, 62 SCRA 275 (1975)).

3. By suspending the privilege of the writ of habeas corpus, the President acquires the power to order the preventive arrest of such persons as he may deem necessary to meet the existing or threatened danger of rebellion or insurrection and to deny them bail which, under normal conditions, they would be entitled to under the Constitution (*Gacia-Padilla, supra;* Morales, *supra*).

4. The question of whether the President complied with constitutional requirements for the issuance of warrants of arrest is immaterial, since the Court cannot review his decision (*Garcia-Padilla, supra; contra,* Morales, *supra*).

It is evident that these rulings run counter to international law (see cases cited in N. Questiaux, *Question of Human Rights of Persons Subjected to Any Form of Detention or Imprisonment*, UNESCO Document E/CN 4/Sub. 2/1982/IS, pp. 15-19). The decision in both *Garcia-Padilla* and *Morales* are pending reconsideration, but the possibility is remote that the Court will change its mind.

Land

Land is vital to tribal and Muslim Filipinos. In *Carino* v. *Insular Government*, 7 Phil. 132 (1906), the Supreme Court denied an application by a highlander for a Torrens title to his land because the petitioner could not show any grant by the State, possession under claim of ownership not being enough, since prescription could not run against the State with respect to public agricultural land. On appeal to the United States Supreme Court, the decision was reversed. The Court ruled that 'when, as far back as testimony of memory goes, the land has been held by individuals under a claim of private ownership, it will be presumed to have been held in the same way from before the Spanish conquest and never to have been public land'; that prescription was recognized by the laws of Spain even against crown lands; and that a contrary doctrine would deny native titles 'for want of ceremonies which the Spaniards would not have permitted and had not the power to enforce'and of which 'presumably a large part of the inhabitants had never heard'(*Carino* v. *Insular Government*, 212 US 449 (1909)). The *Carino* case was followed in *Abaog* v. *Director of Lands*, 45 Phil. 518 (1932).

The rule laid down in these cases, coupled with the rule that, when applicants for land titles have complied with the conditions of the statute of 'open, continuous, exclusive and notorious possession and occupation of agricultural lands of the public domain' for thirty years (Public Land Act, Commonwealth Act No. 141, Sec. 48), they are 'deemed to have acquired, by operation of law . . . a government grant without the necessity of a certificate of title being issued'(*Herico* v. *Dar*, 95 SCRA 437, 443), would seem to recognize native title to lands of tribal and Muslim Filipinos and offer them a simple way of protecting their rights.

This is not as obvious, however, as it may seem for two reasons. Muslim and highlander Filipinos are reluctant to submit their rights to adjudication under national law, because they believe it to be unfair to them. In *Meralco* v. *Castro-Bartolome*, 114 SCRA 801 (1982) and *Republic* v. *Villanueva*, 114 SCRA 875 (1982) followed by *Republic* v. *Garong*, 118 SCRA 729 (1982), the Court ruled that possession for thirty years was not enough — only possession since time immemorial would presume a grant by operation of law. But the major difficulty with these rulings is that they are based on the western, modern concept of private property which requires identifiable owners who are natural or juridical persons. This concept runs squarely against custom law under which tribal lands are predominantly communal land, owned by the tribe which is not a person in law. Modern Philippine law has no concept of communal land. Indeed, anthropologists have criticized efforts by legal scholars to propagate the rules in *Carino* and *Herico*, arguing that these rules betray an ignorance of tribal law and customs. Also inserting these rules into tribal society would insidiously alter tribal ways of life and could make it easier for non-minority groups to acquire tribal and ancestral lands.

If minority rights to land are to be preserved, the need for Philippine law and jurisprudence to develop legal protection for communal lands is urgent. As the Episcopal Commission on Tribal Filipinos said, in 1981, 'Our tribal and Muslim brothers are at a critical juncture in their history. Their very survival is under threat of manifold attack, centred on the very basis of their culture and livelihood — their land.'

Judicial Fact-Finding
It is not the practice in the Philippines to use Judicial Commissions, primarily because, under Philippine constitutional law, Courts exercise judicial power only, and may not be required — and are not allowed — to perform other functions. They are, in fact, prohibited from rendering advisory opinions (*Manila Electric Co.* v. *Pasay Transportation Co.,* 57 Phil. 60 (1932)).

Judicial fact-finding by the Supreme Court, therefore, has been limited to litigation reaching it. In such cases, the Supreme Court has to receive evidence either *en banc* or by a commissioner, and, in exceptional cases, to holding closed door briefings given by the military *Lansang* v. *Garcia*, 42 SCRA 448, 446—467 (1982)). As long as the parties to the case are given the opportunity to hear the evidence or brief, or are notified of the matters the Court proposes to take judicial notice of, and are permitted to present their side, there would seem to be no ground to assail the procedure.

In a working paper on a declaration of basic duties, the Regional Council of Human Rights in Asia proposes the following policy on national minorities:

1. It is the duty of government to recognise that tribal peoples and other national minorities have the same rights as other citizens including

the right to participate on an equal basis in public life. It is moreover the duty of government to enforce respect for the right of such peoples to preserve their identity, traditions, language, culture, heritage and ancestral lands, providing them with all care and facilities to incorporate themselves into modern ways of life, but respecting their right to determine for themselves the pace, manner and extent of assimilation into the larger society.

2. Provided government acts in accordance with this Declaration, it is the duty of tribal peoples and other national minorities to exercise their rights with due respect for the legitimate interests of the national community, respecting their territorial integrity and political unity of the nation.

This policy would not equate integration with assimilation or unity with uniformity. On the contrary, it seeks to establish a unity based on diversity that would be more stable and longer lasting than forcing homogeneity, for it would remove the apprehension of minority groups that they are being pressured into change and that their customs and ways of life are threatened. It would also help reduce the attitudes of distrust and dislike between social groups.

Of course, the best way to adopt the policy is by legislation. The Bar, with its peculiar talent and opportunities for persuasion and education, could play a vital role in helping this come to pass.

There is perhaps one other way in which the Bar and the Bench could bring such a policy into being: by using the equal protection clause, both negatively and positively, not merely to prevent discrimination but to promote equality. The Philippine constitution provides that social justice shall be promoted (1973 Constitution, Art. II, Sec. 6.) Moreover, it commands that 'the state shall consider the customs, traditions, beliefs and interests of national cultural communities in the formulation and implementation of state policies' (1973 Constitution, Art. XV, Sec. II). Equality, social justice, respect for cultural minorities — these are potent weapons for an activist policy by Bench and Bar to promote the well-being of tribal and Muslim Filipinos; for their welfare is also the nation's welfare.

Notes

1. T.J.S. George, *Revolt in Mindanao*, Kuala Lumpur, Oxford University Press, 1980, pp. 13–14.
2. *Statistical Handbook of the Philippines 1976*, Manila, National Census and

Statistics Office, pp. 1, 16; 'Profile of Tribal' in *Tribal Forum*, September–October, 1981, pp. 2 ff; Fredrick L. Wernstedt and J.E. Spencer, *The Philippine Island World*, Berkeley: University of California Press, 1967, pp. 1, 13; Eric Casino, 'Sulayman's Manila' in *Rediscovery*, Cynthia Nograles Lumbera and Teresita Gimanez Maceda, (eds.), pp. 27–8.

3. Leon Ma. Guerrero, 'Encounter of Cultures: The Muslim in the Philippines' in *Rediscovery*, op.cit., p. 464: 'Profile of Tribal and Muslim Filipinos' in *Tribal Forum*, op. cit., p. 25; Fr. Eliseo Mercado, OMI, 'The Moro Struggle in Perspective', in *Sandugo*, 2nd Quarter, 1982, p. 8; Alfonso Felix (ed.), *The Chinese in the Philippines*, Manila, Solidaridad Publishing House, 1966, two volumes, particularly pp. 240–50.

4. H. de la Costa, S.J., *The Jesuits in the Philippines, 1581–1768*, Cambridge, Mass, Harvard University Press, 1961, pp. 12–14.

5. Casino, op.cit.; Guerro, op.cit.; Alfred W.McCoy and Ed C. de Juan, (eds), *Philippine Social History*, Quezon City, Ateneo de Manila University Press, 1982, pp. 361–444.

6. Teodoro M. Kalaw, compiler, *Epistolario Rizalino*, Bureau of Printing, 1930, Vol.5, Part I, p. 669.

7. Book 2, Title 1, Law 4, decree of the Emperor Charles and Princess Regent Joanne, at Valladolid, August 6, 1555.

8. Emma Helen Blair and James Alexander Robertson (eds), *The Philippine Islands 1493–1898*, (Taiwan Reprint), Vol. VIII, pp.–173–96.

9. Ibid., note 8, Vol. XVI, pp. 321–9.

10. Fr. Francisco de Sta. Ines, *Cronica de la Provincia de San Gregorio Magno*, Manila, Chafre y Comp., 1892, p. 591.

11. *Ifugao Law*, Berkeley, University of California Press, 1969; *The Kalingas*, Chicago, Chicago University Press, 1949.

12. Edward P. Dozier, *Mountain Arbiters*, Tucson, University of Arizona Press, 1966.

13. Stuart A. Schlegel, *Tiruray Justice*, Berkeley, University of California Press, 1970.

14. Reproduced in *Rubi* v. *Provincial Board of Mindoro*, 39 Phil. 666, 674–9 (1919).

15. *Rubi* v. *Provincial Board of Mindoro*, 39 Phil, 666, 679–81 (1909).

16. Public Act 2674, Sec.3.

17. *Report of the Department of the Interior 1917*, quoted in the *Rubi* case, *supra*, Note 14.

18. Mamintal Tamano, 'Problems of the Muslim' in *The Muslim Filipinos*, Peter G. Gowing and Robert D. McAmis, (eds.), Manila, Solidardad Publishing House, 1974, pp. 261–2.

19. Cesar Adib Majul, 'The Muslims in the Philippines; An Historical Perspective' in *The Muslim Filipinos*, see p. 11, note 19.

20. T.J.S. George, op.cit., pp. 66–7, note 1.

21. Presidential Decree No. 1414, June 9, 1978.

22. Presidential Decree No. 1083, February 4, 1977.

23. G. Carter Bentley, 'Islamic Law in Christian Southeast Asia' in *Philippine Studies*, 29 (1981) 45–65.
24. Republic Act No. 2260, Sec. 23; PD No. 1414, Sec. 5.
25. Civil Code of the Philippines, Acts 78 and 79.
26. Commonwealth Act No. 141, Secs. 44, 48, 120; PD No. 410.
27. Philippine Bill, Act of July 1, 1902, 32 US Statutes at Large 691, Sec. 1.
28. *Smith Bell* v. *Natividad*, 40 Phil. 136, 144 (1919).
29. *Tolentino* v. *Board of Accountancy*, 90 Phil. 83, 90 (1951).
30. *People* v. *Cayat*, 68 Phil. 12, 18 (1939).

5 PLURALISM AND THE JUDICIARY IN SRI LANKA

H.L. De Silva

The ethnic phenomenon

Some of the most serious challenges to the successful working of democratic government, not only in the developing world, but all the world over,[1] have been the unresolved tensions and conflicts produced by the phenomenon of diverse ethnic groups in societies which are not homogeneous in character. It would be a mistake to regard such phenomena as valueless survivals of a tribal stage of social organizations that will eventually disappear with more urbanization. It would be futile to think that they will become extinct with the growth of more cosmopolitan environments and cultures that arise alongside modern industrial and commercial societies. On the contrary the age-old ties of religion, race, language and perhaps, to a much less extent, caste have shown a remarkable vitality and not simply a capacity for survival. By their continued insistence on their separate existence and distinctiveness, ethnic groups have contributed an extra dimension to the economic and social problems that are already complex enough in the modern world.

Ethnic divisions are an ambivalent value which makes it impossible to adopt a single or consistent attitude in regard to such phenomena. On the one hand, they are intrinsically a highly divisive force in society which impedes the growth of a desirable unity of outlook and vision, which are so necessary if humanity as a whole, and each nation individually, is to cope successfully with the numerous problems that beset them. The tensions which are produced by such differences and the prejudices which are endangered by ethnic differences are a great obstacle to progress and a colossal waste in terms of human effort and available resources.

On the other hand, however, ethnic differences are not a wholly negative factor. Throughout history they have also been a unifying force which has given disparate agglomerations of people a sense of community and a group identity. This sense of a larger unity has enabled the growth of distinctive cultures of great value. This is particularly true in the case of language, which has been a great force for cohesion among people and a vital medium for the expression of human creativity. Likewise the genius of each religion and each particular religious vision has contributed to our understanding of life and contributed to human progress. Ethnic divisions are an integral part of human existence and have by their very diversity and uniqueness contributed richly to the sum total of man's happiness. They symbolise the glories of human civilisation and are therefore worthy of preservation for the future.

The government of plural societies

In any state where ethnic divisions exist under a governmental system based on the democratic principle of majority rule, both the negative and positive aspects of the ethnic phenomenon have to be borne in mind. The problem of government in plural societies is basically one of seeking to do justice between the different groups and communities which exist within the state. While recognising their just claims to autonomy in particular areas, it is necessary to maintain a proper balance between the competing interests of these groups and the integrity and unity of the state.

In particular the task of all the organs of government, including the judiciary, is to seek to translate the theory of democracy into democratic practice, which is no doubt a task of great complexity and difficulty. In plural societies the success of this enterprise not only depends upon the adoption of wise policies of social and economic development which take into account the ethnic factor, but also calls for a proper understanding of the human mind and personality as expressed through the various ethnic groups, each with its own individual ethos. In seeking solutions there is a need to understand and take account of the elemental drives and motivations behind human nature, including the dark irrational element. It is also necessary to analyse the course of prejudice[2] and the apparently deep-seated antagonisms between groups. These antagonisms are thought to have originated in past history, some of which are mythical and some real. It is also important to evince a sympathetic understanding of the fears and apprehensions concerning ethnic identity. No successful adjustment or compromise is possible unless there is an appreciation of all these factors. It is therefore a complex task and the solution of problems of this kind require the combined wisdom and knowledge of all intellectual disciplines and the skills of men of wide and varied experience. Indeed there may be no final solutions, only a continuing problem which one has to live with till the end of time.

Why the judiciary?

The general tasks of government and administration fall within the sphere of politics, and the question may be asked why particular attention is focused on the judiciary as an instrument for their solution. Have the legislative and the executive branches of government been found to be inadequate mechanisms? Can the judiciary, which is the weakest organ in terms of coercive power, be expected to succeed where the other branches of government have so far failed to come up with solutions? Or is its role to be more limited — a complementary one, in conformity with the constitutional theory of the distribution of governmental powers, yet strengthened by the assumption of greater responsibility in this particular task? It need hardly be said that the judiciary cannot presume to supplant the legislature or executive branches in the solution of ethnic problems. It may be said that it cannot even assume a role of dominance. But there are many areas where ethnic problems may have become aggravated by reason of the failure of the judicial branch to function effectively and fulfil its legitimate role and the consequent failure to inspire confidence in its ability to do justice.

Several reasons may explain why the judiciary is in a unique position to be a more effective instrument for the reconciliation of ethnic problems. In most democratic systems the judges enjoy a unique status. Their relative permanence of tenure and irremovability, except for cause, make them less vulnerable to day-to-day pressures and passing waves of passion and this affords opportunities for a more dispassionate consideration of competing claims. Selected as they are from a group of professional men who are specially trained to make decisions in terms of principle rather than expediency, disregarding extraneous matters and irrelevancies, it is said that they are better equipped to deal with these issues which are often overlaid by a highly emotive element.

By and large the higher judiciary is composed of men with a wide outlook and broad interests (who have a greater capacity for balanced judgement on such questions than those who are engaged in the hurly burly of life), who have political impartiality, integrity and independence and have enjoyed a symbolic prestige, standing as they do between citizen and citizen and between the citizen and power of the State in the vindication of legal rights.

Practical realities of the power structure

In any realistic appraisal of the role of the judiciary, however, it is necessary to take into account existing constraints which are part of the constitutional structure and the harsh realities in the practical exercise of political power and their impact on the judiciary. Specifically, we must take cognizance of its limited capacity to exercise coercive powers, its dependence for financial resources, and the general unwillingness on the part of the other organs of government either to give up their powers or even to share them to any substantial extent. While the judiciary has enjoyed a certain prestigious position, which is increasingly becoming more vulnerable in certain states, it is well to recognise its relative impotence in terms of the present realities of the power structure — a condition of infirmity which one dares to hope will not remain either permanent or irreversible.

Objections to an activist role

It is also necessary to consider the objections of those who oppose the idea that judges can and ought to make a more significant contribution to the business of government in situations of conflict, and who resist any attempt on the part of the judges to play a more creative and dynamic role than is the case today. To ascribe such a vital role to a relatively elitist group, it is argued, is to question the fundamental assumptions of democracy under which the elected representatives of the majority exercise supreme power. But are not the assumptions of democracy and the ultimacy of the popular will valid only in a homogeneous community, holding a commonly accepted set of social and cultural values and broadly common economic interests? When that homogeneity of interest is not present, must there not be a countervailing check in the interests of justice? It is therefore necessary for us to consider the rationale for specially assigning to the judiciary a more creative role in the quest for justice among groups with divergent interests arising from their multi-racial and multi-linguistic differences and religious and cultural diversity. It is argued that the assumption of such wide powers is to politicise the judiciary and this would eventually erode its tradition of impartiality and independence. It is even questioned whether members of the judiciary itself can transcend the influence of their own ethnic background and environment, considering that they themselves are drawn from these very groups with their deep-seated cleavages and loyalties that are not so easily jettisoned. In what way can the judiciary assume a more activist role without endangering its credibility as an impartial and independent institution?[3]

Judicial review of legislative and administrative action

One of the essential tasks of the judiciary in plural societies is the protection of the rights of ethnic groups in cases where there are violations of legal rights by the organs of the State — whether legislative or executive. The function of judicial review of the acts of the legislature is sometimes expressly conferred by constitutions which contain guarantees of fundamental rights and freedoms. Yet even there the right of judicial review of legislation, as in a controlled constitution, which may be logically considered to be an essential function of the judiciary, is not beyond controversy.[4] There has been less objection to the judicial control of executive and administrative action. These twin methods of control are the principal modes by which the judiciary is called upon to fulfil its proper role in democratic societies.

The reason why such a function is thought to be appropriately vested in the judiciary is presumably because it is felt that unreasonable attitudes, a narrow and illiberal spirit and the antagonism commonly found among the different ethnic groups that compose society are less frequently found among members of the judiciary than is the case with elected representatives of the legislature and members of the executive. No doubt the assumption is that the judiciary is more likely to be just and fair in ensuring the observance of such basic rights and freedoms. Yet the history of judicial review of legislation and administrative action in many jurisdictions has not always justified this assumption.[5]

Values and the judicial process[6]

The popular notion of a judicial decision is that it is a concomitant of the application of exclusively legal rules or principles through a process of strictly logical reasoning and the ascertainment of a solution which is capable of being arrived at with certainty and as a matter of objective discovery. The part played by judicial discretion in the decision-making process and the sense of justice of the judge himself, (largely a matter of the values he holds sacred, which in turn are partly the result of his own upbringing and experience) is greatly underplayed. Yet many perceptive observers of the judicial process have stressed the individual and subjective element of the judge himself who in a very real sense does make law and does not merely find that which is already made awaiting discovery. What is emphasised is the part played by the values accepted by the judge, what Justice Holmes described as 'the inarticulate major premise of judicial reasoning'. They remain inarticulate because of the reluctance to acknowledge the part they play in decision-making, which would disturb the illusion of an impersonal and objective result which lies at the base of popular confidence in the law.

Yet it would be far more advantageous where ethnic problems are concerned for there to be a frank recognition of the ends or purposes which the legal order is expected to subserve and the ultimate values which the judiciary must seek to uphold. This is especially so because there is no accepted body of legal doctrine or precedents in the resolution of ethnic problems which is capable of being easily applied in the context of these peculiar problems. When there is present before the Court a choice of alternative avenues of approach, what determines the exercise of the judge's discretion is its capacity to realise the ultimate ends of the legal order. This is not always easy to discern because of the many claims of interests which lead to a conflict of the values themselves. The declaration of fundamental rights and freedoms, and the restrictions or limitations which are regarded as permissible on such rights and freedoms, in themselves raise questions of value, not to speak of the directive principles of State policy found in many constitutions, which, though not enforceable, are guiding principles and which cannot be ignored. In fact they are now being relied on in justification of affirmative action programmes which seek to relieve inequality.[7]

Background to ethnic problems

The degree of ethnic heterogeneity in Sri Lanka is in a sense unique for a comparatively small country. With a land area of a little over 65,500 square kilometres, there are four major racially distinct groups (where inter-marriage is unusual) and four major religious communities and two major divisions of language groups. As at 1977 out of a total population of 13.7 million, the Sinhalese comprise 72 per cent, the Sri Lanka Tamils 11.2 per cent, Indian Tamils 9.3 per cent, the Sri Lanka Muslims 6.5 per cent and the balance, 1 per cent, comprise the Burghers and Eurasians, the Indian Muslims, Malays and others. Among the religious groups the Buddhists comprise 67.3 per cent, the Hindus 17.6 per cent, Christians

7.9 per cent and the Muslims 7.1 per cent. Sinhala is the official language of the administration and is spoken mainly by the Sinhalese, while Tamil is spoken by both groups of Tamils and a very large percentage of the Muslims. Together Tamil-speaking persons constitute approximately 27 per cent of the total population. English is a link language spoken by a small though influential section of all races (estimated at less than 10 per cent) as a second language.[8]

The main focus of ethnic rivalry is between the Sinhalese and the Sri Lankan Tamils. During the period preceding political independence the main disputes related to the question of greater representation for the minorities as a whole in order to pre-empt the apprehended disadvantages of a legislature dominated by the Sinhalese majority. With political Independence and the Constitution of 1948 the character of the agitation altered and centred round problems flowing from the policies of the governments that subsequently took office. The problem areas relate to the use of Sinhala as the official language in the transaction of public business without due recognition of the rights of the Tamil-speaking people, employment opportunities in the State services and the public sector, opportunities for admission to the institutions of higher education, Government-sponsored colonisation in the Northern and Eastern Provinces which seeks to alter the demographic character of the areas which are now predominantly inhabited by Tamils, the lack of an adequate programme of economic development for areas inhabited by Sri Lankan Tamils, and the demand for greater autonomy in administration at the regional level in the predominantly Tamil areas.

The demand for a separate state is a latter-day demand and is an outgrowth of the continuous frustration flowing from these unresolved problems. The exacerbation of tensions between the two communities which has led to violence on a mass scale even as at the time of writing, could well result in separatism hardening into a demand in its own right on which compromise may be impossible.

Judicial decisions in the post-Independence period

There is a singular dearth of judicial authority in Sri Lanka concerning the protection of ethnic interests which could be used to illustrate representative judicial attitudes to this problem. Presumably, one reason for this is the lack of any constitutional guarantees of any specific fundamental rights in the Constitution that accompanied the grant of independence (except through the safeguards provided by Section 29 of the Ceylon (Constitution) Order in Council of 1948),[9] which would have enabled the Court to be a forum for such disputes. The strategy of the political leaders of the Tamil community, which was the only significantly vocal group, was in the main directed to securing greater representation in the legislature and the leadership does not appear to have had much faith in legal safeguards for the protection of these rights and interests.

Citizenship and franchise

A convenient starting point would be the decision relating to citizenship and the franchise. The Citizenship Act and the Ceylon (Parliamentary Elections) Amendment[10] drastically restricted the voting rights of a very large number of the Indian Tamil community. It was beyond dispute that the imposition of stringent requirements as to birth in Ceylon (which in some cases required proof that one's paternal great-grandfather was born in Ceylon) resulted in a large number of Indian Tamils being disenfranchised. These two Acts were challenged in *Mudanayake* v. *Sivagnanasunderam*[11] and *Kodakam Pillai* v. *Mudanayake*[12] on the ground that they contravened Section 29 of the Constitution which provided that Parliament should not make any law rendering persons of any community or religion liable to disabilities or restrictions to which persons of other communities or religions were not made liable or confer upon persons of any community or religion any privileges or advantages which were not conferred on persons of other communities or religions. It was in essence a provision which provided for equality before the law and the equal protection of the laws. The Supreme Court rejected the contention that the legislation was *ultra vires* on the ground that the language of these provisions was free from ambiguity and that therefore their practical effect and the motive for their enactment were irrelevant, and refused to permit the admission of affidavits which would have established the harsh operation of these provisions on the Indian community. The Court also declined to look at the Soulbury Report on Constitutional Reform, other State papers and political documents which indicated the object behind this constitutional provision and those relating to the franchise.

The Court's approach was surprisingly narrow considering that it was interpreting a constitutional provision and not an ordinary statute. The Court even doubted whether section 29(2) was intended to be a safeguard for the minorities alone and went on to observe that 'such intention has not been manifested in the words chosen by the Legislature.' It refused to look at the practical effect of the legislation, socially or politically, or consider the motive for their enactment as relevant.

In the final appeal made to the Privy Council[13] the approach was less narrow. The Privy Council accepted the position that there may be circumstances in which legislation, though framed so as not to affect directly a constitutional limitation, may indirectly achieve the same result and that, in that event, the legislation would be *ultra vires*. In the consideration of that question the Privy Council admitted the relevancy of the reports of Parliamentary Commissions, thus differing from the view of the Supreme Court. Yet in the final result they dismissed the appeal on the ground that the maxim *omnia praesumuntur rite esse acta* was applicable to an Act of the legislature and held that they were not prepared to attribute to the leglislature motives or purposes or objects which were beyond its power. In its view there had to be affirmative evidence that the law was enacted as part of a plan to effect indirectly something which the legislature had no pwer to achieve directly.

It is difficult to accept these decisions as being correct upon any realistic appraisal of what was plainly a carefully planned move to alter the balance of representation in the legislature. Both courts did not give serious consideration to the whole object and purpose of Section 29, which was intended to be a real safeguard for the minorities. The Supreme Court thought it fell short of an equal protection clause and distinguished the American cases on what appear to be insubstantial grounds. The Privy Council appears to have thought the evidence adduced to support discrimination as being insufficient and relied on the presumption of regularity.

If the legislation could not be invalidated in these particular cases for lack of sufficient evidence it is somewhat surprising that there were no subsequent challenges upon fuller material, especially when the revision of the electoral registers would have provided ample evidence for the effect of the legislation on the Indian community. These decisions had a profound effect on the subsequent political history of Sri Lanka, as seen by the significant shift of political power after the 1952 election, to the detriment of the minorities. What is more, the rather restrictive view taken as to the efficacy of Section 29 as a safeguard of minority interests appears to have demoralised minority groups to such an extent that they were discouraged from carrying on any further agitation before any judicial forum for many years thereafter. Had these decisions gone the other way, the political history of modern Sri Lanka would in all probability have been quite different.

The schools legislation

A legislative measure which had a great impact on a minority religious group was the Assisted Schools and Training Colleges (Special Provisions) Act of 1961[14] which vested in the State all privately managed schools and training colleges which received grants-in-aid from the State except where the management opted to provide the same service without levying any fees. By reason of the fact that a very large number of the schools so affected were Roman Catholic schools, it was commonly felt that this was a measure directed specifically against the Roman Catholics with a view to reducing the influence of the Church as a centre of power. Unlike the citizenship legislation, this legislation did affect other religious groups as well, though to a very much less extent. No challenge was sought to be made through the Courts and a political compromise appears to have been reached.

The language legislation

The Official Language Act[15] which made Sinhala, the language of the majority community in Sri Lanka, the sole official language was enacted in 1956. Although it led to a great political upheaval and to the communal riots of 1958, it did not give rise to any challenge in the Courts till long afterwards mainly because of the hardships created thereby came to be felt only with the gradual implementation of the legislation. Predictably it arose in consequence of certain disadvantages suffered by a Tamil public officer in the case of *Attorney-General* v. *Kodeswaran.*[16] This took the form of a declaratory action in respect of a Government circular which prescribed a certain degree of proficiency in the official language as a condition of promotion to the higher grades. The circular impugned both on the ground that it was issued pursuant to the Official Language Act, which, it was contended, violated Section 29 of the Constitution and was therefore invalid, and also on the grounds that it was in breach of a fundamental term of contract of the plaintiff with the State (at that time the Crown in Ceylon) which he had entered into prior to the enactment of the Official Language Act. The plaintiff claimed that he was otherwise eligible for promotion and that his increments had been wrongly withheld.

The original court held with the plaintiff on both grounds and granted him a declaration that the circular was invalid and not binding on him. On an appeal by the State, the Supreme Court set aside the judgement on the ground that a Crown Servant had no legally enforceable contract of employment which meant that the plaintiff had no legal right which could be made the subject of a declaration and that accordingly it was unnecessary to pronounce on the constitutional issue. The Privy Council[17] reversed the decision of the Supreme Court on the ground that while a Crown Servant held office at pleasure, it did not prelude him from claiming the salary due to him under the contract. The constitutional issue was thus by-passed, and, as it turned out, the plaintiff in the case retired from the public service. It appears that no interest was shown in pursuing the question of the validity of the Act in terms of the provisions of equality under the Constitution. Such issues remained open questions, considering the view expressed in the District Court.

Section 29 would probably have passed into the limbo of constitutional history as a pathetically inefficient sentinel of ethnic rights, at any rate as interpreted by the Courts, had it not been for an *obiter dictum* of the Privy Council, in the course of the decision in *Ranasinghe* v. *The Bribery Commissioner*[18] which, however, had nothing to do with any ethnic question. In that case Lord Pearce while observing that the provisions of Section 29 'set out religious and racial matters which shall not be the subject of legislation' (i.e. of discriminating kind) went on to add, 'They represent the solemn balance of rights between the citizens of Ceylon, the fundamental condition on which *inter se* they accepted the Constitution and these are unalterable under the Constitution.' This raised a lively controversy on the question whether it really meant that this provision was outside the pale of the amending process in the Constitution for all time. The question was raised whether this was a limitation on the sovereignty of the Sri Lankan Parliament and whether it meant that any future amendment contemplated the concurrence of the Parliament of theUnited Kingdom.

Further, the inconclusive decision in the *Kodeswaran Case* on the validity of the Official Language Act and the far-reaching views expressed by the Privy Council in *Leanage* v. *The Queen*[19] which raised strong doubts as to the extent of the legislative power of the Sri Lankan Parliament led to a strong reaction on the part of the newly formed United Front Government, which came to power in 1970. The United Front Government had little patience with this exhibition of 'judicial valour'. In fact the decision not to have recourse to the amending process provided by the 1948 Order-in-Council and to summon instead a Constituent Assembly was partly motivated by apprehensions concerned such views and with the object of overcoming such problems. The climate of political opinion in 1970 after the landslide victory of the United Front was decidedly unfavourable to any idea of conceding to the judiciary any significant measure of power *vis-à-vis* the legislature. The 1972 Constitution in fact bears clear evidence of a determined strategy to confine the judiciary to a less important role.

Constitutional provisions regarding language (1978)

One of the principal causes for the aggravation of ethnic differences and communal disharmony in Sri Lanka was the failure to accord to the Tamil language, the language of a substantial ethnic group, a recognised legal status in the transaction of official business. This was to a large extent remedied by the constitutional provisions of 1978 which gave Tamil along with Sinhala the status of a national language. These provisions[20] further enabled representatives to the legislature and any local authority to perform their duties and discharge their functions in these bodies in such national language. The Constitution also granted a person the right to be educated through the medium of either of the national languages. It also gave certain rights in regard to the use of the national languages in the institutions of higher education. The Constitution also provided for the use of the Tamil language as the language of administration, for the maintenance of public records and the transaction of all business by public institutions in the Northern and Eastern Provinces. More importantly, it granted to any person the right to receive communications from, to communicate with and to transact business with any official in his official capacity in either of the national languages. It also granted the right to be examined through the medium of either of the national languages at examinations for admission to the public service and to participate in court proceedings in either of the national languages.

Since these constitutional rights also created corresponding public duties, they were enforceable in the courts through orders in the nature of writs of mandamus, and a further special remedy for their enforcement was granted in Article 126. Thus their enforceability and justiciability was put on the same basis as the fundamental rights recognised by the Constitution. Although it is not affirmative evidence of the due observance of these provisions, it is significant that there has been only one instance where a complaint of infringement of language rights has been made to the Supreme Court. Considering that this court is empowered not merely to give directions but also to grant relief, which has now been interpreted to mean damages or compensation for violation of such rights by state officials, it may be said that language rights of the major ethnic groups are granted adequate protection by the courts. The award of damages directly against the public official concerned where he acts contrary to administrative direction will certainly go a long way to eliminate one of the major irritants in the matter of ethnic relations *vis-à-vis* the State.

Problems of university admissions

In spite of the significant expansion of State-funded facilities for higher education during the last decade, it is a fact that a very large number of students who achieve levels of fitness prescribed for entrance to university are shut out for lack of places. There is accordingly very keen competition for the available places. This is a problem[21] which many countries in the developing world have in common with the developed world, although it is much more acute here. The problem has in Sri Lanka come to acquire the character of a major political issue with an ethnic significance chiefly because of the high prestige value attached to university education and the insistent demands made by the Sinhala majority to correct an imbalance in the matter of university admissions. It is generally agreed that this imbalance is partly due to the high proportion of schools equipped to prepare students for the more prestigious courses in the university in the Jaffna district in relation to the rest of the Island. Though this was due partly to historical reasons arising from the pioneering efforts of Christian missionaries in the nineteenth century, it has been held to give Tamil students advantage over students of other communities as reflected in the statistics for admissions. In the mid-1970s, due to strong demands by a certain section of the majority community, the Government adopted a complicated system of standardization of marks on a language basis in order to redress the balance, and this system led to a severe reduction in the number of Tamil student admissions. Presumably because the mechanics of this scheme were not fully explained nor understood, no attempt was made to challenge the validity of this scheme, which had all the external indications of being discriminatory. Although the 1972 Constitution did not provide a special remedy similar to Article 126 of the 1978 Constitution, there is no room to argue that the fundamental rights enacted in 1972 were not justiciable. Yet strangely enough no constitutional challenge was made to this system of admission in the Courts.

With the formation of the new Government in 1977, this form of standardization was abandoned, and the University Grants Commission adopted a new formula which was *ex facie* not directed against any community but sought to achieve (though not overtly) a greater balance as between the different ethnic groups in proportion to their numerical strength.

Under this scheme admission to the university was to be decided on the basis of raw marks obtained at the prescribed entrance examination but according to certain quotas. Thirty per cent of the available places in each course of study were to be filled according to the order of merit reckoned on an all-island basis. Fifty-five per cent of the places in each course of study were to be allocated to the twenty-four administrative districts into which the island was divided, in proportion to the district population, and these places were to be filled according to the order of merit within each district. The remaining fifteen per cent was to be allocated among twelve administrative districts, which were deemed educationally under-privileged, in proportion to their population. Of these districts, four were in areas traditionally populated by persons of the Tamil community.

The new scheme was challenged on the basis that it violated the principle of equality in *Seneviratne* v. *The University Grants Commission*,[22] but not on the ground that there was involved any racial discrimination as such. Yet the overall effect of implementing it was to give added weight to students in areas populated by the Sinhalese. The case is important because of the Court's attitude to the question of affirmative action taken by the State to remedy an existing imbalance, though it is not expressly based on any consideration of ethnic representation as such. The contention was that the limitation of the merit quota to a mere 30 per cent was itself a violation of this principle of equality. Following certain decisions of the Indian Supreme Court, the Supreme Court of Sri Lanka upheld the scheme of admissions. In its view the university had the right to determine the sources from which admissions should be made 'after having made an overall assessment of the needs of the country and taking into account particularly the position of persons or classes of persons who may be underprivileged or handicapped.' The Court held that the criterion adopted was not arbitrary and had a rational relation to the object to be achieved.

The Court was not prepared to hold that the failure to adopt the criterion of excellence in performance at the examination as the sole criterion for admission violated the principle of equality. It held that the UGC was justified in not adopting this as the sole criterion as it would confer an unfair advantage on students in urban areas which had the advantage of better secondary educational facilities. Pointing to the direct connection between the lack of educational facilities and the difficulties in obtaining employment and the causes of social and economic discontent in the country, the Court held that such a policy was justified in the context of the Government's plans for regional development. In this approach the Court appears to have found support in the Directive Principles of State Policy, especially paragraphs (b) and (h) of Article 27(2) of the Constitution. This was probably the first occasion when the Supreme Court of Sri Lanka, following the decision of the Indian Supreme Court in *Kesavananda Shanti* v. *State of Kerala*,[23] accorded the Directive Principles 'a place of honour' in the Constitution and considered them to be the 'social conscience' of the Constitution. The Court went further and observed:

It is a settled principle of construction that when construing a legal document the whole of the document must be considered. Accordingly, all relevant provisions of the Constitution must be given effect to when a constitutional provision is under consideration, and when relevant this must necessarily include the Directive Principles . . . these provisions are part and parcel of the Constitution and . . . the courts must take due recognition of them and make proper allowance for their operation and function.

This seems to imply that as far as Article 12 is concerned, in determining whether there is an infringement of the principle of equality, the Court would take into account any relevant Directive Principle of State policy that is relied on by the executive. If this is so, the party complaining of discrimination could equally invite the Court to consider the question from the point of view of another principle of state policy which is also relevant and on which he relies. The Court would then find itself faced with competing principles of State policy, the consummation of which are all equally desirable but which in the situation are conflicting. This would certainly involve the Courts entering upon questions of policy. It would entail the Court exercising a preference or choice of directive principles and on the whole adopting a markedly activist role in its decisions. It is unlikely that any popularly elected government in Sri Lanka would countenance the judiciary adopting such a role. When the Court takes into account the directive principles of State policy in effect it means taking some step towards their enforcement. How is this possible when Article 29 specifically says that they do not confer legal rights or impose legal obligations and are not enforceable in any court or tribunal? Article 29 is a clear 'no-entry' sign to the judiciary as far as any question of any legislative or executive act being held unconstitutional on the ground that it is violative of a directive principle of State policy is concerned. It is questionable whether the directive principles can be relied on in order to determine the scope or amplitude of a constitutional provision, especially the section on Fundamental Rights.

Furthermore, in the Sri Lankan Constitution, unlike in the Indian Constitution, the operation of the equality clause and the equal protection clause contained in Article 12(1) is made subject to Article 14(7) under which restrictions may be prescribed by law for the protection of the interests therein named. The legislative restrictions on the principle of equality that may be made are of such amplitude that very wide invasions of the principle of equality are permissible, which could in the result evacuate the notion of equality of all significant meaning. For instance, in view of Article 14(7) it would be permissible to impose a restriction on equal treatment for the purpose of securing due recognition and respect for the rights and freedoms of others or of meeting the just requirements of the general welfare of a democratic society. The legislature would have the power to provide, through statute, a programme of affirmative action in the interests of any group, whether it be a minority or the majority, which is in fact preferential treatment of that group, so that any erosion of the principle of equality would be permissible only through legislative action and not through any administrative or executive action. Since such laws do not require a two-thirds majority Article 14(7) by itself substantially reduces the effectiveness of the equality principle.

The views expressd by the Supreme Court in *Seneviratne's* case seem to have opened wide another door to the executive through which far-reaching incursions into the principle of equality may be made, in order to implement directive principles of State policy. The question then arises whether the Court may adopt a similar approach in regard to the interpretation of other fundamental rights and call in the aid of these principles of State policy, in order to test the validity of executive or administrative action. The danger is that even legal concepts, which are reasonably precise, may become so blurred in their practical application that great uncertainty would result from this approach.

The problem of violence

During the last five years particularly, there has been an increasing tendency towards violence and the use of force among certain groups of persons in the North in the agitation for the establishment of a separate state for the Tamils. This led to the enactment in 1978 of a law for the proscription of a group known as the 'Liberation Tigers of Tamil Eelam' and other similar organizations. After its repeal, the Prevention of Terrorism Act was passed in 1979, in which clear restrictions were placed on certain fundamental rights. Departures from the ordinary rules of a criminal trial in the interests of national security and the maintenance of public order were also provided for. The operation of these laws has in turn given rise to allegations of various illegal acts and other excesses of authority on the part of the police and the armed forces, in combating the threats to the maintenance of law and order. The Courts have in judicial proceedings arising from such acts in the main treated these outbreaks of violence and counter-complaints against the armed services in much the same way as other cases of criminal acts which are free of such racial overtones. The main criticism has been against the stringency of the laws themselves and not against any judicial attitude towards such cases.

In the applications made for habeas corpus by *Senthilanayagam and three others*,[24] alleging that their arrest was illegal, that they had been tortured while in custody and questioning the validity of detention orders made by the Minister of Internal Security, the Court of Appeal applied the principles laid down by *Christie* v. *Leachinsky*[25] in determining the validity of their arrest and held the arrests to be legal. The allegations of torture were not substantiated by any medical evidence indicative of such acts, and in the nature of the case there was no corroboration apart from the détenus' own statements. The detention orders were impugned on the ground that where there was evidence of the commission of a defined offence the police were obliged to produce the suspect before a Magistrate and have him remanded until the conclusion of his trial. It was further contended that the concept of 'unlawful activity' in the legislation did not embrace substantive offences and that accordingly orders were permissible only in such cases. The Court did not accept this contention and held that the object was to facilitate investigations and interrogation of both categories of persons and their confederates in order to achieve the object of eradicating terrorism. The Court was of the view that before an order under section 9(1) could be made there had to be objective grounds and a rational basis for belief or suspicion that the suspects were engaged in unlawful activity, and that the Court was entitled to examine the material on which the Minister based his order to satisfy itself of its validity. The Courts have hitherto expressed grave concern where there have been allegations of unlawful invasions of liberty and examined such allegations with scrupulous care.

The question of persons detained in custody being subjected to torture at the hands of the armed services has been brought before the courts in proceedings taken under Article 126 of the Constitution. *In Velmurugu*

v. *The Attorney-General and another*[26] the Court was, *interalia*, concerned with the questions (1) whether the alleged criminal acts had in fact been committed by members of the armed forces (2) whether the Assistant Superintendent of Police into whose custody the complaint had been originally taken was responsible for such acts and (3) whether, in that event if such acts had been done contrary to governmental directions the application was maintainable under Article 126 as being an infringement by 'executive or administrative action.' On the first question the Court found itself seriously handicapped by its own procedural rules which only provided for the production of affidavits and counter-affidavits. The allegations of the petitioner were denied by the respondents, and the Court was divided three to two in rejecting the allegations as unproved mainly because the medical evidence did not support his story. This appears to be quite unsatisfactory procedure where the question naturally turns on the credibility of witnesses and there now appears to be a willingness to allow cross-examination of the deponents of such affidavits. In regard to the second question, too, the Court was similarly divided, the majority rejecting the allegation that the Assistant Superintendent had instigated the alleged acts.

'Executive and administrative action' as a jurisdictional limitation

On the third question there appears to be some uncertainty, as differing views have been expressed. Sharvananda J. observed:

If the State invests one of its officers or agencies with power which is capable of inflicting the deprivation complained of, it is bound by the exercise of such power even if in abuse thereof. The official position makes the abuse effective to achieve the flouting of the subject's fundamental rights. The State has endowed the officer with coercive power and his exercise of its power, whether in conformity with or in disregard of fundamental rights, constitutes 'executive action.' The official's act is ascribed to the State for the purpose of determining responsibility, otherwise the constitutional prohibition will have no meaning.

On this view the State is held to be responsible even though 'what the official did constituted an abuse of power or exceeded the limits of his authority'.

Wanasundera J. while accepting the position that unlawful acts done by a public official through 'over zealousness in carrying out duties' would make the State liable and that the liability extends even to the acts of subordinate officers who 'constitute the decision-making core of the administration' held that, in the light of the affidavits of the three Service Commanders (the Army, the Navy and the Air Force) and also of the Inspector-General of Police who stated in categorical terms that they had at no time authorised, encouraged or condoned unlawful acts or breaches of discipline among their personnel, *such acts could not be regarded as a liability of the State as a matter of law.* Elsewhere in the judgement, however, he has expressed a different view and said that he is inclined to the view that the State should be held strictly liable for any acts of its high State officials, and that if in the case before him the allegations against the Assistant Superintendent had been proved, they would have constituted an act of the State itself and would have entailed the liability of the State for such acts. He has stated specifically:

The liability in respect of subordinate officers should apply to all acts done under colour of office i.e. within the scope of their authority, express or implied and should also extend to such other acts that may be *ultra vires* and given in disregard of a prohibition or special directions provided that they are done in furtherance or supposed furtherance of their authority or done at least with the intention of benefiting the State.

In the light of these observations it would be difficult to sustain the final conclusion reached by him on the question whether it would constitute exclusive or administrative action on the evidence of affidavits alone. The other two judges who formed the majority expressed no view on this question in view of their findings on the facts. It is not clear whether these views expressed here were limited to cases of infringement of Article 11, which has 'a preferred position' among other fundamental rights in the constitution. Article 11 requires for its amendment not only a two-thirds majority but also approval at a Referendum.

On the other hand, the Supreme Court has taken an inexplicably narrow view as to whether acts done by public corporations carrying on commercial business and not performing traditional governmental functions constitute 'executive or administrative action' for the purposes of Article 126. Thus in *Wijetunga* v. *the Insurance Corporation*[27] it was held that the Insurance Corporation of Sri Lanka, which took over almost the entirety of insurance business in Sri Lanka after nationalization (and not only the insurance of State property and government liability risks), was *not an organ of government or an instrumentality of the State* so as to make it amenable to the Courts' jurisdiction. The petitioner's complaints of violations of his freedom of speech and expression and freedom to join a trade union were thus rejected on the jurisdictional issue. Such a narrow view is not justified by the provisions of the Constitution itself and has ominous implications in a plural society where complaints of discrimination on ethnic grounds are not infrequent. Considering the vast areas of commercial trading activity in the hands of Government corporations it would be anomalous to exclude them from the protection of Article 126.

Right of protest and demonstration

The freedom of thought and conscience, of speech and expression, of peaceful assembly and association are the mainsprings of democracy and are especially so in a plural society. The successful working of democracy depends on the practical effectiveness of these guarantees and not on their elaborations in constitutional documents. Judicial sensitivity to these questions of ultimate concern is therefore of vital importance because the erosion of these freedoms by any authoritarian regime takes subtle forms and rarely does it assume the form of an undisguised frontal attack. Although there is a strong tradition of freedom of speech at political meetings in Sri Lanka, there appears to be a lesser degree of tolerance of demonstrations of protest which take less conventional forms. Even non-violent forms of protest in the shape of publicly undertaken fasts, public acts of *satyagraha* and peaceful picketing appear to invite unlawful interference by opposing groups, leading to their abandonment, without any protection from the authorities responsible for law enforcement. The conventional forms of action and the technical requirements as to evidence and proof result in there being no judicial protection for these rights. This is an area of rights which calls for judicial innovation by affording an adequate remedy. The current judicial view as to the responsibility of state officials for the violation of fundamental rights, even when contrary to express directions, suggests a basis for their extension to cover cases of omission or failure to provide protection to demonstrators.

The prevailing judicial attitudes to these rights are on the whole conservative. In *Dr Neville Fernando and others* v. *Leanage*[28] the petitioners who were the shareholders of the 6th Petitioner-Company complained that the printing works established by the 6th Petitioner-Company had been closed and sealed up on the orders of the Secretary to the Minister of State under the Emergency Regulations and that they were prevented from engaging in the business of commercial printing in violation of their freedom to engage themselves in association with others in any lawful occupation, business or enterprise which was guaranteed to them under Article 14(1)(g). When the petitioners sought leave to proceed with their application the Court, *ex mero motu*, rejected the application on the ground that they lacked standing. The Court observed:

No one except those whose fundamental rights are directly infringed by executive or administrative action can complain of such infringement in proceedings under Article 126. A complainant cannot succeed because someone else in whom he is interested has been hit by such an act. Articles 17 and 126 make it competent only to the person whose fundamental rights have been infringed by executive or administrative action to avail himself of the special remedy provided by Article 126.

The 6th Petitioner was held disentitled on the ground that the right under Article 14(1)(g) was given only to a citizen and as it was a company it had no such rights. The 1st to 5th shareholders were held to be disentitled on the ground that having regard to the fact that the company had a separate legal personality the shareholders had no direct proprietary right in the company's property. The Court elected to follow the decision of the Indian Supreme Court in *State of Gujerat* v. *Ambica Mills*[29] in preference to the view expressed in *Bennet Coleman & Co.* v. *Union of India*.[30]

Unfortunately this view places greater emphasis on a doctrine in company law which has been evolved for the purpose of that law, and fails to give full meaning and vitality to the fundamental rights in the Constitution, which is the very bedrock on which the legal super-structure stands. There is often a lamentable failure to pay heed to the famous words of Chief Justice Marshall, 'We must never forget that it is a Constitution we are expounding.'[31] In more recent times the Privy Council[32] in interpreting the provisions as to fundamental rights in the Constitution of Bermuda gave expression to a similar view. Lord Wilberforce observed that they '. . . call for a generous interpretation avoiding what has been called "the austerity of tabulated legalism" suitable to give to individuals the full measure of the fundamental rights and freedoms.'

The strict view taken by the Supreme Court has serious implications for the exercise of many other fundamental rights where the right is limited to citizens. This is specially so where freedom of speech and expression which includes publication is concerned. In the world of today individual rights of expression are often submerged by the mass media, and it is only the organised expression of views which can effecitvely influence public opinion. To deny this to a group which has resorted to the available legal procedures such as incorporation, for the greater protection and safeguarding of these rights, is a great disadvantage and an impediment to minority groups seeking to protest through constitutional channels. Likewise incorporated bodies of trustees of places of religious worship would be faced with problems of standing when asserting their freedom to manifest their religious beliefs in worship, observance, practice and teaching under Article 126.

In *Dr. S.N. Fernando* v. *The Attorney-General*,[33] the petitioner, who joined in a demonstration of protest against the arrest and detention of certain Christian clergymen and others taken into custody under the Prevention of Terrorism Act, complained of the denial of freedom from illegal arrest and freedom of peaceful assembly. The Respondents denied the allegations and countered that the petitioner was a member of an illegal procession which when ordered to disperse, attacked the police leading to his arrest and detention. The Court did not accept the petitioner's version of these events and held that he had taken part in an illegal procession in contravention of certain provisions of the Referendum Act. The procession was also held to be illegal because no notice of it had been given to the police in terms of Section 77(1) of the Police Ordinance. Although the police had in making the arrest acted on the basis of certain emergency regulations, which were not in force at the time, the Court held that the police had in fact 'the power to act in the way they did and [that] it did not matter if they purported to do it with reference to the wrong provision of law', relying on its own decision in *Vijaya Kumaranatunga* v. *Samarasinghe*.[34] The Chief Justice observed:

> The Petitioner was informed that he was part of an illegal procession and that is sufficient reason for the arrest. The Police do not have to quote chapter and verse from statutes and legal literature to justify the arrest. There is no obligation on the Police to quote the law applicable.

A stricter view appears to have been taken in *Vivienne Goonewardene* v. *Hector Perera and others*.[35] The petitioner was leading a procession on Women's Day carrying banners of protest against the American presence in Diego Garcia, the high cost of living and other matters. She was arrested by a Sub-Inspector of Police (not any of the named Respondents) for participation in a procession without a permit and refusing to disperse when ordered to do so. The court held that the Sub-Inspector of Police had no legal authority to order the processionists to disperse, since he was below the rank of an Assistant Superintendent and that the processionists were within their rights to ignore such orders and the arrest was illegal. The Court held that the State had adopted the action of the Sub-Inspector and was liable for such infringement. The Court agreed with the formulation of the principle of State liability as expressed by Sharvananda J. in *Velmurugu's case*. The Court took the view that with the enactment of the fundamental rights 'the Constitution has created a new liability in public law,' adopting a view expressed by Lord Diplock in *Maharaj* v. *The Attorney-General of Trinidad and Tobago*.[36]

Commissions of inquiry

The Commissions of Inquiry[37] enables the appointment of a Commission to inquire into and obtain information, *inter alia*, as to any matters in respect of which, in the opinion of the President of the Republic, an inquiry will be in the interests of public safety or welfare. It empowers the recording of evidence of witnesses and permits the admission of evidence which might be inadmissible in civil or criminal proceedings. If summoned to give evidence, attendance before the Commission is compulsory and a refusal to attend or answer questions is punishable as contempt by the Supreme Court. There appears to be only one instance of such a Commission being appointed to deal with ethnic problems and that was in November 1977 following a widespread outbreak of communal violence between the Sinhalese and the Tamils in the months of August and September that year. A former Chief Justice of the Supreme Court, Mr. J.C. Sansoni, was appointed to ascertain the circumstances and the causes that led to the acts of violence, death and injury to persons and the destruction and damage to property during this period.

The hearings lasted nearly eighteen months, 953 witnesses testified before Sansoni and the appearance of over 100 lawyers was noted! The record of proceedings ran to over 15,000 pages. The report[38] itself is mainly concerned with an examination of the immediate causes which led to the outbreak of the incidents and reveals a frightening picture. There is a remarkable degree of objectivity in handling controverted issues of fact which is no doubt attributable to the Commissioner's judicial training and his own eminence as a judge. Although an examination of the underlying causes of communal conflict has not been attempted in any great depth, the Commission has afforded a valuable opportunity for an open-ended expression of views which is of undoubted value. What is more, an objective appraisal of disputed facts is often a useful starting point for dialogue and remedial action.

The inquisitorial method of inquiry which this kind of proceedings envisages is well suited for the understanding of problems of ethnic conflict, in regard to which there is a great deal of ignorance and prejudice. The success or failure of this kind of inquiry, particularly when it is by one man, depends a great deal on his capability for impartial and independent judgement, and since this is not always realised in practice, this procedure may not always be found to be acceptable.

Concluding comments

In any appraisal of the role of the judiciary the basic assumptions and expectations of the ordinary man centre round its qualities of integrity, impartiality and independence. At any time and in any place its high prestige must rest on these foundations. Even its capacity for erudition in the various disciplines apart from the law and clearness of vision appear to be less important considerations. Its uniqueness and value depends on the possession of these near-divine qualities which are not in any realistic degree expected of those who inhabit the world of politics. The judiciary's claim to play a greater role in decisions that affect the community depends on the realization of these virtues. It is these very qualities that are constantly under threat from every side, and unfortunately not least from the weaker brethren within the institution itself.

The present situation in Sri Lanka is the gradual outcome of historical events that began with the attainment of independence and the consequent release of the new political and economic forces which followed with independence. Yet in the last two decades there have appeared symptoms of a crisis which has ominous consequences for the future. The new Constitution of 1978, despite the enactment of some forty-two Articles which relate to the judiciary, has the same basic weakness in regard to the vesting of the judicial power which afflicted its predecessor — 1972 Constitution. In Article 4 of the Constitution it is stated that the judicial power of the people shall be *exercised by Parliament* through the Courts, tribunals, and institutions created and established by law, subject to a reserved area in which it may be exercised directly by Parliament, viz in respect of its own privileges and immunities. In contrast the executive power of the people, including the defence of Sri Lanka, is directly exercisable by the President of the Republic elected by the people. It may be asked why, if the executive power is directly vested in the President, the judicial power should not be similarly vested in the judiciary which is also an organ of State power?

The argument that both Parliament and President are directly elected by the people is not a convincing one for distrusting the judiciary, which is another organ of government whose independence and integrity is specially sought to be safeguarded in the Constitution, quite apart from the final sanction of removal for misbehaviour. What is more, it is their very independence from the transient changes of popular opinion that make for impartiality and integrity of thought and decision by the judiciary. Sensitivity to popular opinion is not always a safe basis for doing what is fair and just and can often be an impediment.

Most governments in any part of the world do not like the idea of sharing power and are suspicious, if not intolerant, of challenges from competing sources. While they profess to value judicial independence, in practice their actions create the impression that they desire a subservient judiciary with only the trappings of independence. Governments are averse to subjecting themselves to external scrutiny and are not anxious to submit their acts to any objective judgement. Hence the frequent appearances of restrictions on judicial review in recent legislation. The desire to continue to enjoy power without fetter or restraint is the besetting sin of governments and this is reflected in all those who wield political power.

It is an undoubted fact that every administration tends to resent decisions which cause them a loss of political prestige, and despite possessing vast powers to secure any desired end, they are nevertheless anxious to appear morally just before their own people and world opinion. Even if they do not obtain the moral advantage of a judicial verdict in their favour they are at least concerned to avoid judicial criticism or censure, which would be hurtful to their public image, even when their actions are far from righteous in the view of any right-minded person. It is the moral authority which attaches to their office and the judicial imprimatur which the judges must seek at all costs to preserve and not cheaply barter away for a 'mess of potage'.

On the other hand political parties in opposition when bereft of political power are champions of judicial independence. Often they find that even their just claims and the recognition of their basic rights, and sometimes even the possibility of their political survival, are in jeopardy because of the weakened state of the judiciary to which they themselves contributed while in office. A government which while in office has undermined judicial independence, whether it is by acts of harassment or blandishment, cannot reasonably expect an independent judiciary when out of office. Likewise it must be remembered that an opposition which has suffered at the hands of a weak and ineffective judiciary cannot be expected to respect genuine independence when in the seats of power.

The greater its sense of resentment by being denied protection when in opposition, the more extreme will be its attitude towards the judiciary, which it has ceased to respect, when it assumes power.

Such attitudes on the part of governments and politicians must inevitably destroy independence and kill for ever what is surely among the most precious and cherished of our institutions. Of course in this process it is not only the government that has to bear responsibility and blame. Judges are equally responsible if they display weakness at time of crisis in their differences with the government. Any deviation from the strict norms of independence and impartiality will render the whole institution vulnerable and ultimately bring about its final liquidation and absorption as an arm of the executive.

Judicial independence is a value which stands above the conflicts and stresses of the political arena. While it is true that judges are sometimes inevitably drawn into the maelstrom of politics in the course of the performance of their functions, both politicians and judges have to recognise the fact that the permanent values of impartiality and independence need to be safeguarded and not sacrificed for temporary ends.

Certain observable tendencies in the relations between the government and the judiciary in Sri Lanka, especially during the past decade, do not augur well for the future. The situation is likely to deteriorate if all political parties do not agree on a *modus vivendi* which would ensure a place of respect and dignity for the judiciary, which is an institution of immeasurable value in the whole democratic system. This is of vital importance and an essential precondition if the judiciary is to play any significant role in the resolution of ethnic conflicts and tensions in our society.

Notes

1 Anthony D. Smith, citing Walker Connor, gives the following pattern of ethnic diversity: of the 132 independent states in 1971, only 12 were ethnically homogenous, representing 9.1 per cent of the total, while another 25 (or 18.9 per cent) have a single ethnic community comprising over 90 per cent of the state's population. A further 25 have a single ethnic community comprising 75–90 per cent of the population and 31 have an ethnic community representing 50–74 per cent of the state's population. On the other side, in 39 states (or 29.5 per cent) the largest ethnic group comprised less than 50 per cent of the popultion; while in 53 states (40.2 per cent) the population is divided into more than five significant groups. Accordingly he concludes that ethnic pluralism rather than ethnic homogeneity appears still to be the norm.

The Ethnic Revival in the Modern World, Cambridge, Cambridge University Press, 1980, pp. 9–10.

2 Gerhart Saenger, *The Social Psychology of Prejudice*, New York, Harper & Brothers, 1980.

3 J.A.G. Griffith, *The Politics of the Judiciary*, London, Fontana Press, 1985 (3rd ed.).

4 K.C. Wheare, *Modern Constitutions*, Oxford, Oxford University Press, 1960.

5 J.A.G. Griffith, ibid. pp. 189–202; The Judgement of Justice Marshall in *Regents of University of California* v. *Bakke* (1978) 98 Sup. Ct. 2733, at pp. 2799–805.

6 R.W.M. Dias, *Jurisprudence*, London, Butterworth, 1976, Chapter 9.

7 *Seneviratne* v. *The University Grants Commission*, S.C. Application No. 88 of 1980 S.C.M. 27.10.80.

8 *Statistical Pocket Book of Sri Lanka, 1977*, Department of Census and Statistics, 1977.

9 *Legislative Enactments of Ceylon* (1956 edition), Vol. XI Chap. 379.

10 *Lesislative Enactments of Ceylon* (1956), Vol. XI Chaps. 349 & 381.

11 (1953) **53** NLR 25.

12 (1954) **54** NLR 433.

13 *Ibid.*

14 Act No. 8 of 1961, *Legislative Enactments* — Supplement (1966) Vol. 2 p. 732.

15 Act No. 33 of 1956, *Legislative Enactments* — Supplement (1966) Vol. 2 p. 1.

16 (1967) **70** NLR 121 (S.C. Decision).

17 (1969) **72** NLR 337 (P.C. Decision).

18 (1964) **66** NLR 73.

19 (1965) **67** NLR 193.

20 Articles 19 to 25 of the Constitution of the Democratic Socialist Republic of Sri Lanka.

21 C.R. de Silva, 'The Politics of University Admissions — A review of some aspects of the admission policy in Sri Lanka (1971–1978)', **1** *Sri Lanka Journal of Social Science*, no. 2.

22 S.C. Application 88 of 1980 decided on 27.10.80.

23 (1973) A.I.R. (S.C.) 1461.

24 H.C. Application Nos. 10/81 to 13/81 decided on 10.9.81.

25 [1947] A.C. 573.

26 S.C. Application No. 74 of 1971 decided on 9.11.81.

27 S.C. Application No. 87 of 1982 decided on 29.11.82.

28 S.C. Application No. 116 of 1982 decided on 14.12.82.

29 (1974) A.I.R. S.C. 1300.

30 (1974) A.I.R. S.C. 106.

31 *M'Culloch* v. *The State of Maryland*, U.S. Law Reports 4 Law Ed. 597, 602.

32 *Minister of Home Affairs* v. *Fisher* [1979] 3 All E.R. 21.

33 S.C. Application No. 2 of 1983 decided on 16.3.83.

34 S.C. Application No. 121 of 1982 decided on 3.2.83.
35 S.C. Application No. 20 of 1983 decided on 18.6.83.
36 [1979] A.C. 385.
37 *Legislative Enactments of Ceylon* — Vol. XI, Chap. 393.
38 Sessional Paper VII of 1980.

6 THE SRI LANKAN JUDICIARY AND FUNDAMENTAL RIGHTS: A REALIST CRITIQUE

Radhika Coomaraswamy

> To accept jurisprudential adulthood the question is not any longer whether or not judges make law. Rather the questions are: what kind of law, how much of it and in what manner
>
> Upendra Baxi

For six years during the period of the Republican Constitution (1972–8) not one case for fundamental rights was decided on by the Supreme Court. The Constitution of the Democratic Socialist Republic of Sri Lanka was enacted in 1978. Of the twenty reported cases on fundamental rights filed before the Supreme Court during the period April 1979 to December 1981, only one case was decided in favour of the citizen or groups of citizens who brought their grievances before the judiciary.[1] Subsequently, however, four important cases, including *Vivienne Goonewardene* v. *Hector Perera* and *Ratnasara Thero* v. *Udugampola*, were decided in favour of the petitioners. The first led to a violent demonstration in front of the houses of the deciding judges. The second led to the promotion of one of the respondents cited in the case as being responsible for violating the rights of the petitioner.[2] The other two important cases which have been decided in favour of the petitioners are *Kapugeekiyana* v. *Hettiarachi* on illegal detention and the other, *Guna-ratne* v. *The People's Bank*, on the freedom of association.

Both the 1972 Constitution and the 1978 Constitution contain Bills of Rights, though those enumerated in the latter Constitution are more elaborate and comprehensive. But, what do these rights mean in real terms? What do the judges actually do in fact? The quality of fundamental rights is not determined so much by the potentialities inherent in a piece of formal legislation but in the reality of specific cases decided by actual courts. It is in this spirit that the present critique is written. It is motivated by a realistic concern over the nature and quality of actual fundamental rights protection in post-independent Sri Lanka.

What are the cases before the court?

Those cases which have come before the judiciary in recent years with regard to fundamental rights litigation appear to have the following characteristics. The most popular type of case is found under the *equal protection* clause. These cases usually concern allegations of discrimination in the area of education and employment. Promotions, transfers and demotions are prevalent in these grievances. In a developing society, these types of complaints are especially important as they deeply affect employment possibilities as well as status in society. It is therefore perhaps natural that many of the fundamental rights cases are concerned with these issues, and the court's experience in this area has allowed for the growth of judicial doctrine.[3] The Court has recognised equal protection in terms of the need for 'reasonable classification' and the application of that classification to particular cases of fact situations.

The second most popular area is that of *trade union* action, whether in terms of the right to join a trade union or with regard to the right to strike and peaceful assembly. The courts have remained reticent in their interpretation of these rights. However, in a 1986 decision *Gunaratne* v. *People's Bank*[4] the Court spoke out clearly recognising the right to association as a fundamental right which cannot be contracted away. Still the liberal attitude has not yet extended to the right to strike and the right of peaceful assembly.

A third area of importance is that associated with *freedom of press and freedom of expression*. The sealing of presses for public security purposes is the main type of action which has appeared before the Courts. Again, the Courts have been reticent to question the judgement of the Competent Authority. However, in the *Visuvalingam case*[5] they did recognise a recipient's right to information as part of the rights associated with freedom of speech and the Press.

A growing area of concern is the area of torture and criminal procedure. Only a few cases have been brought under the Prevention of Terrorism Act, or the Code of Criminal Procedure. This is primarily due to the fact that the Sri Lankan Constitution does provide for judicial review and does not contain a 'due process' clause — a standard by which to judge existing laws and values of criminal procedure. Nor have the Courts seen fit to read in such a clause into executive and administrative actions as part of fundamental rights. Though there have been allegations of torture in numerous cases in the North and the South of the country and though Article 11 is absolute, most of these cases have been dismissed 'on balance' for lack of evidence or because the Courts have held that individual acts of torture by officers do not constitute a violation of fundamental rights because they are not 'state action' and therefore trial should take place in a lower Court. Even as recently as 1986, the Supreme Court in *Elmo Perera* v. *Jayawickrema et al.*[6] stated that the chapter on fundamental rights does not have due process provisions and that arbitrary and capricious acts by state authorities cannot be challenged in themselves and have to be linked to a specific provision of fundamental rights. This is the position, despite the weight of opinion in other Commonwealth jurisdictions, which state that arbitrary state action or abuse of power can in themselves violate the rights of individuals.

It is also interesting to consider what type of fundamental rights cases did *not* appear before the Supreme Court during this post-1977 period. Despite the enormous social cost of the current ethnic conflict, only one case involving ethnic rights has appeared before the courts — that which challenged the writing of a cheque in Sinhalese to a Tamil recipient.[7] In addition, there has yet to be a fundamental rights case involving issues with regard to women's position in society. There has never been a judicial determination of equal protection with regard to the rights of women. Ironically, in the United States, the United Kingdom and India, the areas of minority rights and women's rights have been in the forefront of fundamental rights litigation, and have provided for the dynamic growth of judicial doctrine.

What is the role of the Supreme Court?

The role of the Judiciary within a given political framework has changed over time. The changes have been encouraged by new techniques of interpretation as well as new jurisprudential concepts as to the principled intervention of the judiciary in certain areas of constitutional law.

The classical role of the judiciary assigned to it by positivist jurists, such as Austin, is that of mechanical interpretation of the law as passed by the supreme legislature. This particular vision of the judiciary arose in Victorian England, where a stable government faced with a homogenous population enacted legislation according to custom and convention recognised and respected by all political actors whether in power or in the opposition. Such a judiciary was only concerned with the 'plain meaning' of legislation and gave extreme deference to the value judgements of the legislature. Only in very exceptional cases, did courts go against the judgement of Parliament. Even in the United States, the home of judicial review, at the height of Positivist influence only in 78 cases did the Court hold against the government[8] during a period of 200 years.

Independent Sri Lanka inherited this tradition of mechanical jurisprudence from its colonial masters. As a result the Sri Lankan judiciary is a restrained judiciary without the power of judicial review. This restraint was coupled with mechanical styles of interpretation. The decisions of the Soulbury Supreme Court displayed the twin directives of 'deference' and 'plain meaning'. Without a Bill of Rights, except for Section 29, the Supreme Court saw no reason to engage in any form of judicial 'policy-making'. For example, H.L. De Silva in reviewing the citizenship cases of *Mudanayake* v. *Sivagnanasunderam* and *Kodukm Pillai* v. *Mudanayake*, where it was alleged that post-independent citizenship requirements discriminated against the Indian Tamil population, states, 'It is difficult to accept these decisions as being correct upon any realistic appraisal of what was plainly a carefully planned move to alter the balance of representation in the legislature. Both Courts did not give serious consideration to the whole object and purpose of Section 2a.'[9] The Court held that the legislature in its language did not discriminate against Indian Tamils, so the provisions were valid under the Constitution. The intention of the legislature, the actual facts of the case, the social impact of the law were irrelevant.

'Realistic Appraisal', 'objects and purpose' were not seen as part of the judicial process of reasoning. Refusing to cast doubt on the motives of the legislature, the Court adopted a style of interpretation reserved for the analysis of contracts. Because the words of the law were considered 'unambiguous', the Court refused to consider evidence with regard to the practical impact of the legislation before it or even before the Soulbury Commission Report on constitutional reform which clearly outlined the intention of the Commission in adopting section 29.

This formalistic method of interpretation served to foreclose the Sri Lankan Supreme Court from its inception as an important arena for debate on constitutional values and standards. Pieces of legislation were rarely challenged and even when they were, the Supreme Court found justification for deferring to legislative opinion.

Only the Privy Council located in Britain appeared to give some consideration to the nature of legislative accountability. The retroactive, 'bill of attainder quality' of the legislation passed to try and convict the *1962 coup* participants was in many ways legislation which went against all accepted principles of natural justice. Despite the far-reaching provisions, which would have shocked most jurists,[10] the Supreme Court gave its endorsement to the legislation without much difficulty. When the Privy Council finally handed down its judgement in *Queen* v. *Liyanage*[11] the issues of natural justice were quickly superseded by a nationalist sense of outrage that a British Court could sit in judgement over a sovereign Sri Lankan Parliament. This case not only raised nationalist fears but also led to a deep suspicion of the judiciary and judicial power as protectors of vested interest and neo-colonial power structures. If our own Supreme Court had made principled interventions from its inception, those issues which were so prominent in *Queen* v. *Liyanage* might have been perceived in a different light.

Many in Sri Lanka would argue that the Soulbury Judiciary was an ideal court because it was 'non-political' — it only interpreted the Constitution and did not create law. But, today, jurists would agree that the Soulbury Judiciary was very much a political and partisan court which with specific purpose gave constitutional legitimacy to the acts of the legislature at the expense of individual and group rights. A case which illustrates this point is perhaps *Attorney-General* v. *Kodeswaran*[12] which challenged under Section 29 a government circular requiring proficiency in the official language for promotion. The lower courts held that with *Kodeswaran* — a 'plain meaning' interpretation of Section 29 appeared to warrant such a decision.[13] But 'plain meaning' was also used only as a judicial tool, even in its heyday. As a result, the Supreme Court avoided the issue by stating that the Crown did not enter into 'legally enforceable contracts of employment' and therefore Kodeswaran was not entitled to relief. A realist critique would naturally point to the fact that the Court, like most supreme courts of those times, used the 'plain meaning' justification when it was convenient and *avoided* issues when the 'plain meaning' required confrontation with the State. It is therefore only an illusion to consider the Soulbury Supreme Court as non-political. A realist would argue that if one were to strip away the technical-legal form, the politics of the Court becomes very clear.

What jurists such as Upendra Baxi argue today is that law and jurisprudence should move away from 'bottom line' questions such as whether courts are political institutions or not, whether courts make law or not and address more fundamental issues — what kind of policy-making should be reserved for the judiciary? Which functions does it perform best? How can it maximize its role in the constitutional hierarchy? Only a sophisticated judiciary would be able to grapple with the complex problems of under-development.

Since the mid-twentieth century, courts throughout the world have moved away from the mechanical interpretation which influenced them in early years. In making constitutional decisions they have gone beyond form and language and have increasingly looked at the 'spirit of the constitution' and its actual impact on social and political life. In addition in recent years, courts have begun to carve out areas of 'activism', where the level of scrutiny and analysis of government action is more extensive and where judicial orders have compelled executive compliance with certain procedures articulated by the Court. The judiciary has begun to carve out a specific role for itself as the protector of certain values inherent in a democratic political order.

The Sri Lankan Supreme Court has not remained untouched by these developments. Especially after 1978, there appear to be some judgements which have been influenced by these new ideas in judicial decision-making. The initial decisions of the post-1978 Supreme Court reflected the continuing influence of the positivist school of mechanical jurisprudence. The doctrine of what constitutes *State action* is a case in point. For example, the courts in earlier cases have held that action by a public corporation such as the State Insurance Corporation does not constitute State action.[14] In addition, in the first torture case to be brought before the Supreme Court,[15] the Court held that the petitioner had to prove the existence of an actual *administrative or executive practice* of torture approved by the State for there to be state action. A single act by an officer was not sufficient. If the police, for example, held a formal internal inquiry, that in itself constituted proof that there was no such 'administrative practice' and therefore torture could not be State action but only the criminal liability of an individual officer. This narrow reading of what constitutes State action was perhaps relevant in early western society where the State was purely concerned with public administration and where private companies controlled economic life. Today, however, especially in developing societies, the State is involved in many types of activities and without the competition of the market-place, it is far less accountable for its actions. The concept of State action is therefore one means devised to ensure compliance with certain constitutional norms at least by those institutions set up with public funds and administered by public officials.

Recent decisions of the Supreme Court display a move away from mechanical jurisprudence at least with regard to the interpretation of State action. In the 1986 decision *Gunaratne* v. *The People's Bank* the Court went beyond form and adopted the 'functional test' for what constitutes State action. The Court looked to the powers exercised by government over the People's Bank and secondly to the nature of the function as it relates to the facts of the particular case. Here, as it was an employment contract, the Court on an analysis of the facts, held that there was State action. This broad fact-oriented reading was a determination to go beyond the narrow technical interpretation of 'executive and administrative' action and to develop a broader theory of liability[16] more consonant with present-day reality.

Even in the United States, where *laissez-faire* remains the dominant economic doctrine, courts have broadly construed the concept of State action.[17] In the area of civil rights, not only have they accepted State action when private bodies which have State shareholding have violated fundamental rights, but have employed the withholding of grants to private bodies which do not comply with certain constitutional standards.[18] In India, the same broad interpretation has already taken hold. In the hallmark ASIAD case, the actual violations of fundamental rights were the product of the actions of private contractors, but the State was held responsible because it had chosen to enter into contract with those who violated fundamental rights.[19]

The technical non-fact-based interpretation of provisions of the Constitution is however present in other areas of constitutional law. For example, the Supreme Court of Sri Lanka has held that only *individuals* are entitled to fundamental rights and not corporate bodies,[20] despite the fact that constitutional doctrines with regard to freedom of speech and the Press around the world have evolved around cases brought by the various media industries. Famous cases such as *New York Times* v. *Sullivan*[21] in the United States and cases involving the *Indian Express* in India accept the principle of a company being entitled to fundamental rights. To limit the scope and application of fundamental rights on 'plain meaning' without reference to the facts of the case or its actual social impact is reminiscent of the earlier classical approach. The same type of mechanical interpretation was present in the *Kandasamy Adiapathan* case where the Court held that a cheque was not a communication under Article 22 of the Constitution and therefore a Tamil citizen was not entitled to receive a State cheque in Tamil.[22] Though no one can really challenge the logical consistency of the argument made by the Supreme Court, the truth remains that when a Tamil-speaking member of the public receives such a cheque, he will have to turn to his Sinhala neighbour to find out whether the cheque is actually in his name. One must therefore ask, is this judgement really within the spirit and intention of Article 22?

Despite the Supreme Court's cautious approach to fundamental rights and its positivistic approach to language, in recent years there has been a qualitative difference in the language and style of the Court's opinion indicating the gradual influence of recent developments in constitutional jurisprudence. However, these progressive and conservative approaches often contradict each other and run side by side. The Court has yet to consciously define its role in the constitutional hierarchy and not only adopt strategies which mix and match approaches and styles on an *ad hoc* basis.

While in *Dr. Neville Fernando*[23] the Court upheld the conservative position, that a company is not entitled to freedom of the Press and expression, in a later case, *Visuvalingam* v. *Liyanage*,[24] the Court held that 'right to receive information' is within the purview of the freedoms associated with speech and the Press as envisioned by the Constitution. The right to information is a modern right well beyond the 'plain meaning' of the specific constitutional provision. In *Seneviratne* v. *the University Grants Commission*,[25] the courts upheld the admission scheme to University which gave only 30 per cent of the seats to those who pass on merit. The Court, again, did not rely on the plain meaning of the equal protection clause but, using the method adopted in the Indian case of *Kesavananda*,[26] appeared to imply that the non-justifiable Principles of State Policy could be used to limit constitutional challenges under equal protection. Ironically *Seneviratne* is an example of a judiciary which uses policy analysis not to give full effect to the policy and intent of underlying fundamental rights provisions but to *actually limit* these rights and to give constitutional justification for an adverse state policy of the moment.

The case of *Seneviratne* then highlights the problem of *ad hoc* judicial policy-making. The Sri Lankan Supreme Court has made some unusual decisions but its interventions when studied over time do have the appearance of being *ad hoc*, case by case judgements, not animated by any vision of the proper role for the judiciary in the constitutional hierarchy. For example, in *Vivienne Goonewardene*[27] the Court came out strongly for the petitioner stating that even though she had not complied with the Police Ordinance, she had the right to ignore arrest orders given by a Superintendent as she could only be arrested by an Assistant Superintendent, a decision very specific to the facts of the case. Earlier in *Dr. S.A. Fernando*[28] the Court had declared that the police were correct in arresting Dr. Fernando because no notice of a procession was given to the police. Each of these decisions may be justified in terms of the facts before the Court but what insight do they actually throw on the freedom of assembly and freedom of speech provisions of the

Constitution? The important questions of principle remain — though the Police and the State have the right to regulate the time, place and manner of a public assembly and public expressions of speech, can they do so with procedures which effectively deny the exercise of these rights? At what point and in what circumstances should the balance be achieved? Despite the brave decision in *Vivienne Goonewardene*, a lawyer or general member of the public remains mystified as to the actual nature of the rights protected under Article 14(b).

To escape the *ad hoc* nature of judicial policy-making, it therefore becomes essential for the Supreme Court to define its institutional role within the constitutional hierarchy. Only then can it intervene effectively and consistently to preserve and protect the constitutional values and to restore checks and balances in the political system.

The general subject of constitutional jurisprudence and the attempt to outline the 'proper role for the judiciary' has concerned scholars throughout the twentieth century. However, in recent years, it has become the primary preoccupation of jurists the world over. From John Hart Ely at Harvard, to Ronald Dwarkin of Oxford, to Upendra Baxi at the University of New Delhi, to Professor Christy Weeramanthri of Monash, the constitutional role of the judiciary has become the primary area for jurisprudential analysis. What is remarkable is that despite their diversity, both in location and interest, they appear to agree that the legitimacy of the judiciary is greatly dependent on its ability to defend and protect fundamental rights. A judiciary that fails to accept this role will not enjoy high levels of respect in society. Though each of these jurists outlines different methods of judicial analysis, they do envision an activist judiciary in certain areas of constitutional law — i.e. those areas of constitutional law where values cannot be vindicated by the legislature or the executive.

The Supreme Court of Sri Lanka plays a dual role of being the highest Appeal Court and the Court with exclusive jurisdiction over fundamental rights cases. Upendra Baxi argues forcefully in his book on the Indian Supreme Court[29] that the Court as the defender of constitutional values must recognise that as the final interpreter of constitutional provisions it has a very particular function in the political system. It is entrusted with the duty to ensure that the legislature and the executive conform to certain constitutional values. In certain areas extreme deference to the wishes of the legislature and the executive will be counter-productive. It may only encourage what Upendra Baxi describes as 'government lawlessness'.[30] John Hart Ely in *Democracy and Distrust*,[31] considered to be the most outstanding book on American constitutional jurisprudence since Bickel's *The Least Dangerous Branch*,[32] argues forcefully that the constitutional function of the Supreme Court is to make democracy more effective. In other words he argues in favour of an activist judiciary which clears away the bottlenecks and allows for equal participation of all members of society especially those who have historically been denied equal opportunity. He argues for an engaged judiciary which will allow for a special level of scrutiny with regard to cases involving such issues as for example, the right to vote, the right of minorities and the equality of women.

Ronald Dworkin has consistently articulated the need for a strategy of constitutional policy-making by the judiciary. In *Taking Rights Seriously*,[33] he argues that the Supreme Court should not decide constitutional cases on the facts alone but should insist on developing consistent constitutional principles which would be clearly understood by lawyer and layman alike. The Court should first decide on areas in which there is a constitutional duty requiring activism and thereafter be consistent in developing doctrine which would not only convey the spirit of these constitutional provisions, but which would make them actually effective in the daily lives of citizens. Many have argued that the Burger Court in America did not turn out to be as conservative as predicted in the early years and has upheld the activist principles of the Warren Court especially in the area of women's rights and minority rights. Dworkin argues that consistency in constitutional policy-making and principled decision as to which areas require activism is more effective than *ad hoc*, piecemeal intervention.

The Sri Lankan Supreme Court has worked with a Bill of Rights which has been clearly justiciable only for the last seven years. As a result it is still in the process of developing and evaluating judicial doctrine. We can only hope that in the future it too will carve out a special role for itself and give a central place to constitutional policy-making with regard to fundamental rights.

What the judges do in fact — judicial doctrine and fundamental rights in Sri Lanka

The most popular area of fundamental rights litigation in Sri Lanka is Article 12 — the equal protection clause. Given the broad interpretations in other jurisdictions, the Supreme Court of Sri Lanka has in relative terms only allowed for a narrow reading of quality. However, in *Perera* v.

UGC,[34] the Court appeared to open the gates of litigation with an activist interpretation of equality.

In the *Perera* case, the Court held that in the case of university admissions when two sources are integrated into one class there can be no reference to the original source in choosing individuals for admission. However, the dicta in the case gave rise to greater expectations with regard to constitutional approaches to the equality principle. The *Perera* opinion quoted from well-known cases in the United States and India and the standards which were articulated were those which have developed over time in Anglo-American jurisprudence: i.e. that a classification in law must be reasonable and that it must have a rational relation to the object sought to be achieved by the law. However the *Perera* opinion is a very detailed one with a comprehensive study of the facts. Given the close nature of judicial scrutiny, it was expected that 'reasonableness' and 'rational relation' would always be strictly interpreted to maximize government accountability. A large number of cases involving university admissions were filed soon after the *Perera* decision.

Within months, the Supreme Court closed the flood-gates which it had unwillingly opened. In *Seneviratne* v. *UGC* (see earlier) the strict scrutiny of facts in *Perera* gave way to general policy notions of 'overall assessment'. The broad directives of State policy with general clauses such as 'the promotion of the welfare of the people' were allowed as justifications by the state against allegations of the violation of fundamental rights. The interpretation of equality in *Seneviratne* was reminiscent of Article 18(2) of the 1972 Republican Constitution which allowed for broad limitations within the chapter of fundamental rights. Within a period of one year, the Supreme Court's approach to the doctrine under equal protection underwent a reversal — strict scrutiny of facts in the style of the American Courts gave way to deference to broad and loose justifications of State policy which are unverifiable given the nature of available empirical data. Since then the Supreme Court has held against the petitioner in many equal protection cases. Was *Perera* v. *the UGC* only an aberration in the modern history of the Supreme Court or was it an initial foray into the realm of strict factual scrutiny — a realm which suddenly proved to be unmanageable when the Court calendars were filled with similar cases seeking the vindication of fundamental rights?

The dilemma of the Court with regard to equal protection was no more apparent than in *Elmo Perera* v. *Motegu Jayawickrema et al.*[35] Here the Court spelt out the equal protection doctrine in classical terms — the need for reasonable classification by the State to distinguish among groups. However, it held that in this particular case because the individual had not actually pointed out a class or group similarly situated which was better off or against whom his discrimination could be measured, the case must fail. In addition the Court held that suits based on notions of State 'arbitrariness', 'capriciousness', 'abuse of power' are not violations of fundamental rights in themselves but must be linked to the violation of actual fundamental rights provisions elaborated in the chapter of fundamental rights. This strange technical and linguistic juggling mixed with a special concern for the petitioner's state reflects in a nutshell the vulnerability of a third world Court which desires to shed the shackles of formal law and appear just but which is also afraid to open up the Pandora's Box.

In the second most popular area of constitutional litigation, freedom of association and peaceful assembly, the Supreme Court has been singularly unsympathetic to the rights of trade unions and their workers. This lack of sympathy has also prevented development of what may be termed 'poverty law' — issues with regard to social welfare and basic needs. In this sense the concerns before the Supreme Court have been to some extent very elitist. Not one decision in the period 1978–84 has helped vindicate the rights of trade-union members, members of the rural poor or the unemployed.

One important and controversial decision was made with regard to trade-union processions which resulted in demonstrations before the houses of the deciding judges. In *Vivienne Goonewardene* v. *Hector Perera*[36] the Court upheld Mrs. Goonewardene's right to peaceful assembly on a technicality — that the person who arrested her was below the rank of an Assistant Superintendent as required by the Police Ordinance. Despite the trouble generated by this decision including citations in all human rights evaluations of Sri Lanka, there was no real significant development of judicial doctrine. As mentioned earlier, despite *Vivienne Goonewardene* v. *Hector Perera* we still remain ignorant as to the quality of the rights protected by Article (14)(b) and in what manner the right may be regulated by the authorities. Even if Mrs. Goonewardene had complied with police regulations and given notice of requested permission for her procession could the procession have been prevented without a reasonable justification? By what constitutional standards should one judge the discretion of the police officer in granting or withholding permission with regard to peaceful assembly and procession? These broader questions of constitutional principle have yet to be addressed in the Sri Lanka context.

Despite the nature of the present political crisis in Sri Lanka, only a few cases with regard to torture, arrest and detention have come before the Sri Lankan Supreme Court. In the case of torture every case has been dismissed on the grounds that there was insufficient evidence. The standard for evaluating facts adopted by the Court was a 'balance of probabilities' even though Article 11 is in language absolute.[37] In such a context only an extreme case of torture (where there is physical mutilation of the body certified by a doctor) will ever be decided in favour of the petitioner. Amnesty International and other human rights organizations have written extensively that new torture methods do not leave tell-tale marks on the human body.

The problem of 'custodial violence' is a new and important area of developing country law. In India, in certain types of cases, the difficulty of getting corroboration in a situation where an individual is in custody and at the mercy of custodial officers has led to new approaches with regard to burdens of proof especially in the area of rape. If a prima facie case of custodial rape is established, the burden shifts and it is up to the custodial officers to prove that such violence did not take place. In *Velumurugu* v. *Attorney-General* where the Sri Lankan Court was divided 3–2 on whether there was sufficient evidence of torture such an approach might have led to a different result if the custodial officers had had the burden of proof.

Despite the Draconian provisions of the Prevention of Terrorism Act (PTA)[38] there has been only one constitutional case challenging its applicability in a particular situation.[39] The case was dismissed by the Supreme Court on a reading of the term 'unlawful activity', a broad provision which is not present in, for example, the U.K. act and also even though the alleged activity of the petitioner took place before the enactment of the PTA. In an ugly case of contract murder in Kegalle however, the Supreme Court did hold that the suspect had been subject to illegal detention — a period of three days — when the Criminal Code of Procedure required that he be produced before a magistrate within 24 hours.[40]

In many other countries, criminal procedure is the most important area of constitutional litigation, and this is especially true of the United States and the United Kingdom. In fact many feel that it is the backbone of the whole framework of fundamental rights. Yet, in Sri Lanka it does not have high constitutional visibility. The reason for this lies in the fact that the Sri Lankan Constitution does not contain a 'due process' clause. Any procedure is valid so long as it is according to the law, even if the law itself shocks the conscience. Without the higher standard of due process, constitutional litigation under Article 12 will always be minimal. The Indian Constitution does not have a due process clause but the Indian

Courts in Meneka Gandhi[41] read the 'due process standard', into the Constitutional provisions as implied. The Sri Lankan Supreme Court in *Elmo Seneviratne* refused to do so, stressing the differences in the two constitutions, in that the Indian Supreme Court has the power of review, a power unavailable to the Sri Lankan Court.

In the area of freedom of expression and freedom of speech the approach of the Court has been more complex. In *Dr. Neville Fernando* (see earlier) the Court refused to give companies — i.e. all the media industries — *locus standi* to allege fundamental rights violation — a very restrictive interpretation given the actual nature of how these freedoms are exercised. On the other hand, in *Visuvalingam* v. *Liyanage* (1984)[42] the Court seemed to imply that readers of newspapers have a right to receive information — a far-reaching doctrine if taken to its logical limit. Despite this broad reading of the scope of these freedoms, the Court held against Visuvalingam, giving deference to what it felt was the reasonable opinion of the competent authority in using his discretion pursuant to Emergency regulations. Ironically in earlier cases, the Supreme Court has been sensitive to freedom of speech issues — having limited the scope of parliamentary privilege in one of its first cases.[43]

In studying the pattern in recent judgements, it may be said that the Court has accepted a new style of judgement writing. The judgement initially spells out a broad and comprehensive right but is then limited by strict technical and procedural interpretation in a specific context. This allows for the articulation of norms but without individual remedy or recourse.

In *Ratnasara Thero* v. *Udugampola*, the Court declared that the seizure of pamphlets advocating positions against the 1962 referendum was illegal and violated freedom of speech and expression. The right of individuals to hand out leaflets and communicate with the public directly was seen as an important aspect of freedom of speech.[44]

In the three cases mentioned above in which the Court found for the petitioner, the Court ordered compensation of Rs.10,000. In accepting compensation as a remedy the Sri Lankan Supreme Court is ahead of other jurisdictions which are content with granting far-reaching court directions against state bodies which violate fundamental rights! Very little comment needs to be made against this type of 'government lawlessness', a lawlessness which strikes at the roots of legitimacy of any political system.

Judicial competence and fundamental rights

H.L. De Silva in his article on 'Anomalies in the Enforcement of Fundamental Rights in Sri Lanka' [45] has outlined the procedural problems associated with fundamental rights litigations in Sri Lanka. There is no right of judicial review and therefore only executive and administrative action is accountable. Exclusive fundamental rights jurisdiction in the Supreme Court has also created major problems of fact-finding with decisions having to be made only on the basis of affidavits. In one case, the Court appears to have allowed oral evidence but there is no generalized procedure with regard to constitutional fact-finding [46] at the level of the Supreme Court.

The American Courts, for example, have no such problems, because fundamental rights cases originate in the lower courts. However, though the Indian Supreme Court does not have exclusive jurisdiction over fundamental rights in many cases, it is the Court of original jurisdiction. Over the last few years under the leadership of such Justices as Krishna Iyer, Chandrachur, and Bhagwati, the Court has improvised on new procedures of fact-findings. The new methods rely on 'Commissions of Inquiry' [47] appointed by the Court to research into the disputed facts. This is especially relevant in situations of custodial abuse, corporate and State malpractice. The Independent Commissions report to the Supreme Court and the Court often accepts their recommendations. [48] The Commissions of Inquiry procedure bypasses the old strategy of adversarial haggling and allows for a more comprehensive understanding of the facts upon which argumentation may be based. In addition it allows the Court to be advised by the expertise of other disciplines in the social and natural sciences especially with regard to the implications of the orders which it feels compelled to make.

Another problem with regard to fundamental rights litigation in Sri Lanka is that Article 126, which allows for action against administrative and executive bodies, has a time limit of one month. Many of the cases listed in the attached schedule were dismissed because they were filed after the *one-month* time-limit. In addition in developing societies it is well accepted that only those who are aware of their rights can bring their grievances before the Courts. Many of our citizens are ignorant of our law and as Gananath Obeysekera has pointed out in many of his studies they often prefer to take their grievances to the Goddess Kali than to the Sri Lankan Supreme Court. [49]

Again Indian experience in recent years may be relevant to this problem of access. The concept of 'epistolary jurisdiction', where any

Table 1 Cases on fundamental rights — April 1979 to December 1981

Name of case	Article of Constitution	For or against petitioner	Holding
W.P.R. Wickramasinghe and others v. Attorney-General and others	Article 12 — equality discrimination in Job Bank Scheme for political reasons	Against petitioner	Petitioner no standing because he is not one of the class eligible for nomination in Job Bank Scheme
W.K. Nimala Wijesinha v. Attorney-General	Article 12 — equality termination of services by Cabinet for political reasons — without being charged	Against petitioner	Acts of Cabinet prima facie lawful — need not hold an inquiry
K.C. Adiapathan v. Attorney-General	Article 22(2) — language Tamil refusing to accept a cheque written only in Sinhala	Against petitioner	A cheque is not a communication, so case does not fall within Art. 22(2)
G. Thenabadu v. University of Colombo v. others	Article 12 — equality discrimination against external students doing law	Against petitioner	Insufficient evidence
K.D. Perera and others v. R. Premadasa	Article 12 — equality malafide acquisition of land	Against petitioner	Insufficient evidence
K.S.S.E. Ranatunga v. Jayawardene and others	Article 126(1) — threatened infringement challenging appointment of a sub-post master	Against petitioner	Beyond time limit of one month

Gunatilleke and Sirimanne v. Attorney-General	*Article 12(1)* — discrimination on land acquisition	Against petitioner	Insufficient evidence with regard to facts
K.S. Ranasinghe and another v. Ceylon Plywood Corporation and another	*Article 12(2)* — cancellation of promotion because of political victimization	Against petitioner	Insufficient evidence
Weeratunga v. Attorney-General and another	*Article 14 — right of association* trade-union official should not be transferred from office site	Against petitioner	Transfer is not a fundamental rights issue unless *malafide* is proven
E.P. Jayasena and others v. K.R.S. Soysa and another	*Article 14 — right of association* intimidation of trade-union members	Against petitioner	Insufficient evidence
Perera v. University Grants Commission	*Article 12* — university admissions — two sets of examinations for one year's entry	For petitioner	Integrated class-equality requires that there be no reference back to the original source
A. Thadcharmoorthi and others v. Attorney-General	*Article 11* — allegation of torture at a police station	Against petitioner	Beyond time limit Insufficient proof Not State action because not approved at the highest levels — no administrative practice
Gamini Samarasinghe v. Bank of Ceylon	*Article 12* — discrimination in a bank promotion scheme	Against petitioner	Insufficient proof

(continued)

Table 1 (*continued*)

Name of case	Article of Constitution	For or against petitioner	Holding
D.A. Yasapala v. Ranil Wickramasinghe	*Article 12 —* *Article 14 —* *Right to strike* discrimination against strikers who were fired after July strike	Against petitioner	Emergency Regulation — under Public Security Ordinance. President's sole discretion. Right to strike not a fundamental right
B.M. Jayawardene v. Attorney-General	*Article 126(1)* abuse of executive discretion	Against petitioner	Beyond time limit
A.K. Velmurugu v. Attorney-General	*Article 11 —* torture allegation at army camp	Against petitioner	3-2 decision Insufficient proof But State action *dissent —* Sufficient proof
G.A. Eheliyagoda and others v. Janatha Estate Development Board	*Article 126 — abuse of discretion* abuse of executive discretion in demoting petitioners	For petitioner	Unfettered, unregulated discretion without jurisdiction
Mrs. U.N.S. Pieris v. E.B. Abeysekera and others	*Article 12 — equality* political victimization. *Article 14 — trade union right* petitioner transferred because she joined union	Against petitioner	Insufficient evidence

Case	Article	Decision	Notes
Neville Fernando and others v. Liyanage	*Article 14* — freedom of speech and association. — sealing of press by government	Against petitioner	Companies have no fundamental rights. Only individuals
Vivienne* Gunawardene v. Hector Perera and others	*Article 14* — freedom of peaceful assembly and speech — march on women's day	For petitioner	Arrest by someone less than Assistant Superintendent. Arrest illegal. Rs.10,000 compensation
Dr. S.N. Fernando v. Attorney-General	*Article 14* — freedom of peaceful assembly and speech. — procession to protest arrests under PTA	Against petitioner	No notice given to police under (77) of ordinance. Illegal procession
A.K.T.J. Gunawardena and others v. E.L. Senanayake	*Article 126* — abuse of executive discretion	Against petitioner	Beyond time-limit
Ratnasara Thero* v. Udugampola	*Article 14* — freedom of speech and expression— illegal seizing of pamphlets *Article 126(4)* — compensation for FR Violation	For petitioner	Handing out of pamphlets to vote against referendum a fundamental right Compensation Rs.10,000

* Those two cases were decided after December 1981 but have been included for the sake of information.

Source: *Fundamental Rights April 1979 to December 1981*, Lake House Printers, 1984.

Table 2 Post 1984 — important cases

Name of case	Article of Constitution	For or against petitioner	Holding
Wijeratne and another v. People's Bank and another	*Article 12 — equality* discrimination on employment promotion	Against petitioner	Action by People's Bank is not State action — *test* 'commercial activities'
Visuvalingam and others v. Liyanage and others SC 6/84	*Article 12 —* regulating Article 14 Freedom of speech and Press Sealing of *Saturday Review* under New Emergency Regulations	Against petitioner	Freedom of Speech includes the freedom of the individual to receive information Test for censorship sealing etc., by Competent Authority is reasonableness and was reasonable
Tampoe v. Ragasingham and others	*Article 14 —* freedom of Assembly. Procession and meeting to Galle Face by trade Union — Reg.12 of Emergency Regulations	Against petitioner	Going through private lanes in groups of five is a 'procession' within the meaning of Emergency Reg.12.

Case	Issue	Decision	Outcome
Kapugeekiyana v. Hettiarachchi and two others	*Article 11* — torture *Article 12* — equality *Article 13* — criminal process *Article 14* — right to profession and arrest and detention illegal under Code of Criminal Procedure	Against petitioner on all grounds save * — illegal detention	Insufficient proof of torture. Arrest was legal, can be arrested without warrant if 'reasonable'. Detention was illegal. Remedy Rs.10,000 compensation
Gunaratne v. People's Bank	*Article 14* — right to association	For petitioner	Right to association cannot be contracted away by the employer
Perera v. Jayawickrema	*Article 12* — equal protection. Arbitrary capricious action of part of state	Against petitioner	Not equal protection, petitioner must show the class which benefits while he is discriminated. Freedom from arbitrariness not a fundamental right in itself. Constitution does not have due process clause

Source: * 2 SRLR, Volume I, Part I.

member of the public acting bona fide can address a letter to the Supreme Court outlining incidents of fundamental rights violations, allows for the greater realization of fundamental rights. The Court will treat the letter as a writ petition. This exercise in 'judicial populism' may actually allow the poorer elements in society to bring their grievances to the Supreme Court.

It is fair to say that the success of social action litigation in India in recent years has as much to do with the activist quality of the Bar as with the creative intervention of the judiciary. Groups of committed lawyers have organized themselves so as to go and seek out cases of fundamental rights violation whether in Madras or Rajasthan. On the other hand, the Sri Lankan Supreme Court is actually faced with a very passive Bar, a weak legal aid programme and lack of commitment on the part of the new and more youthful members of the legal profession.

In contrast, there have also been many instances in India, the United Kingdom and the United States where Courts, after reading newspaper items and conducting initial investigations, have on their own motion opened up inquiries into the violation of fundamental rights. In recent months gruesome stories have appeared in the Sri Lankan newspapers about the Anuradhapura Women's Prisons, about the treatment of Ministry of Fisheries' Officials by members of the police force, about the abuses and malpractices in our public hospitals etc. And yet, neither the Bar nor the judiciary have attempted to bring these tragic issues before the Courts. Without proper ventilation these issues naturally go underground and become part of the mythology of recounted injustices. The inability of any political system to remedy these wrongs only serves to delegitimize it in the eyes of the general public as being both ineffective and callously unconcerned with the real nature of justice in society. Judicial activism is in fact one possible avenue for limited non-violent social change, especially in societies where cleavages of class and community allow for the easy use of violence. By strengthening the ability of the judiciary to resolve some of the more important conflicts in society, one naturally strengthens the non-violent democratic institutions of government.

Activism with regard to a developing country judiciary is no simple matter. Nor is it often a matter of choice. Scholars have always warned that in defining the role of the judiciary one must not go beyond the practical limitation of man and material. Enough consideration must be given to matters of judicial administration. Judicial activism can only be successful if it is combined with a pragmatic assessment of judicial capabilities. However, issues of administration, time and cost cannot in themselves be seen as justification for the abdication of constitutional duties. A written Constitution requires a judiciary to interpret it. In this act of interpretation lies the power of vindicating the rights of wronged individuals as well as the power of instilling constitutional values in the lower judiciary, in the legal profession and among the more aware members of the general public. Unless the judiciary is truly effective in protecting these values, a democratic ideology will not easily take hold in a multi-ethnic, multi-religious developing society.

In writing these words, one must of course accept that the Sri Lankan judiciary does not exist in political vacuum. The cases of *Vivienne Goonewardene* and *Ratnasara Thero* and their aftermath indicate the vulnerability of the judiciary especially when it is faced with an unyielding and hostile executive. However, as long as there are democratic forms of government, and a system of checks and balances, the judiciary will always have a creative role to play if it decides to accept and act upon its constitutional responsibilities.

Notes

1. *Perera* v. *University Grants Commission*, SC Application 57/80.
2. *Vivienne Goonewardene* v. *Hector Perera*, SC Application 20/83 and *Ratnasara Theor* v. *Udugampola and others*, SC Application 125/82.
3. *Kapugeekiyana* v. *Hettiarachchi*, SC Application 80/84.
4. *Gunaratne* v. *People's Bank*, SC Application 58/84.
5. *Visuvalingam* v. *Liyanage* (1984) 2 SR L.R. Part 1, p. 123.
6. *Perera* v. *Jayawickrema et al*, SC Application 134/84.
7. *Kandasamy Adipathan* v. *Attorney-General et al.* (1984) 2SR L.R. Part 1.
8. L. Friedman and H.N. Scherber, *American Law and the Constitutional Order*, Cambridge, Harvard University Press, 1978, p. 397.
9. *Mudanayake* v. *Sivagnanasunderam* **53** *New Law Reports*, 25 and *Kodakam Pillai* v. *Mudanayake* **4** *New Law Reports* 433 and also see H.L. De Silva 'Role of the Judiciary in Plural Societies' unpublished, ICES, 1983, p. 16-17.
10. See for example: 19 and 21 of the Criminal Law (Special Provisions) Act, No. 1 of 1962 which is retroactive and specific to crimes on a special date.
11. *The Queen* v. *Liyanage* (1962) **64** *New Law Reports* 313 and **65** *New Law Reports* 73 and (1965) **67** *New Law Reports* 193.
12. *Kodeswaran* v. *The Attorney-General* (1964) **72** *New Law Reports* 337.
13. The legislative history of section 29 shows that the provision was intended to protect the interest of minority groups though the section could also be read as an equal protection clause.
14. *Wijetunga* v. *The Insurance Corporation*, SC Application 87/82.
15. *Aiyathurai Thadchanamoorthi* v. *Attorney-General and others; Vedivel*

130   *Radhika Coomaraswamy*

Mahenthiran v. *Attorney-General and others*, SC Application 63/80 and 68/80.

16. *Gunaratne*, see note 4.
17. See Choper, 'Thoughts on State Action. The Government Function and Power Theory Approaches', 1979 Wash. ULQ 757.
18. See *Ascherman* v. *Presbyterian Hosp.*, 507 F2d 1103 (9th as 1974) and *Himes* v. *Cenla Community Action Committee*, 474 F2d 102 (5th on 1973).
19. *People's Union For Democratic Rights* v. *The Union of India* — Writ Petition 8143 of 1981.
20. *Dr. Neville Fernando and Others* v. *Liyanage* — SC Application 116/81.
21. See for example *N.Y. Times* v. *Sullivan*, 376 US (US Reports) 255, 1964.
22. *Kandasamy's*, see note 7.
23. *Dr. Neville Fernando and Others*, see note 20.
24. *Visuvalingam* v. *Liyanage* (1984), 2 SRI L.R., Part 1, p. 123.
25. *Seneviratne* v. *The University Grants Commission* — SC Application 88/80.
26. *Kesavananda Shanti* v. *State of Kerala* AIR 1973 (S.C.) 1461.
27. *Vivienne Goonewardene* v. *Hector Perera and others*, SC Application 20/83.
28. *Dr. S.N. Fernando* v. *Attorney-General*, SC Application 2/83.
29. See U. Baxi, *The Indian Supreme Court and Politics*, New Delhi, 1980.
30. See U. Baxi, *The Crisis of the Indian Legal System*, New Delhi, Vikas 1982.
31. John Hart Ely, *Democracy & Distrust*, Cambridge, 1981.
32. A. Bickel, *The Least Dangerous Branch*, New Haven, 1962.
33. R. Dworkin, *Taking Rights Seriously* — Cambridge, 1977, 1978.
34. *Perera*, see note 1.
35. *Perera*, see note 6.
36. *Goonewardene*, see note 2.
37. *A.K. Vel Murugu* v. *Attorney-General* — SC Application 74/81.
38. Prevention Terrorism Act of 1979.
39. *Senthilanayagam and the Three Others*, HC Applications 19/81 and 13/81.
40. *Kapugeekiyana*, see note 3.
41. *Meneka Gandhi* — AIR 1978, SC Application 597/77.
42. *Visuvalingam*, see note 24.
43. See articles written by Mr. S. Nadesan in *The Sun*, February 27 to March 2, 1978.
44. *Ratnasara Thero* v. *Udugampola and others* — SC Application 125/82.
45. H.L. De Silva, 'Anomalies in the Enforcement of Fundamental Rights in Sri Lanka' in *Mooter*, Volume 1, 1984, p. 12.
46. *Kapugeekiyana*, see note 3.
47. *Sheela Barse* v. *State of Maharasthra* — Writ No. 1053-1054.
48. Note the position of Dr. Desai in the Sheela Barse Case.
49. Gananath Obeysekera, 'The Goddess Pattini and the Parable on Justice', Punitham Tiruchelvam Memorial Lecture, Colombo, 1983.

7 THE JUDICIARY IN CONTEXT: THE CASE OF TANZANIA

M.K.B. Wambali and C.M. Peter

The individual looks to the law and to the Courts to right any wrong that he has suffered, and does not take law into his own hands. It is therefore essential for the efficient running of our judicial system that the judiciary and in assessing a judge the public will have regard not only for his judgements in court but also as to his way of life. Like Caesar's wife, they must be beyond suspicion.

Sir William Duffus[1]

There are jobs in our society which can be done by indisciplined people and people whose personal integrity can be called into question; being a Judge or Magistrate is not among them.

President Julius Nyerere[2]

Introduction

The judiciary is one of the three arms of the modern state. The other two are the executive and the legislature. Among the main functions of the judiciary are adjudication of cases, interpreting the law made by the legislature and checking abuse of power by the executive. To be able to function properly and be effective, the judiciary must be independent of the other arms of the State and especially the executive. Therefore, independence of the judiciary has developed into one of the most sacred principles since the rise of the modern nation-state. This principle has evolved together with that rule of law and the Supremacy of Parliament.[3]

There is currently a debate as to whether the judiciary should restrict itself to its traditional role of applying the law made elsewhere, or whether it should move out of this cocoon and make legal and policy pronouncements which amount to law. Blackstone, the great English jurist, is among those who insisted that the judiciary should merely enunciate or discover the existing law.[4]

However, the current approach to judging recognizes that judges do make law. Sir Chalres Newbold, the President of the now defunct Court of Appeal for West Africa, in support of this school of thought says, 'For myself, I consider that a judge's decision is law because he says it; and not that he only says it because it is law'.[5] The realist school of jurisprudence has gone further to assert that the judiciary is the real source of law. A leading realist, Justice Oliver Wendell Holmes of the US Supreme Court, once declared that 'the prophecies of what the Courts will do in fact and nothing more pretentious are what I mean by law'.[6] Another realist, John Chipman Gray, supports him by treating judge-made law as primary and legislative law and precedent as secondary materials at the disposal of the judge. In his own words, 'It has been sometimes said that the law is composed of two parts, legislative law and judge-made law, but in truth all law is judge-made law'.[7] This being the case Judge Jerome Frank, the most flamboyant of all realists, concludes that, 'Until a court has given its judgement on the facts no law on the subject is yet in existence. Before that decision the only law available is a lawyer's opinion, that opinion is not actually law but only a guess as to what a court will decide.' [8]

The arguments by the realists to a great extent augment the importance of the judiciary as a source of law. This is in conformity with the concrete reality of the present epoch. Courts have played a great part in the evolution of legal rules in the common law systems and this cannot be easily ignored. The creativity and contribution of the courts is illustrated by the decisions in *Donoghue* v. *Stevenson*[9] in negligence and *Rylands* v. *Fletcher*[10] in strict liability.

Judiciary in a historical perspective

The judiciary we have today has not always been there. It is in one sense a product of a protracted class struggle. One of the main demands made by the rising bourgeoisie from the absolute monarch was for an independent judiciary. This was important because under an absolute monarchy the new rising class had no breathing space. All powers were concentrated in one person, the king. He was the law-maker, the administrator of the law and its enforcer. In England this was the situation during the reign of King Henry VIII. It was thus essential to use popular slogans in order to get the support of broad sections of the population. These slogans included 'freedom of contract,' 'freedom of movement', 'freedom to own property' etc. At the same time there were demands for independence of the judiciary, separation of powers, supremacy of the parliament and rule of law.

These demands were achieved with the 1688 glorious bloodless revolution in England which marked the final victory of the bourgeoisie over feudalism and the assumption of Parliament as the most supreme organ of the state. However, ironically, the bourgeoisie and the colonial masters did not export their laws and legal systems to the colonies during the initial imperial phase.[11]

Ideals such as rule of law, independence of the judiciary or supremacy of parliament could on occasions undermine their purposes and thus they were often left behind in the home country. Thus in the colonies brutality often reigned for the sake of capitalism and imperial power. To cut costs and ensure total obedience, colonial administrators acted as magistrates as well. There was no independent judiciary in the then Tanganyika, both during the German and British colonial rule. Race was a determinant factor in accessibility to legal institutions. Native Courts were for Africans, while Magistrate Courts were for non-Africans.[12] This system existed with few inconsequential modifications throughout the colonial period which ended in December, 1961.

Independence in 1961 was a legal act in which political power was transferred from the colonial state to the nationalists. The Republic in 1962 did not bring substantial changes in legal structure for it only substituted the Governor-General for the President, as the executive head of the State.

Judiciary after independence

After Tanzania received independence, steps were taken to separate judicial and administrative functions. During the colonial period District Commissioners acted as magistrates as well. This changed after independence. In 1963 the Magistrates' Court Act[13] was enacted which introduced a three-tier system. The chief Court was the High Court, beneath which was the District Court (which included the Resident Magistrates' Court). The Primary Court remained at the bottom of the hierarchy. Appeals from the High Court lay in the Court of Appeal for Eastern Africa. Appeals to the Privy Council in England ceased after independence. Other than those changes, the judiciary remained intact, performing the same functions and applying the same colonial laws which were retained through the Judicature and Application of Laws Act.[14]

Party supremacy versus parliamentary supremacy

There were additional developments that affected the judiciary and other state institutions in the country. Firstly, the country was formally declared a *de jure* one-party state in 1965.[15] Secondly, there was a departure from the principle of parliamentary supremacy to party supremacy. This was a novel invention by Tanzania. It has been noted by lawyers that even in socialist states the party is not supreme.

Party supremacy was officially institutionalised in 1975 by Act No. 8 of 1975 which amended Section 3 of the Interim Constitution, 1965. The amendment provided that 'All political activities in Tanzania shall be conducted by or under the auspices of the Party' and further that 'The functions of all the organs of the State of the United Republic shall be performed under the auspices of the Party.'

This amendment has been incorporated in the 1977 permanent Constitution of the United Republic which declares Chama Cha Mapinduzi (CCM) the only political party in Tanzania.

Supremacy of the Party over the Executive was explained and emphasized by President Nyerere in the following terms:

For the truth is that it is not the Party which is the instrument of the government. It is the governent which is the instrument through which the Party tries to implement the wishes of the people and serve their interests. And the Party has therefore to determine basic principles on which government should act, it has to determine the policies its government will follow.[17]

The effect of this was to shift policy making duty from the parliament to the National Executive Committee of the Party (NEC). However, it should be noted that this did not in any way make NEC decisions legal. To have legal force and thus be binding on the courts, they still had to pass through the parliament for 'rubber-stamping'. This point was well made by the late Sir Biron, J. in 1973:

The fact that NEC made policy did not mean that it followed without saying that whatever came out of it was law. No! Where an important policy matter had been issued without a corresponding parliamentary endorsement by the way of legislation, the courts of law are not bound to enforce it.[18]

Despite this need for formal approval, there is no doubt that the Party has systematically stripped the Parliament of all its powers. Under Article 54(1) of the Constitution the Parliament remains a mere committee of the National Conference of the Party as provided by Article 59(ii) of the CCM Constitution.

This background is necessary to enable us to appreciate the limitations of a judiciary which has to operate within this framework. Is the judiciary independent in Tanzania? Does it perform its functions smoothly without interference and are its decisions and orders respected? These are some of the questions we shall hereinafter attempt to answer.

Appointments in the judiciary

The government and the Party play a vital if not a decisive role in determining who will man various positions in the judiciary. This in a way has a bearing on the work of this important institution.

Part five of the Constitution provides for the judiciary which is to be guided by the Constitution or any other law. Appointments to the highest levels of the judiciary are made by the head of the executive. Article 61(1) of the Constitution provides that the Chief Justice will be appointed by the President. The puisne judges are also appointed by the President in consultation with the Chief Justice. The Constitution also provides safeguards to the judges, such as charging their salary directly from the consolidated fund and requiring elaborate procedure to be followed before a judge is disciplined or removed. The President himself boasts about these safeguards: 'The Tanzanian Constitution makes it very difficult indeed for any judge to be dismissed.'[19]

However, experience has shown that these safeguards are formal enactments and are not all that water-tight. Judges have been transferred from the judiciary and given other responsibilities in the government service.[20]

The very fact that the executive makes appointments has at times tended to make members of the judiciary subservient to the executive and the Party. This is indicated by a circular issued by a former Chief Justice some time ago, directing that all cases involving Ujamaa Villages should be sent to him directly as, according to the circular, he was the only person with jurisdiction to entertain them. This circular brought the Chief Justice under fire at the Judges and Magistrates Conference in Dar es Salaam in 1973. At that Conference the late Sir Biron, J. categorically asserted that:

The Chief Justice cannot issue circulars ordering members of the Judiciary to abide by political or executive whims . . Judges are supposed to act independently of political or executive pressures and thus to dispense justice without fear or favour.

The late Justice of Appeal Yona Mwakasendo made it clear that until parliament enacts law for establishment of Ujamaa Villages, judges and magistrates will not obey the Chief Justice's circular requiring that cases involving Ujamaa Villages be sent to him.

Despite disagreements with brother judges, the former Chief Justice made public his support for the party in power and government policy setting up Ujamaa Villages. He is reported to have urged the judiciary to identify itself with the policies of the government and to do everything in its power to further the aims of Ujamaa. He was afraid that the judiciary would be used to oppose what he saw as 'progressive' changes. In his opinion, 'Since Tanzania believed in Ujamaa then, the interest of many people in land cases should override those of some few individuals. The judiciary could not be used as a tool to oppose Ujamaa . . . as citizens and TANU members, the courts are bound to further Ujamaa'.[21] Professor Rudi James argues that in his dual capacity the Chief Justice creates a dilemma to the judges and magistrates who are by the Oath Act[22] committed to solve disputes according to the law.[23]

The lower level of the judiciary is not insulated from the influence of the Executive and the Party either. The Party is involved in the appointment process of judicial officers at all levels. For a person to be appointed as primary court magistrate, he has to be recommended by the District Judicial Board, which is chaired by the Regional Party Secretary. After considering the candidates, the Board sends its recommendations to the Judicial Service Special Commission, which advises the Minister for Justice, who makes the appointment.[24] The Minister for Justice allocates Resident Magistrates to the judiciary from the list of the newly graduated lawyers from the University of Dar es Salaam who are supposed to undergo a one-year internship programme at the Attorney-General's chambers.[25]

Also Assessors who are important in Primary Court's proceedings are nominated by the Party branch Executive Committee as provided by the Primary Courts (Assessors) Regulations, 1972. The final selection of the panel is done by the District Executive Committee of the Party.

Harassment of the judiciary

Although the Executive and the Party are very instrumental in determining the composition of the judiciary at all levels, it does not always follow that their wishes are respected. However, where the directives of these two institutions have been ignored, it has often led to interference with the work of the judiciary and at times to the harassment of the judicial personnel. Sometimes interference and harassment is used to pre-empt an anticipated anti-establishment verdict. A few cases will illustrate the point.

The first reported incident in which a member of the judiciary was harassed by the executive took place in Taboro back in 1968. This was in the case of *R. V. Kassella Bantu and others*.[26] In this case a District Magistrate in his judicial capacity released the first accused, Joseph Kassella Bantu who was then Member of Parliament for Nzega East Constituency, on bail pending his trial with sixteen others for murder of cattle thieves. As a result of granting bail the Magistrate was detained.[27]

As interesting exchange between the judiciary and the executive/Party took place in Dodoma in 1979. This was in the case of *R. V. Iddi Mtegule*.[28] The respondent Iddi Mtegule stood charged with the offence of disobeying a lawful order contrary to Section 124 of the Penal Code before Mpwapwa Primary Court. He was alleged to have offered Mandazi for sale, in disobedience of an order issued by the Mpwapwa Area Commissioner, banning the sale and/or consumption of edibles in a bid to prevent the spread of cholera. The order which was issued in writing on February 19, 1979 contained a list of all prohibited articles. As Mandazi were not among the prohibited articles, the Primary Court Magistrate acquitted the accused.

The decision angered the Area Commissioner. He wrote an emotional letter to the Magistrate accusing him of bias and deliberate attempts to thwart the efforts of the authorities to stamp out cholera. He went further than that. He asked the trial Magistrate to explain why he had acquitted the accused. He even threatened to take stern action against the Magistrate. The Magistrate, however, was strong-minded and did not give in. He responded immediately, and went on to lecture the Area Commissioner on the provision of the Constitution relating to the independence of the judiciary. The matter went to the District Court in revision where the District Magistrate quashed the proceedings of the Primary Court, ordered re-arrest of the accused and a re-trial by another Magistrate of competent jurisdiction. At the High Court, Chipeta, J. restored the Primary Court decision commenting that it was his hope and the hope for all those who cherish the rule of law that such flagrant interference with the independence of the judiciary would not recur and were it to do so, it would receive the appropriate condemnation by the authorities concerned.

At least in the foregoing case the Primary Court Magistrate was brave enough to defend his position when attacked by the Area Commissioner. This was not the case in *James Bita* v. *Iddi Kambi*.[29] In this case, which was in Musoma, the District Party Secretary wrote a letter to the District Magistrate informing him that the dispute over allocation of land which was pending in his Court was a political issue and therefore the Party had to be consulted. The Magistrate was therefore asked to shift the dispute from the courtroom to the village council. The Magistrate complied with this order. In receipt of the results of the village council deliberations on the dispute, he reluctantly wrote a routine judgment abiding by the decision of the village council.

Contempt of court orders

For the judiciary to be effective, it must have the cooperation of the other organs of the state, especially the police and the Prisons Department. It is very awkward when the Court makes a decision and the executive refuses to enforce it. This happened in the United States of America under President Andrew Jackson. To show displeasure over a decision of the Supreme Court, the President decided to ignore it saying 'Well, John Marshall has made his decision, now let him enforce it.'

This has happened many times in Tanzania. Court orders have been completely disregarded or ignored by those supposed to enforce them. These are many cases which indicate this tendency. For example in *Sheikh Mohamed Nassoro Abdullah* v. *The Regional Police Commander Dar es Salaam*[30] the applicant, a religious leader, was arrested at his house in Mabiba in Dar es Salaam, 'whisked away in a Land Rover to Police custody' and later deported to Zanzibar on the orders of the President. This deportation was challenged on the ground that the President has no power under the Deportation Ordinance to deport a person from any part of Tanganyika to Zanzibar, and thus by deporting the applicant the President had exceeded his powers. The application was upheld and the order of habeas corpus issued. However, the authorities ignored the Court order and to date the applicant's presence is still restricted in Zanzibar.

Similar circumstances applied in *Lesinoi Ndeinai or Joseph Saleyo Laizer and Masai Lekasi* v. *Regional Prisons Officer and Regional Police Commander.*[31] In this case the two applicants were arrested by police in August 1979 pursuant to orders of the officer commanding the District. From the police they were transferred to prison and no charges were preferred against them. Being naturally desirous of resumption of their liberty, they filed application for habeas corpus. The High Court granted the application and ordered immediate release of the two detainees.

However, the unexpected happened. On stepping outside the courtroom as free men, the two were immediately re-arrested and returned to prison. The order of the Court that they be released as their detention was illegal was totally disobeyed by both the police and prison officers.

Possibly the worst case of this abuse occurred in *Edward Mlaki and Lision Matemba* v. *Regional Police Commander Kilimanjaro Region and Secretary Regional Security Committee Kilimanjaro Region*.[32] The applicants in this case had their two saloon cars, which they were using as taxicabs, seized by police. They applied for order of mandamus so that they could be released. The two respondents, the Regional Police Commander and the Secretary of the Regional Security Committee refused to accept service of summons from a duly constituted process server of the Court.

This blatant refusal by both respondents depicts the degree of hostility which can exist between the judiciary and other state and Party organs. It greatly worried Justice Mwesiuma who commented that:

This defiance to the Court process by the two highly placed government officials though prima facie directed at this Court is in fact directed to the laws of this country and therefore to the Constitution and the government of this land. In reality it is tantamount to watering down the whole legal system of the country.

On the part of the Regional Police Commander, the judge wondered how such a person who needs the co-operation of the public in getting witnesses to court in his duty of maintaining law and order could set such an example to others. Alarmed by the sharpening of the conflict between judiciary and other other state and Party organs, the Chief Justice Mr Francis Nyalali, while touring the Kondoa District in 1980, called for frequent meetings between officials of the police and the judiciary to discuss how best to collaborate in the enforcement of law and order.[33]

Side-stepping the judiciary

Having realised that the judiciary is not always on its side, there have been attempts by the State to discredit certain acts by the courts of law. This has been made public by the executive openly airing its distrust for courts. For example during the crackdown on 'racketeers and economic saboteurs' in April, 1983, President Nyerere said:

We have a problem on what to do with these people. However, we have not yet decided on the course of action . . . *I ask magistrates to forgive us if we hesitate to*

take culprits to courts of law. At times racketeers have been taken to courts where they either receive light sentences or have been set free . . . In the courts the racketeers could use their ill-gotten money to engage lawyers or use that money to twist the law in their favour.[34]
(emphasis added)

It should however be noted that this tendency of avoiding courts of law is not peculiar to Tanzania. It is often an aspect of the colonial legal system superimposed on our societies so that only the rich can make use of legal proceedings. Various methods have been devised to avoid courts of law in sensitive issues which may jeopardize the interests of the state. Among these methods are the introduction of 'ouster' clauses and resort to administrative tribunals.

Ouster clauses are statutory provisions excluding application for perogative remedies in the courts of law. These clauses thus make the administration immune from judicial review. Others have called this method as being 'judge proof.'[35] Those who might think of challenging administrative action are thus effectively disarmed. An example of an ouster clause is Section 7(5) of the Tanzanian Interim Constitution of 1965 which provides that 'Where a person has been declared by the Electoral Commission to have been elected President, his election shall not be questioned in any court.'

Ouster clauses take various forms and are related to what are called 'finality clauses', which provide that a certain decision is 'final' or 'final and conclusive'. Where the state thinks fit to oust the jurisdiction of the courts, then it resorts to clauses of this nature.

Administrative tribunals, also sometimes referred to as 'Kangaroo Courts' for quick justice, are another method used by the state as a substitute for the normal courts of law. Again these tribunals are concentrated in the areas classified as sensitive to the economy and thus likely to cause political and social instability. The proceedings of most of these tribunals are held in camera to avoid publicity. Areas covered by tribunals include land, house rent, economic sabotage, labour matters and so on.

Democratic-minded citizens who advocate respect for the rule of law have always indicated their dislike to such tribunals. One of the most unpopular tribunals is the Anti-Economic Sabotage Tribunal in Tanzania established under the Economic Sabotage (Special Provisions) Act, 1983. However, it has been justified by the executive as a necessary instrument to curb certain economic and social evils, in the words of President Nyerere:

Successive governments in this cournty have sometimes been forced to pass laws which in practice can be very dangerous for justice . . . the recent Economic Sabotage Acts, together with setting up of tribunals could be cited and there may be others. The reason for these laws is known. People can differ about whether or not they are necessary, but it is obvious that those who proposed them, or agree to them, thought that they were necessary and I am among those who saw their importance.[36]

The Economic Sabotage Act completely excludes the jurisdiction of the courts in all offences termed economic sabotage.[37] This has been interpreted as an indication of lack of confidence in the judiciary and the judiciary has responded accordingly. Judges have at times condemned laws which seek quick decisions at the expense of justice.[38]

However, mounting criticism and failure to achieve what was anticipated through the tribunals has forced the government to return to the judiciary. Issues of credibility/legitimacy have forced a reappraisal of the judicial role. The Economic Sabotage Act has now been repealed and replaced by another act which allows the High Court to entertain what are categorised as 'economic crimes.'[39] At the same time the executive and Party seem willing now to provide audience to and entertain advice from the judiciary at various forums including lecturing the National Executive Committee (NEC) of the Party on rule of law.[40] This indicates the crisis of confidence which exists in the country.

The contribution of the judiciary

The record of the judiciary in Tanzania, especially the High Court and the Court of Appeal, in advocating for individual liberty and rule of law is not really ascertainable. Though working under an extremely complicated political climate, the judiciary appears to have managed to weather the storm. It has continued to contribute considerably to the development of the law and particularly in interpreting the law in favour of the under-privileged and oppressed sections of the population.

This is clearly established by the various incidents discussed in this chapter where the courts of law in appropriate cases have not hesitated to grant applications for habeas corpus. Also, in cases where the State has, without justification detained persons, the courts have awarded heavy damages for false imprisonment. A good example is the case of *Feyya-Mipawa* v. *The Honourable Attorney-General and Assistant Superintendent Lazaro Kambi*.[41] In this case the plaintiff was claiming special and general damages for trepass to the person because on three occasions he was without lawful causes and of malice pretence, spitefully arrested, detained and prosecuted by or at the instance of the second defendant and that he suffered loss and injuries as a result. Mapigano, J. awarded general and exemplary damages at 400,000 shillings and special damages at 21,452 shillings. At one stage in his judgment the Judge observed that 'Indeed, if nothing else, this could be a textbook example of how the powerful can with a total scorn for civil rights and the singleness of purpose cause the machinery of criminal law to operate against a completely innocent subject.'

Another area in which the courts have made a remarkable contribution is the rights of children, where the courts have developed the 'welfare principle' and applied it rigorously for the future of children. This principle provides that in case of divorce, custody of children will be granted to the spouse with the ability to provide a conducive climate for proper upbringing of the children so that they can grow to be responsible citizens. This rule has been very helpful and there are suggestions that it should be extended to cover illegitimate children as well.

On rights of women, the courts have made very progressive decisions and pronouncements. The epoch-making decision is that of the Court of Appeal of Tanzania in *Hawa Mohamed* v. *Ally Sefo*.[42] The bone of contention in this appeal was interpretation of Section 114 of the law of Marriage Act, 1971. This section provides for division of matrimonial property at divorce. The question was whether domestic housework done by a housewife such as cooking for the husband and the family and caring for the children could be regarded as contributing in the acquisition of property by the family and thus entitling the wife to a share of the family assets at divorce. The High Court Judges were divided on this. There were two schools of thought, the liberal and conservative. The liberal school of thought held that domestic duties entitled the wife to a share of family property. The conservatives believed that for the housewife to be entitled to family property, she had to make direct financial or material contributions towards the acquisition of the property.[43]

The Court of Appeal upheld the liberal point of view that domestic duties performed by the housewife are important and entitled her to a share in the matrimonial property. The Court observed that:

Bi. Hawa, the applicant in looking after the matrimonial home, must be regarded as working not only for her current needs but also for her future needs and such future has to be provided from the matrimonial or family assets jointly acquired during the marriage in keeping with the extent of her contribution.

The decision has been hailed as a landmark pronouncement from the highest court of the land. This is because it recognizes the economic rights of women, most of whom being not salaried workers, used to invest their entire youthful and active years in the marriage only to be told at divorce that they could have no share in the family assets because they were mere wives who performed 'wifely duties' for free.[44]

Conclusion

There is no doubt that the judiciary as an organ of the State serves the interests of the ruling class. However, the capitalist system is a living contradiction. While the bourgeoisie would like their interests safeguarded by the judiciary, at the same time they advocate its independence, to render credibility to their system. However, any attempt to assert this independence is seen as 'mischevious' in the eyes of those who control the State. This is in fact the ultimate irony. The situation is worse in post-colonial States where the State is shaky, insecure and unstable. It is, therefore, easily threatened by any challenge or contractions from other organs of state. This explains the suspicion and hostility which can exist between the judiciary and the executive arm of the State. Therefore, a progressive and popular judiciary manned by principled and honest men will always be operating a very delicate balance. The interests of the people and those of the State have to be carefully balanced. That is not an easy task as nobody can pretend to be neutral. You are either with the people or with their oppressors. The judiciary has to choose which side to support.

Notes

1. Duffus, Sir William, 'The Judiciary and the Public' 3 *Dar es Salaam University Law Journal*, December, 1971.
2. Nyerere, J.K., Speech to the meeting of Judges and Resident Magistrates at Arusha on March 15, 1984. See *Daily News* (Tanzania) March 16, 1984.
3. For a discussion on these principles. See Phillips, O.H., *Constitutional and Administrative Law*, London: Sweet and Maxwell, 1973; Manchester, A.H., *A Modern Legal History of England and Wales 1759–1950*, London: Butterworths, 1980; and other works on administrative and constitutional law.
4. See Hansbury, H.G., 'Blackstone in Retrospect' (1950) 66 L.Q.R. 318 or Blackstone's *Commentaries on the Laws of England*.
5. Newbold, Sir Charles, 'The Roles of a Judge as a Policy Maker', 2 *Eastern Africa Law Review*, no. 2, August, 1969.

6. Holmes, O.W., *Collected Papers*, 1920, p. 173.
7. Gray, J.C., *Nature and Sources of the Law*, New York, 1938, p. 125.
8. Frank, J., *Law and the Modern Mind*, New York: Tudor Publishing Company, 1935.
9. (1932) A.C. 562.
10. (1865) 3 H & C 774.
11. For a thorough treatment of the development of capitalism to imperialism see Lenin, V.I. 'Imperialism, The highest stage of Capitalism: A popular Outline' *Selected Works* Volume I, Moscow: Progress Publishers, 1976.
12. See Du Bow *Justice For The People*, Ph.D. Thesis, University of California at Berkeley, 1973.
13. Chap. 537 of the Laws of Tanzania.
14. Chap. 453 of the Laws of Tanzania.
15. See the Interim Constitution, 1965 Chap. 596.
16. See Ng Maryo, E.S. and Mawalla, J.R.W.S., 'Strengthening the Power of the People'. A paper presented at the Tanganyika Law Society Seminar on proposed Constitutional changes held in Dar es Salaam in July, 1983.
17. Nyerere, J.K., 'The Party must speak for the People' *Uhuru Na Maendeleo*, Oxford University Press, Dar es Salaam, 1973, p. 30.
18. See the Proceedings of the Judges and Magistrates Conference held in Dar es Salaam in May, 1973.
19. President Nyerere's speech to the meeting of Judges and Resident Magistrates held in Arusha on March 15, 1984; see *Daily News* (Tanzania), March 16, 1984.
20. For example Justice Manning was appointed Minister for Justice in 1975, the late Justice of Appeal Vona Mwakasendo, then a Puisne Judge of the High Court was appointed Chief Corporation Counsel of the Tanzania Legal Corporation in 1976, and Justice Patel was appointed Counsellor at the Tanzania High Commission in New Delhi, India in 1978. See Fimbo, G.M., 'The Court of Appeal of the United Republic of Tanzania'. A paper presented at Faculty of Law Staff Seminar on Saturday February 20, 1982.
21. See 'Put Ujamaa First' *Daily News* (Tanzania) September 26, 1972.
22. See The Official Oaths Act, 1962 (Chap. 506).
23. James, R.W. 'Implementing the Arusha Declaration – The Rule of the Legal System' 5 *Dar es Salaam University Law Journal*, December 1973.
24. See Administration of Justice (Miscellaneous Amendments) Act, 1971 (Act 26 of 1971).
25. For a longer discussion on the Internship Programme which every lawyer graduating from the University must undergo for one year see Rwelamira, M.R.K., 'The Tanzania Legal Internship Programme: A New Horizon in Legal Education', 6 *Dar es Salaam University Law Journal*, April, 1977.
26. (1969) HCD 170.
27. See *The Tanzania Standard*, Friday, September 27, 1968.
28. High Court of Tanzania at Dodoma, Criminal Revision, no. 1 of 1979.
29. 1979 LRT no. 9.

30. This incident is cited by Justice Nassora Mnzavas, J.K. in *Ally Lilakwa* v. *Regional Prison's Officer and Regional Police Commander*, High Court of Tanzania at Arusha, Miscellaneous Criminal Cause, no. 21 of 1983 (unreported).

31. High Court of Tanzania at Arusha, Miscellaneous Criminal Cause, no. 22 of 1979.

32. High Court of Tanzania at Arusha, Miscellaneous Civil Application, no. 38 of 1979.

33. See *Daily News* (Tanzania) Friday, January 25, 1980.

34. See *Daily News* (Tanzania) Wednesday, April 6, 1983 also quoted in Malingumu G.R. Rutashobya 'On Professional Misconduct and Legal Ethics: A Lawyer's view'. A paper presented at Tanganyika Law Society Seminar held in January, 1984.

35. See Oluyede, P.A. *Adminstrative Law in East Africa*, East African Literature Bureau, Dar es Salaam, 1973, p.195.

36. President Nyerere's speech at the meeting of Judges and Resident Magistrates held in Arusha on March 15, 1984 See *Daily News* (Tanzania) March 16, 1984.

37. See Mwanukuzi, P.G. and Mjemmas, G.J. 'A Socio-Economic and Legal Critique of the Economic Sabotage (Special Provisions) Act, 1983'. A third year compulsory research paper, Faculty of Law, University of Dar es Salaam, 1984.

38. For example see the paper by Justice of Appeal Robert H. Kisanga, 'The Lawyer and the Society: The Challenge of the Professional and the Academic in Tanzania' delivered to the University of Dar es Salaam Law Society at the Main Campus on November 2, 1983.

39. The new Act is the Economic and Organised Crime Control Act, 1984.

40. The Chief Justice of Tanzania, Mr Francis Nyalali and the Chief Justice of Zanzibar Mr Augustino Ramadhani presented a paper on the country's legal system to the National Executive Committee (NEC) of the Party on May 28, 1984, see 'NEC Stresses Rule of Law', *Daily News* (Tanzania), Thursday May 31, 1984.

41. High Court of Tanzania at Dar es Salaam Civil Case, no. 254 of 1981.

42. Court of Appeal of Tanzania at Dar es Salaam Civil Appeal, no. 9 of 1983.

43. The Liberal School is articulated by Makame, J. (as he then was) in *Rukia Diwani Konzi* v. *Abdallah Issa Kihenga* High Court of Tanzania at Dar es Salaam, Matrimonial cause, no. 6 of 1977 (unreported). The conservative school is adopted by Patel, J. in *Hamid Amir* v. *Maimuna Amir* 1977 LRT no. 55 and by Mapigano, J. in *Zawadi Abdallah* v. *Ibrahim Iddi* High Court of Tanzania at Dar es Salaam Civil Appeal no. 10 of 1980.

44. See Rwezaura, B.A. 'Division of Matrimonial Assets under the Tanzania Marriage Law' *Verfassung Und Recht in Ubersee* 17 Jahrgang – 2 Quartal 1984 pp.177 – 93.

8 THE LEGAL PROFESSION, PLURALISM AND PUBLIC INTEREST LITIGATION IN TANZANIA

R.H. Kisanga

Introduction

The concept of *Public Interest Litigation* is only a recent development. It is a new approach being adopted for the enforcement of social or collective rights as distinct from individual rights. The need for the new approach has come about following the emergence of the social welfare state. Most countries in the world today recognise that all their subjects are entitled to certain basic social and economic rights. They do not stop there; they go further and seek to protect or guarantee such rights by statute law or the Constitution. However, it is one thing to proclaim legal and constitutional rights for all, but it is quite another as to whether or not all the subjects actually enjoy those rights.

For quite some time, a common feature in most of the developing countries has been that justice is open to a few privileged persons such as the rich and the educated. The large masses of the population have no access to justice because of their social, economic or other disabilities. In other words, by reason of such disabilities, these weaker sections of the community are unable to come to court and enforce the social and economic rights which they possess. Yet it is quite clear that the whole idea of states protecting and guaranteeing social and economic rights for all is of no practical value if the large masses of the population cannot translate those rights into a practical reality.

This state of affairs, where only a few privileged persons have access to justice, is no longer compatible with the current thinking and aspirations of many people in the world. Today it is increasingly clear that the right of access to justice is the key to the enjoyment of other social and economic rights, inasmuch as that right makes it possible to enforce other rights. The concept of public interest litigation is being developed with a view to achieving that end. If the large masses have access to justice that would make more meaningful the concept of the rule of law. This concept is widely accepted as an essential feature of a just and democratic society, something which we are all striving to create in our countries.

In this chapter it is proposed first of all to examine, in some detail, some of the factors which constitute a hinderance or obstacle to the socially and economically disadvantaged groups having access to justice. Then an attempt will be made to show how the approach of public interest litigation was evolved or developed, and how, through that approach, the legal profession tries to to surmount such obstacles. Finally, a few observations will be made on the factors which are likely to influence the development and effective working of this approach. The discussion will be based, as far as possible, on the experiences drawn from the Tanzanian society.

Some obstacles to having access to justice

There are various groups of disadvantaged persons in our present societies: these include the poor, the uneducated, the industrial, the agricultural or domestic workers, the women and the children, to mention only a few examples. In Tanzania, attempts have been made to protect the rights of these groups by legislation such as labour laws and, more recently, by the Constitution. Thus a Bill of Rights is now entrenched in the fourth amendment to the country's Constitution whereby it is sought to guarantee various types of freedom and equality for all, including for example the right to work, to receive just renumeration, the right to receive education, the right to hold property, the right not to be discriminated against, the right of an accused person to be presumed innocent until proved guilty, the right of a fair trial and the right of appeal.

In practice, however, a large number of people do not really exercise these rights. They merely possess them but are unable to enforce them for various reasons. The main obstacle is of course the factor of poverty. Tanzania is one of the poorest countries in the world. The vast majority of the population cannot afford the costs of enforcing these rights. Justice is an expensive process. This is so especially when it involves litigation in the district or superior courts. For instance, civil litigation in such courts often entails the parties and their witnesses travelling over considerable distances. This in turn imposes financial constraints. There is the question of paying for the services of an advocate. The vast majority cannot afford to pay advocate fees. Yet, the importance of an advocate in our system of justice cannot be over-emphasised. So long as poverty continues to be a predominant feature among the members of the society, the various rights as recognised and guaranteed by the State will continue to remain solely on paper.

Another serious obstacle to the exercise of basic rights by the masses is their lack of awareness about the existence and enforceability of those rights. It is clear that if people do not know their rights, they cannot be expected to exercise or enforce those rights. Tanzania has made considerable achievements in the field of literacy which is at present 85 per cent of the population. Although this is a big step forward, legal issues require more than a programme for general literacy. They require, among other things, some machinery which is designed to educate and guide the people on particular legal issues. For reasons which will be apparent later in this discussion, there is very little of such machinery at the moment in Tanzania. Thus despite the relatively high degree of literacy in the country, the large masses of the people remain ignorant of the rights which they have, and of the steps needed to be taken in order to exercise those rights effectively.

Even where such persons are aware of their rights, there is still the problem of lack of confidence to come forward and assert those rights. Take, for instance, the provision in our Permanent Labour Tribunal Act which empowers the workers to refer trade disputes to the Tribunal established under that Act for settlement.

Experience shows that this provision is rarely made use of. This is not because there are no trade disputes. The explanation seems to be that the workers feel threatened and scared to confront the employer for fear of reprisals. Such action is also seen as ineffective as the employers will in any event engage an advocate who is more competent in dealing with the legal disputes. A similar situation arises in relation to domestic workers. Many of them receive less wages and work for longer hours than the law prescribes. Some of them might not know of their entitlement under the law, but even when they do, they often do not vindicate their rights for fear of reprisals, such as losing the job or incurring the hostility or displeasure of the employer.

It is often said that this lax attitude towards the enforcement of legal rights has led to the exploitation of child labour. This happens especially in the rural areas where children are employed on the farm, say, to pick coffee. Some of these children are below the statutory working age. In pursuance of such employment some of the children have their education interrupted temporarily or even permanently. In some instances they are unpaid or overworked. They represent a denial of education, a basic right which is guaranteed under the Constitution, and violation of employment regulations as sanctioned by the labour laws of the country. By reason of their social disability such as youth, ignorance and dependency, however, the children are unable to protest against such injustices.

Social attitudes towards women is another area where this approach is prevalent. Tanzanian society is to a large extent male dominated, with a traditional bias against women. For instance, women in the rural areas work just as hard as men, if not harder, towards the upkeep and maintenance of the family unit. They participate fully in producing cash crops, such as coffee, which earn the family its cash income. But when the crop is sold, women have practically no control over the money that is realised from it. The man, as the head of the family, takes sole charge of the money and deals with it as he thinks fit; and very often the woman does not get an opportunity to receive her share. This is so notwithstanding the right enshrined in the country's Constitution that each one is entitled to receive a just reward for his or her labour.

Again, in some areas, there are customary laws which militate against the women. For instance, under the customary laws of the Bahaya and the Wachaga tribes, the women have no right to own or inherit clan land. Such land always devolves on the male members to ensure that it remains within the clan. Besides custom which discriminates against women, women in the country are discriminated against also when it comes to equality of opportunity, of employment, and eligibility for promotion. Women are not always treated equally with men in such matters. Again this is unfortunately so, despite clear guarantees in the country's Constitution that all persons are born equal, that all persons are equal before the law with an equal right to own property and the right not to be discriminated against on any ground. All these are clear instances of injustices to women. Yet women, especially those in the rural areas, often feel inhibited to protest against such injustices and to vindicate their constitutional rights.

Allied to all these obstacles is the general problem posed by the complex nature of legal procedures. Court procedures are so complicated that even the average educated man often finds them difficult to understand. There are a vast array of rules governing the conduct of a case from the very time of drawing up the plaint or petition to the end of the suit. Non-compliance with such technical rules may easily lead to the action being thrown out. For the most part, prospective litigants in the disadvantaged groups do not have the capacity to comprehend and comply with such rules and procedures, and this in turn serves to discourage or put them off completely.

More illustrations could be given of what constitute the obstacles to socially and economically disadvantaged groups enjoying their legal and constitutional rights in Tanzania today. What makes the matter even more serious however is that this problem is not limited to a small minority, but involves the vast majority of people in developing countries. This discussion therefore centres around the question: what role does the legal profession in third world societies have, in delivering justice to the disadvantaged groups of the community? What procedures can be adopted to ensure that such groups can enforce their legal and constitutional rights through the judicial process? It is to this aspect that I now turn.

Evolution of public interest litigation

The traditional approach to the problem of access to law has been to operate legal aid schemes which offer free legal service to poor persons who cannot afford to hire the services of counsel. In Tanzania there are two types of legal aid services — statutory and voluntary.

Statutory legal aid is provided by the State and is confined to criminal cases of serious nature such as homicide. Voluntary legal aid is operated by two institutions: the Tanganyika Law Society, consisting of advocates in private practice and the Law Faculty of the University of Dar es Salaam. Both institutions offer legal aid almost wholly in civil matters only. This traditional approach has many limitations however, ranging from being too selective to problems of finances and manpower. Such services are increasingly inadequate to meet current needs. In particular they offer assistance on an individual basis only. They were not designed to cater for group or collective rights. In these days when the concept of the welfare state is close to an accepted norm of everyday life, the traditional approach which focused attention on the individual is proving to be rather too narrow. It has therefore been necessary to search for new ways to accommodate these new developments. Consistent with that search, the view that is now emerging is that today something ought to be done to see that such weaker groups have their grievances redressed through legal process. This is the essence of the whole concept of public interest litigation. Perhaps the highest water mark of this view is to be found in the recent decision of the Supreme Court of India in the case of *People's Union for Democratic Rights* v. *Union of India* AIR 1982 S.C. 1433 where the Court held:

Public Interest Litigation is intended to promote and vindicate public interest which demands that violation of constitutional or legal rights of large numbers of people who are poor, ignorant or in a socially and economically disadvantaged position should not go unnoticed or unordained. Public Interest Litigation is essentially co-operative or collective effort on the part of the petitioner, the state or public authority and the court to secure observance of constitutional or legal rights, benefits and privileges conferred upon vulnerable sections of the community and to reach social justice to them.

The Indian Court was able to adopt this new approach because of yet another innovation. By reforming its procedural and jursidictional rules relating to the doctine of *locus standi*, it has given greater access to the vulnerable sectors. The doctrine of *locus standi* in its original form says that only a person to whom a legal injury is caused can move the court for judicial redress. This was considered too narrow and acceptable only when private law dominated the legal scene. However, as expanded by the Indian Court that doctrine now provides that:

Where there is a denial of the constitutional or legal rights of a class of persons who by reason of their poverty or disability or socially or economically disadvantaged position cannot approach a court of law for vindicating their rights, any member of the public or social action group acting bona fide can approach the courts for judicial redress on behalf of the poor and this need not be done by filing a regular writ petition through a lawyer, though that would be preferable but in appropriate cases, it may be done even by addressing a letter to the court.

This type of Public Interest Litigation is an important innovation by the Indian Courts. Through this approach, group demands of the socially and economically disadvantaged can now be brought before the courts and the courts can hear them in an endeavour to bring justice to such groups. Such developments bring hope to the disadvantaged by seeking to extend the frontiers of justice. For instance, where grievances could not be brought to the court because the aggrieved was or were poor or ignorant of their rights, a suit can now be maintained by some other person or persons on their behalf. Where the oppressed were afraid of suing for fear of reprisals by their powerful opponents such as employers, a suit may now be brought on behalf of such groups by another person or persons who have no cause to fear the possible consequences of such action. Where discriminatory tradition or custom of a particular society inhibits the discriminated members of that society to sue (for example the custom barring women from inheritance), it is now open to any person even outside such a community to maintain a suit on behalf of such discriminated groups. Again under the new approach, the procedure governing presentation of a complaint has been greatly simplified so that a letter of complaint addressed to the court by a layman is now sufficient to move the court. In a real sense one can say that through public interest litigation the legal and judicial process is becoming an instrument for establishing the claims and demands of the weaker sections which are struggling to find expression. Such claims and demands consisting principally of the effective access to justice are necessary for the enforcement and effective exercise of social and economic rights. In this connection, the role played by the legal profession has been, and will continue to be, of great significance.

Conditions for making public interest litigation effective

While public interest litigation has great potential as an instrument for the deprived sections of the community to have their social and economic rights vindicated, it seems that the effective working of that doctrine may have to depend on a number of factors. First and foremost, perhaps, is the willingness of members of the public to act for members of the disadvantaged groups. This is of prime importance because the essence of public interest litigation is that someone acting bona fide has to move the court. The doctrine does not provide that the court itself can initiate the proceedings. Thus, for this innovation to succeed in any country, groups within the community must be public spirited. There must be people who have the interests of the community as a whole at heart; people who take a broad view of development to mean development not only for the individual and his family but for the community as a whole, and who strive to achieve that end through legal and social action.

In this regard the role of the legal profession cannot be understated. For the purposes of this chapter, the legal profession in Tanzania includes the judiciary, the Bar, the law lecturers and professors. All these are involved, one way or another, in the administration of justice in the country and the problem now at hand presents a challenge to them all. The profession has a key role to play in the matter. Its members are much better placed than anyone else in the community to tackle these issues. Through their knowledge of the law they know the various social and economic rights of the groups concerned; they know where these rights have been denied or violated and they are conversant with the proper procedures of seeking redress in the courts or other tribunals in the event of denial or violation if such rights. Not only that, they know how best to put the case before the court or the appropriate tribunal. For, it is recognised that although a party may have a good case, the success or failure of the action depends to some extent on how the case is prepared and presented before the court. Thus in those countries where the legal profession is well established and thriving, public interest litigation has greater chances of succeeding. In this respect is seems that Tanzania is not so well placed. Here, the legal profession is relatively very young. The history of the indigenous legal profession in our country can properly be said to have started only in 1961 with the establishment of the Law Faculty of the then University of Dar es Salaam. Because of the economic constraints affecting the country, especially since the 1970s, it is not possible to train as many lawyers as are needed. As a result there is a shortage of lawyers in the country generally, a shortage which is likely to continue so long as the country's economic difficulties persist.

The development of public interest litigation will also depend on how much freedom of expression there is in any particular country. The doctrine is likely to thrive in a country where a person feels free to criticise the government or public authority without fear of reprisals. In other words, there are better chances for this doctrine in a country where a person has the courage to stand up and point out the faults or weaknesses of the government or public authority, for example, by showing that the government or public authority has deprived a said group of its rights. However, it may be difficult to agitate in such a manner in a country whose system of administration is, or tends to be, autocratic or totalitarian. Under such a regime, although a person sees the need for such agitations, he may prefer to keep quiet for fear of being persecuted as a political opponent.

There is yet another consideration which is closely connected with the scope for public interest litigation in our societies. The effective working of public interest litigation will depend also on the willingness of the government to be sued. In some countries, it is more difficult to sue the government than in others. In Tanzania, the matter is governed by statute. Under the Government Proceedings Act, 1967 as amended by Act no. 40 of 1974, no civil proceedings may be instituted against the government without the previous consent in writing of the Minister for Justice. On the face of it, there may be perfectly good reasons for this provision. For instance, it could be a means by which the government seeks to discourage or exclude frivolous litigation against it. It could also be a means of expediting conclusion of a matter and of minimizing costs by giving the government sufficient opportunity to consider and settle the matter out of courts where the claim is genuine. But on the other hand, the provision appears to pose a problem.

Psychologically, the provision tends to discourage or scare off prospective litigants. Ordinarily, it requires a lot of courage to sue a powerful opponent such as the government, but it is even more discouraging when such a powerful opponent has to consent to being sued. In other words, the right of a party to sue the government becomes more of a favour because whether or not that party can in fact sue depends on whether the government will consent. There is no guarantee that the government will always consent. Furthermore, experience shows that even where consent it given, it is not given in time. It often involves such long delays that the party suing almost despairs, thus rendering the party's right to sue practically illusory. Such a state of affairs serves to frustrate public-spirited persons who might be interested in acting on behalf of disadvantaged groups.

Lastly, there is the question of the world economic order which is today characterised by vast inequalities in the distribution of wealth among the nations. It is submitted that this issue is of some relevance to the effective working of the approach of public interest litigation. Essentially it seeks to assist the socially and economically disadvantaged sections of the community, to enforce the rights which they have under the law and the Constitution. The success of that approach, however, will depend on whether or not the party against whom such rights are being enforced has the ability or means to satisfy the claims being made against him. Today, there are a considerable number of people in the developing countries who are uneducated. This should provide a suitable area in which to urge the governments concerned to provide education for such groups. In Tanzania, for instance, the right to education is guaranteed under the Constitution. It is clear though, that the government cannot afford to provide facilities for all its people to get education, or to pursue education in the field of their own choice and to the degree they desire, as guaranteed by the Constitution, so that it would be a futile exercise to try, through public interest litigation, to enforce against such a government, the right of the uneducated section of its people to education. This is only one example, but one can think of others in which governments, being poor, cannot meet the demands for basic rights of some needy sections of their populations, even if they were compelled to do so.

This issue of poverty has a wider implication. Many of the governments in the third world countries are poor. Because of their poverty they are not in a position to do something to uplift the social and economic conditions of their subjects; so their subjects continue to live in poverty. Thus, one way of making public interest litigation effective is to try to eradicate or reduce poverty.

It seems, therefore, that the situation calls for a concerted effort by the international economic community to try and find ways of redressing the present global economic imbalance. That task requires, in particular, close co-operation with understanding among the world political leaders. If they succeed in bringing about the change, by alleviating the poverty of the less fortunate members of the third world countries, then the doctrine of public interest litigation will be more meaningful and can be used as a device for ensuring justice for all.

Conclusion

The approach of public interest litigation is an innovation by the court in an attempt to find ways of enforcing group or collective rights. The innovation of this approach goes to show that the court is dynamic in the sense that it interprets and applies the existing laws to meet the society's needs of the day. It adapts the law to the changing needs of the society. Collective rights are likely to feature prominently in the days to come, as the idea of a welfare state becomes an accepted factor of our daily lives. In these circumstances, public interest litigation has great potential as a means of helping the weaker and disadvantaged groups or sections of the community to have their grievances redressed by the courts. The legal profession has played, and must continue to play, a significant role by innovating and developing the approach of public interest litigation to cope with the emergence of group or collective rights.

The development and effective working of this doctrine will depend on a variety of factors, such as the strength of the legal profession, the readiness of members of the general public to act for the disadvantaged groups, the readiness of the governments to be sued and so on. It is apparent that the presence of such factors will vary from country to country. This means that the development of this doctrine and the effective working of it is also likely to vary depending on it context. However, it is a doctrine which serves the noble and useful purpose of trying to help the less fortunate members of the community realise their rights. It is a doctrine which ought to be given every encouragement to develop.

9 MOZAMBIQUE: PLURALISM, COLONIALISM AND THE LAW

Gita Itonwana Welch

Mozambique, as with other sub-Saharan countries, emerged from the settlement of Bantu people after the great migrations which our continent has seen over the last thousand years.[1] More recently, at the beginning of the nineteenth century, a Zulu migration began which resulted in further settlement in the southern part of our country. The northern coast also witnessed a strong Arab-Muslim influence which, from about the tenth century, expanded into the interior towards Lake Niassa. In the nineteenth century also came the Portuguese colonial penetration, first along the coast, and then at the end of the last century into the interior.

The result of all this is that Mozambique presents a complex linguistic, cultural and racial picture. At least twenty national languages are spoken, not to mention countless dialects. Even though all share Bantu roots, each has its own grammatical and etymological characteristics. Thus we may refer to the principal linguistic–cultural groups as being: the Maraves (including the languages Nyanja, Swahili, Ajava, Makua, Makonde) to be found principally in the northern provinces of Niassa, Cabo Delgado, Nampula and Zambezia; the Chuabos, found in the southern part of Zambezia; the Tswara in the north-east of Tete Province; the Nguni, Nyungwe and Shona in parts of Tete; Manica and Sofala in the centre of the country; the Sena in Sofala; and finally, the Tsonga in the southern provinces of Inhambane, Gaza and Maputo. Each province on its own and all the provinces together have to be considered as a mosaic.

Before colonial penetration, each linguistic–cultural group had its own forms of social organization, its own forms of art, crafts and culture, its specific forms of production and distribution, in short its own social structures and values.

Legal pluralism in colonial times in Mozambique

We cannot, for reasons of a practical order, grant to the natives the rights established in our constitutional instruments. We cannot subject the natives' individual, domestic and public life — if we may put it that way — to our political laws, our administrative, civil, commercial and penal codes, to our judicial structure.

We reserve for them their own legal order in keeping with their faculties, their mentality as primitive people, their feelings, their life, without excluding the need to guide them, in whatever ways possible, to even higher levels of existence . . . It is laid down that private courts be created to give simple, rapid and effective justice to the natives. This function is conferred upon the local administrators acting with the collaboration of elements drawn from the local population and with the attendance of the native chiefs, who know the special law of the natives and who are accordingly reliable informants of the uses and traditions of the tribe which need to be referred to in the administration of justice.

(Extract from Decree no. 12.533 of November 27, 1926 to establish the political, civil and criminal status of natives in the Portuguese colonies of Angola and Mozambique.)

In practice, how was this 'respect' of the colonialists for the customs and mentality of the 'natives' expressed?

Colonialism is by definition the institutional form whereby a nation exploits the riches and the labour of the people of another nation, holding back the social, economic and cultural progress of the latter for its own benefit. It is inherent in the system of colonialism to consider the inhabitants of the colonies as inferior beings, as uncivilised and primitive natives, lacking the social and cultural accomplishments of the Christian man of the west. It is the very socio-economic and cultural base of colonial exploitation and domination which underlies the pluralism fostered by a colonial power.

Portuguese colonialism, which for five centuries exploited and oppressed the peoples of what today is the People's Republic of Mozambique, constituted a particularly atrocious form of colonialism, because of the great cultural underdevelopment and backwardness of the productive forces of Portugal itself, in comparison with other European colonial powers. We may add that a large part of the Portuguese population itself, especially during most of this century, was subjected to brutal repression by the same backward regime.

At the level of law and the administration of justice, the discriminatory practices of Portuguese colonialism in Mozambique translated them-selves into a dualistic legal system that, far from having the intention of conferring special rights on the 'natives' was designed to give to the colonists the same rights that their compatriots enjoyed in the Metropole, while conserving and enlarging sources of cheap labour in the colony, thereby furthering the economic interests of colonialism. This is to say that as far as we Mozambicans are concerned, any form of pluralism under colonialism inevitably meant subtle or not so subtle forms of discrimination between various persons, within the context of a legalised and institutionalised status based on racial or ethnic origin, religious persuasion or social position.

The concern expressed by Portuguese colonialism 'not to shock the native mentality nor to impose on the native a foreign culture, but rather to give him complete freedom of action within the framework of his own institutions, gradually introducing him into the habits of the civilised', was a weak cover, used by the Portuguese government in the period after the Second World War, to justify the profound racial and social segregation which it practised for reasons of practical advantage and in terms of ideological conviction.

This process of adaptation took place over time. In May 1933, shortly after the rise to power of the dictator Salazar, the Colonies Act, Legislative Decree 22.465 was published which determined clearly the territorial demarcation of the Portuguese Colonial Empire, and provided that:

In the colonies, in keeping with the state of evolution of the native people, there will be special statutes for the natives to establish for them under the influence of the public and private law of Portugal, legal regimes in harmony with their individual, domestic and social uses and customs which are not incompatible with morality and the dictates of humanity.

In 1951, however, with the revision of the 1933 Salazarist constitution, Portugal made its first great attempt to update itself as a colonial power, and transformed what it had formerly called its 'colonies' into what it now called 'Overseas Provinces'.

In practice little changed, despite the change of denomination. The legal system throughout this period was characterised essentially by the existence of one set of laws for the colonists on the one hand, and another for the 'natives'. In respect of the latter, traditional or religious legal rules were supposed to be applicable. Yet in the eyes of the colonists, these local laws never rose above the status of mere uses and customs, which were either ignored by the administrators when inconvenient (for example when the colonists wished to dispossess the people of land) or else merely tolerated even when they did not go contrary to the so-called dictates of humanity and Christian civilization. At the level of the administration of justice, the courts, and the whole apparatus of judges and lawyers, existed only for the colonists. For the 'natives', the administration of justice was little more than an aspect of 'native policy' and local government. It was the colonial administrator with little legal training, but extensive training in how to attend to the 'native affairs', who did justice in terms of the 'native laws'.

In practice, 'native laws' for the Mozambicans meant the inhuman and discriminatory pass and tax laws, it meant the barbaric law that imposed forced labour. In respect of labour conditions, the relations between the indigenous employee and the colonial master were governed by the Native Workers Code and the Rural Workers Code, which, in truth, established work regimes not far short of slavery. In the spheres of civil and criminal law, the political, civil and criminal status of 'natives' ensured that, because of their primitiveness, the statutes, laws and codes applied to the colonists, would not be applied to them. Only a tiny class of persons of indigenous descent were assimilated as 'colonists'.

As for the day-to-day problems that arose among the people, these were resolved accordingly to the so-called uses and customs of the area. They were administered by the chiefs and headmen, acting as faithful servants of colonialism, who often ensured that even these uses and customs were filtered according to the interests of the colonial administration.

Unity, the central theme in the struggle for national liberation

It was without doubt the peculiarities of the type of colonialism imposed by Portugal (an underdeveloped colonialism, as it has been called) that required us to achieve our independence by means of a ten-year armed struggle and military confrontation.

Since Mozambique is a vast country, manifesting great ethnic, linguistic, religious and racial complexity, an immense amount of popular mobilization was necessary to bring about the successful outcome of the national liberation with the creation of the broad front. For FRELIMO, the question of national unity came to be a dominant question in the process of achieving national independence. Pluralism had been manipulated by the colonial power as a means of divide and rule. National liberation required unity in diversity. We would like to quote an extract from a text by Samora Machel in relation to preparation for the agricultural year in 1971, issued at the height of the armed struggle. It illustrates the importance given by the leadership of FRELIMO to unity:

When I a Nyanja, am working the soil side by side with an Ngoni, my sweat runs down as his sweat runs down; we value the effort each of the other and, I feel a bond of unity with him. When I from the North learn from a Comrade from the South to construct an orchard, to irrigate tomatoes, red and plump, when I from the Centre learn from a Comrade from the North how to grow mandioca, which I never knew before, I am learning about unity with these comrades, I am living in a concrete way the unity of my country, the unity of my class, of the working people. I am destroying with each and every one of them prejudices of tribe, of religion of language, everything that is secondary and that divides us. With each plant that grows, with drops of sweat and of intelligence which we stir into the soil, so we grow our unity.

It is this question of national unity which profoundly underlay the whole process of national liberation in Mozambique and constituted in itself an important battle won by the Mozambican people in the course of their struggle for national independence.

It was in the liberated zones in the midst of this struggle that the people took power on various fronts, organising themselves into producers' co-operatives, building their own schools, crèches and hospitals, and resolving in a collective way the social problems and conflicts which emerged.

We say today that our legal system is based on the notion of popular justice, since the people participate directly in the administration of justice, jointly with the organs and entities to whom the State attributes a judicial function; but it was in the liberated zones that for the first time since the advent of colonialism the people exercised judicial power by means of their participation in the Disciplinary Commissions of FRE-LIMO. These disciplinary organs operated at the grass-roots level and resolved matters involving the guerrillas as well as the population in the criminal civil and security spheres and in relation to military discipline. In addition, the disciplinary committees attended to ideological–political questions that arose, not in relation to abstract questions of doctrine or belief, but in relation to concrete questions about what the objectives of the struggle were, what was meant by unity, and what was involved in the struggle against tribalism, regionalism and racism.

In this way, the identity of outlook in relation to principles and objectives which FRELIMO sought to evoke on the part of its militants and the special care and attention given to these concrete ideological questions, questions of perspective, was a factor which systematically and progressively helped to consolidate national unity and minimise points of difference : language, cultural ways, ethnic origin, religion, race and tribe.

We may refer to the words in this regard of Jose Moiane, veteran of the national liberation, today Governor of the Province of Maputo, when he gave an interview recently to the journal of the Ministry of Justice, *Justica Popular*:

By means of the activity we developed to resolve concrete cases with the participation of the people, by means of the process of re-education, of political explanation, of the actual organization of life and society in the liberated zones, people developed a partriotic consciousness and understood the importance of the tasks which each moment of struggle brought their way.

And, of course, later in those zones people began to marry without thinking about tribe; fighters from Maputo and Gaza (in the south) married young girls from Tete and Niassa (in the north) and integrated themselves into the culture of these regions. I myself, when I operated in Niassa and Tete Provinces, felt myself completely at home. So much so, that I know those Provinces better today than I do my own Province of origin, which is Gaza. It was the struggle itself that taught us how to assume (take on the dimension of) national unity.[2]

The judicial system in Mozambique today

The People's Republic of Mozambique was born at zero hour on June 25, 1975, fruit of the liberation struggle led by the Front for the Liberation of Mozambique (FRELIMO). The Front, in its turn, had been created in 1962 by means of the unification of various groups of Mozambicans who for varying reasons had been actively opposed to Portuguese colonialism.

The People's Republic of Mozambique is a unitary State, just as the Front for the Liberation of Mozambique was unified during the process of achieving national independence. How is this principle reflected at the level of law and in relation to the administration of justice? It is necessary to analyse, even if briefly, the Courts Act of 1978, which regulates the creation and functioning of the Popular Tribunals.

The new court system established in 1978 created a series of Popular Tribunals hierarchically arranged in accordance with the administrative divisions of our country.[3] Thus we have Popular Tribunals at the level of the base (localities, neighbourhoods and communal villages); District Popular Tribunals; Provincial Popular Tribunals and in contemplation, a Supreme Popular Tribunal. In addition we have the Procurator-General's Office, something akin to the Attorney-General's Office in other countries. All the courts function by means of the judges acting collectively, trying to reach consensus where possible, otherwise by majority vote, each judge being equal.

With the exception of the courts at the level of the base, where there are no professional judges, in all other courts the sessions are presided over by trained judges. Even in the higher courts, however, the majority of the judges are elected from the local population, such elections being conducted in public on the basis of the moral integrity of judges, their civil awareness and their respect for the principles and values of the new society as set out in the Constitution.

In the past years we have witnessed the gradual simplification of procedure, so important for the functioning of a popular justice without long delays prejudicial to litigants and the accused. It is not only these formal aspects which characterise our new system of justice. On the contrary, the main change is in the substance, in the very content and meaning of justice. The participation of the people in the system of justice, particularly at the community level, is a reality. By means of encouragement from the Women's Movement and the Youth Movement, and also from the Assemblies of the People, the people in the neighbourhood go in large numbers to the courts not only to have their own cases heard but also to attend cases that arise at their places of work or residence, helping the judges in terms of what they knew about the matter. The District and Provincial courts sit as often as possible in the actual site where the crime was committed, for example, in the case of thefts at the Airport, the Court sits in the Airport building itself with as many airport workers as possible present. The same might happen in a case of homicide with a background of imputed sorcery — the Court will try to hold its hearings in the area where the offence took place, so as to permit the people from the area to attend. In this way the Court enters into a direct relationship with the people, and its hearings become a school in which the people learn to understand and voluntarily accept our laws, and in which the people became involved in the struggle against crime.

It is especially at the level of the base where the popular tribunals in reality constitute the greatest innovation.[4] In these tribunals procedural formalism is reduced to a minimum. In effect, it is the population, knowing the case arose in their community, which serves as witness for the prosecution or offers the Court vital information without which, it would not be easy to arrive at a just decision. In these courts, although the procedure does not obey formal rules, although there is no prosecutor or counsel for the defence, it is the people who exercise these functions, drawing on a long democratic tradition of popular participation in resolving disputes, but doing so in terms of new values and goals.

As we have already stated, there are no professional judges in these lower courts. The judges are elected from the local population. They are known and respected in the community. They in turn know the community, they know its problems. Their procedure is flexible, and open, and these are the courts to which the people have the most direct and immediate access. In truth, these grass-roots courts are a direct outcome of our revolutionary process and serve as an inspiration for new ideas in relation to the whole justice system, so as to make it increasingly responsive to the interests of the people. It is in these courts, completely free from the influence of the laws and formalism of the colonial system, where the cultural values of the people are best expressed as well as their popular sense of justice. We now have about seven hundred of these courts in operation throughout the country, involving about five thousand elected judges, operating one or two days a week, and attending to the great bulk of family disputes, neighbour's problems and problems of day-to-day infractions of the law in the community. These courts can give divorces in the case of persons not married in the civil registry, award custody and maintenance and division of property where the value is not high, determine compensation or damages in civil matters and order fines, perform public criticism or give sentences of up to thirty days' community service for crimes (they have no power to order imprisonment).

To deal with cases of a more complex nature, or involving civil claims for higher amounts, or criminal offences in which prison is a possibility, there exist the District and Provincial Courts, each with its respectively defined jurisdiction. In these courts, the judges determine cases according to the written law, both in terms of substance and procedure. A system of appeal exists from the lower to the higher courts, and this is one way of attempting to guarantee a uniform system of justice for the whole country. But probably more important in practice is the holding of Judicial Seminars at which judges from the lower courts meet and exchange experiences with judges from the higher courts, and receive in broad outlines indications of how certain problems should be dealt with.[5] These orientations have a function similar to that of judicial precedent in other systems, save that the judges in the lower courts have a more active role in raising their problems and offering their opinions. Thus by means of Seminars, visits from the judges in the higher courts, and special courses for judges in the lower courts, as well as through the system of appeal, we seek to realise the Constitutional injunction to establish a uniform system of justice that is equally available to all, whether in the towns or the countryside, irrespective of the ethnic or racial origin or the religion of the violater or the violated, from the Rovuma to Maputo.

Ethnic–cultural diversity and legal unity

We have tried to show how in a country like Mozambique instead of being a source of opposition, ethnic–cultural diversity acts in a complementary way. For us the degree of national unity thus achieved is a source of great pride; we do not ignore the ethnic and cultural particularities of each region of our country, but on the contrary regard them as our riches, as the heritage of the whole people. Each is a partial aspect of our global culture, of our overall personality as Mozambican and African men and women. The formation of the Mozambican nation as we know it today is the culmination of centuries of unification, of various kingdoms, of various tribal and ethnic groups, in relation to which the brutal impact of colonialism was only one factor (it was not colonialism that created Mozambique, but the common struggle against colonialism).

After Independence, this sentiment of national unity has been increased. There is intense cultural interchange between the North, the South and the Centre. In nursery schools and high schools, in cultural and literary associations, in the media, we find expressed the songs, dances, stories and oral tradition of all the zones of our country. The recently held Extraordinary Conference of the Organization of Mozambican Women, for example, was the culmination of a year-long process of research and interaction through the length and breadth of the country. It involved meetings, largely in the rural areas, in which perhaps half the women participated and expressed their opinions on various social and traditional practices, such as initiation rites and marriage settlements.

From what we have said legal pluralism is not the only way to recognise and express the ethnic–cultural diversity of a country. We do not for a moment suggest that all African countries (in the great majority, followers of pluralism) should immediately adopt unitary systems. We just wish to say that as far as we are concerned the creation of a unified legal system was an important step in the guaranteeing of the real equality of all our duties for men and women which is guaranteed in general terms in constitutions in Africa, an equality which had previously been diluted by the inequalities of pluralist systems introduced by colonial administrators.

The role of traditional law in the context of a unitary legal system

Traditional law in Mozambique, as traditional law in all African countries, has a dynamic and vitality of its own. It is not composed of rigid, compartmentalised and impersonal norms. Reflecting its character as part of the oral tradition, as part of the symbolic life of the people, of social interaction and mutual aid, traditional law is, in addition to being law, an important part of our cultural heritage.

In his well-known study on 'The Evolution of Law and Government in Africa', T.O. Elias states succinctly:

We should not minimise the advantages which African Courts and their procedures may possess:

(1) Justice was popular, in the sense that the people understood the mechanism and objectives of the judicial process and the law applied. The people controlled the courts.

(2) Justice was local and rapid.
The main concern of traditional African Courts was to do justice in the local community, rather than to have administrative efficiency or carry out the will of central organs.

(3) Justice was simple and flexible.
There were no elaborate procedural codes or complex forms of proof although in practice there were certain practical rules in relation to evidence. The judges did not merely carry out the law, above all sought solution for disputes.

(4) The apparatus for extra-judicial arbitration was always there.

At the same time, while recognising these considerable virtues, there are aspects to the rules and principles of traditional law we may consider negative, especially when they reflect the class bias of feudal society and inasmuch as they were designed to reinforce social and other inequalities between men and women. We are compelled to move away from their application in the day-to-day life of the courts, while recognising their historical cultural value as part of our past and recording and preserving them as part of the culture of our people.

Conclusions

For us Mozambicans, pluralism has been historically defined as the interaction of two or more legal systems within a single state. In the context of Mozambique it is directly related to Portuguese colonial oppression. In fact, the pluralist relationship meant a relationship of subordination and domination. Traditional pre-colonial law was tolerated to a certain degree, but in a distorted form and only to the extent that it did not inconvenience the colonists. Its application by chiefs and headmen holding junior positions in the colonial administration and exploiting such positions for gaining petty privileges ensured that it bore little real relationship to the pre-colonial law.

Hilda and Leo Kuper bring out neatly this kind of relationship between pluralism and colonialism when they write:

> In the colonial system pluralism did not constitute any threat to colonial power; on the contrary, it facilitated and perpetuated colonial administration. In this way, the multiplicity of legal systems reflected in the pluralism of colonised societies, served to help colonial domination, maintaining to a certain degree, the divisions between the multiple segments of society. Colonial power was threatened more by unification between the different segments than by the eventual secession of one of the plural parts. On the contrary, pluralism represents a latent threat of conflict in independent states. The law may either be used to create a society more homogenous or else to reinforce differences.

Notes

1. Article 26 of the Constitution declares that: all citizens of the People's Republic of Mozambique enjoy the same rights, and are subject to the same duties, independently of their colour, race, sex, ethnic origin, place of birth, religion, level of education, social position or occupation. Any act calculated to prejudice social harmony, create divisions or situations of privileges on the basis of colour, race, sex, ethnic origin, place of birth, religion, level of education, social position or profession, shall be punishable by Law.
2. Article 9 of the Courts Act.
3. Unlike the District and Provincial Popular Tribunals, Courts at the level of the base had no counterparts in colonial times. They are a direct result of the experience of justice in the Liberated Zones during the armed struggle for national liberation, an experience which continued in a new form after Independence under the initiative of Dynamising Groups, groups set up at the grass-roots level to attend to political, administrative and judicial functions in villages, neighbourhoods and blocks.
4. A majority of judges of the local Popular Tribunals are illiterate. In the adult literary campaigns launched by the Ministry of Education and Culture, elected judges, together with elected deputies and other persons in the 'structure', are given absolute priority. It is estimated that from 1978 until today about one-half of the elected judges have been involved in literacy

courses or else other adult education courses. Illiteracy is one of the great scourges left behind by colonial domination. In 1975 about 95 per cent of our population was illiterate, a figure which by 1983 had been reduced to 70 per cent. But even apart from this fact, using clear and simple language in our laws is part of the fundamental principle that all legislation should be clearly understood and accepted by the people.

5. The Rovuma is the river which marks the country's northern border, while the Maputo is the most southerly of the country's major rivers.

Sources

Official Documents of the People's Republic of Mozambique
(1) The Constitution.
(2) The Courts Act, 1978 (literally, the Law on Judicial Organization).
(3) Report of the Central Committee to the IV Congress of the FRELIMO Party, 1983.
(4) *A Nossa Luta* (Our Struggle) — National Institute of Books and Records, INLD, 2nd ed., Maputo.
(5) First General Census of the Population in Mozambique — 1978.

10   ON THE SHAME OF NOT BEING AN ACTIVIST: THOUGHTS ON JUDICIAL ACTIVISM

Upendra Baxi

The fact that appellate justices make law, and not merely interpret it, is now fully acknowledged amongst the *cognoscenti*. But there are many, including the appellate justices, who even at this day and age contest this simple proposition. They do this in a manner reminiscent of the Three Sisters in Salman Rushdie's *Shame* who until the mysterious happened to them (or more accurately to *one* of them though, alas! no one will even know *which* one) firmly believed that 'fertilization might have been supposed to happen through the breast' through "bizarre genitalia" such as holes in the chest into which their nipples might snugly fit' (Rushdie, 1983, p. 13). Those who wish to preserve their jurisprudential pubescence are entitled to such fantasies; but the shame of belated discovery would haunt them, like the Three Sisters, forever, with some sinister and some very tragic results.

If we, then, accept jurisprudential adulthood, the question is not any longer whether or not judges make law: rather the questions are: what *kind* of law, how *much* of it, in what *manner*, within which self-imposed *limits*, to what *willed results* and with what tolerable accumulation of unintended results, may the judges make law? These kinds of questions direct immediate attention to the ineluctable policy and political choices which judges have to make in their daily administration of justice and to the problem of accountability for their actions (see Baxi, 1982).

It is only natural that judges wish to exercise power but do not wish to be particularly accountable to anyone. It is natural, too, for them to begin to indulge themselves in the honest fiction that they are merely carrying out the intention of legislators or discovering the immanent something called the Law. The tradition of the law and the craft of jurisprudence offer such judges plenty of dignified exits from the agony of self-conscious wielding of power. This stance suits, equally, also the lawyer and the scholar who also find it more convenient to deal with immediate issues of technique and substance, rather than look back to more fundamental questions of the role of the judge and the lawyer in a changing (often traumatically so) society. Hence, the conspiracy of the Great Blackstonian Lie; and hence, to borrow the felicitous phrase of Picasso, the incredibly persistent attempt to convince the people of the truth of the lie that judges do not make law.

These questions concerning power and accountability have been extensively discussed in literature (e.g. Bickel, 1962; Weschler, 1959; Miller & Howell, 1960; Stone, 1964, 1966; Dworkin, 1977; Baxi, 1980; Ely, 1982). They will continue to be discussed for a long time to come, with or without any satisfactory final answer since there cannot be, in the very nature of things, a universal theory of the nature of judicial process (Baxi, 1980).

But with all its richness and promise, even the present framework of discussion continues to be confined to the problematic of the power of judges to make law and its justification. It ignores other powers which justices exercise which are not patently legislative and yet are almost as important. Let us call these powers *'faute de mieux* executive powers of appellate justices'. These deserve study by all those interested in the judicial process as a species of political process.

The 'executive' power of judges involves at least seven distinct sets of powers. Most of these powers may even result in a decision not to proceed to a decision! The executive powers thus extend to:

(i)   powers of admission;
(ii)   powers of scheduling cases for hearing;
(iii)   powers to form benches or panels;
(iv)   powers of granting 'stay' *pendente lite*;
(v)   powers of 'suggestive jurisprudence';
(vi)   powers of scheduling reasoned judgements and
(vii)   powers of allowing/disallowing a review.

Except in category (vii) where occasionally at least a judgement needs to be written, there are, at least in India, no guidelines on how the rest of the discretionary executive powers should be used. In each of these categories the powers of appellate justices, and especially of the Supreme Court, are absolute, without a trace of accountability.

In regard to the first facet, take, for example, a prayer of a citizen before the Supreme Court of her country that the imposition of martial law or emergency or dissolution of a legislature or emergency should be allowed to be legally contested: the Court allowing such a challenge, regardless of the ultimate decision, would indeed be exercising its discretionary admission powers to allow space for political action. Take the less dramatic issue of *locus standi*: in deciding who shall have the right to activate the Court, the Court will undoubtedly make some law. Not so however, when it, in a non-speaking order, just dismisses the petition *in limine*. A group of citizens may be denied political voice just by refusal to hear them, even on the issue of why they should be heard.

The power of scheduling cases is also fraught with immense potential for good and bad use. Hearings on imminent violations of fundamental rights may be scheduled after their large-scale violations have taken place! Challenges to suspension of habeas corpus or the legality of military rule or the Emergency may be scheduled for hearing after the horrible realities of detention without trial and torture without redress have become *faits accomplis*. At less dramatic levels, courts could so organise their dockets as to hear late cases which should be heard early, given their social or political importance; and vice versa. This may happen through design or default, intention or inertia. The result, overall, is the same. Justices do not lag behind editors and proprietors of newspapers; these latter have the power to 'kill' stories. Justices have the power by simple or devious docketing exercise, to kill controversy, contention and social relevance of cases before them.

In the third category, peculiar only to countries where the Court as a whole does not sit, the Chief Justice possesses enormous powers to constitute benches or panels of justices to decide matters. There are no guidelines for the exercise of this discretionary power; it has unfettered and hitherto unreviewable administrative discretion, open to malign and benign uses. In any case, the Court becomes fragmented, shifting panels of judges decide cases and in many cases the Court as an institution loses its corporateness and craftspersonship. From the point of view of the citizen, the Court as an institution becomes merely a panel of a few justices selected unaccountably by the Chief Justice from time to time.

The power of granting stay, *ex parte* and upon hearing till the disposal of the matter, is also a very potent power, which can be used to great mischief or great service, depending on the specific litigious and overall political context. To decline to give stay against demolition of twenty thousand hutments of pavement dwellers one day may mean bulldozing of their lives and livelihoods; and to grant a stay the next time round would be to allow them to continue to cheat their way to survival. To allow governments to transfer incorruptible officials in favour of more 'pliable' ones by refusing stay might cancel all the possible gains of upholding on 'merits' after some years their plea against transfer. In the meantime, effective enforcement of legislation (say, land reforms) beneficial to the masses may be suspended by the *de facto* placement of a corrupt official. The examples can be multiplied. The fact remains — a decision to exercise judicial power to favour or restrain redistribution is made when stays are allowed or disallowed. The decision, howsoever masked in terms of 'balance of convenience' and related 'tests', is ultimately grounded in some political choice, favouring either status quo or redistribution. Undoubtedly, this is an important power, especially in countries like India where population explosion seems not unrelated to docket explosion (Baxi, 1982; Dhavan, 1978). It is the Indian experience, at least, that justices cannot be hurried, based perhaps on the maxim 'Justices hurried are justices buried'!

Powers of 'suggestive' jurisprudence often result in compromise, settlement, abandonment of a case or evolution of jurisprudence *ex concessionis*. Justices have ways of communicating to counsel, in a variety of explicit and implicit ways, the anticipations they have of how the case might be decided by them, and good counsel decide often accordingly. This is not an insignificant power at all. The career of an important constitutional conception or an elaboration of a doctrine could be aborted by, for example, proceeding on the basis that the so-called ratio of a case is what counsel for the instant case agree it to be (as partly happened in the *Indira Nehru Gandhi* v. *Raj Narain* in regard to the 'ratio' of the basic structure in *Kesvananda Bharati*: see Baxi, 1978). The same result, more or less, might ensue when a case is withdrawn on the basis of compromise, led by justices. Once again it needs saying that suggestive jurisprudence is not in itself good or bad; but its possible uses and abuses do need attention.

It is not to be assumed, at least in India, that upon the completion of the hearing on merits a reasoned judgement will follow in reasonable time. In the Supreme Court of India, judgements take a long time to come; unaccountably, they are held up by some justices for months and years together. Sometimes, orders are given but reasons deferred, and these are delivered after long lapses of time. The time-context in which a judgement is rendered is often charged with political or social significance, and unreasonable delay, planned or inadvertent, affects the course of public opinion and social action on the issues involved.

Much the same can be said concerning the powers of courts to review their own decisions. For example, following the 'Open Letter to the Chief Justice of India' (see Baxi *et al.,* 1979), national women's organizations insisted that the Court review its verdict of acquittal in that rape case. The review was actually taken in hand after about two years and quietly dismissed. The power and procedure for review of its own judgements by the Supreme Court of India are subject to no specific discipline and accountability; almost all is left to the 'good sense' and power of the deciding justice.

This rapid review does suggest that the 'executive' powers of appellate justices are as important as their law-making powers and, importantly, there appears to be an even greater degree of unaccountability in their exercise of the executive powers. For example, by the fairness standards the Supreme Court of India has itself developed, concerning the exercise of administrative judicial powers (see Baxi, 1982), many of these powers are too wide and confer uncanalized discretion and their actual exercise violates many of the fairness requirements! *Quis custodiet ipsos custodes?*

Discussion on judicial activism has hitherto focused merely on the exercise of judicial lawmaking powers. But 'activism' also has an important role to play in the exercise of judicial executive/administrative powers discussed in the preceding paragraphs. In each of the seven categories identified by us (and there indeed might be some more still to be identified), judges have the choice of exercising their powers militantly in favour of constitutional values or of behaving merely in a bureaucratic manner, looking at issues presented before them strictly as routine managerial tasks. One would expect that an activist justice will be inclined to take the former view in exercise of executive powers as she is inclined to do in exercise of her judicial legislative powers. But this correlation has to be empirically established. There might also be dissonance in judicial behaviour in these two realms.

II

'Activism' is one word, but does not have one meaning for all those who use the term. An activist judge, to my mind, is a judge who is aware that she wields enormous executive and legislative power in her role as a judge and that this power and discretion have to be used militantly for the promotion of constitutional values. Such a judge realises that the legal system is, to some extent or other, relatively autonomous both from the economy and the polity and that this autonomy is a function of the very nature of the coalitions of the ruling class which have acquired the powers of national governance.

An activist judge knows that the constitutional value proclamations are an aspect of the ideology-maintenance apparatus of the state and are designed to enhance or reinforce the legitimacy of the ruling classes. By the same token, such a judge also knows that the ruling class is divided in its pursuit of constitutional values, since an authentic pursuit of these values will bring about a change in the very class character of the state. Elaboration of constitutional values by justices assists the process of legitimation of the ruling classes; at the same time, it tends to expose them to new demands, new uncertainties, new sources of discontent and fresh challenges to their legitimacy. The dual character of judicial elaboration is always pre-eminent to the mind of activist justices and that itself is the source of strength and legitimacy of judicial activism. An activist judge is thus one who has developed a heightened political consciousness concerning the structure of her society and the nature of transformation processes. The scope of her activism depends on how the ruling groups perform through the ensemble of state institutions. In what follows, we look at this aspect a bit closely.

If the legislature is in effect discharging its job of legislating, the scope for judicial legislation is constricted, and vice versa. Let us take some concrete examples from the domain of relations between labour and capital in India. Parliament did not legislate on the legality of the scope of the contract labour system; the Supreme Court in 1960 laid down conditions under which contract labour is legally and constitutionally permissible. It is this decision which led Parliament to enact the Contract Labour (Regulation and Abolition) Act, 1962.[1] Similarly, when owners ask for voluntary winding-up of a company, the workers have no standing under the Companies Act even to contest the petition. Suggestions have not been lacking for the reform of this excessively pro-capital legislation. At last in 1982, some activist justices of the Supreme Court held that labour is not just a marketable, vendible commodity, but rather an equal partner with capital and changed the law to require that workers be heard.[2] Similarly, the Supreme Court radically redefined the concept of 'industry' under the Industrial Disputes Act, finding that Parliament had been inactive for over two decades and it had not altered the definition which was unclear and misleading in the first place.[3]

In other words, an activist judge will consider herself perfectly justified in resorting to lawmaking power when the legislature just doesn't bother to legislate. Whatever may be said in the First World concerning this kind of lawmaking by judges (see Dworkin, 1977; Ely, 1982), it is clear that in almost all countries of the Third World such judicial initiatives are both necessary and desirable. At least in the Indian experience, it does not appear that legislators have resented much the judicial takeover of their burdens, since it liberates them to attend to other tasks of *realpolitik*.

There are other kinds of situations in which a legislature of a multi-ethnic society acts, but it often acts in such a way as to preserve anti-constitutional traditions and practices of a minority group. For example, while amending the provisions of the Indian Criminal Procedure Code relating to maintenance, Muslim spouses were excluded, not because the system of *mahr* was considered to ensure adequate maintenance to Muslim women but because the ruling coalition apprehended alienation of Muslim male-dominated constituencies. Justice Krishna Iyer valiantly reinterpreted the relevant provisions to apply to Muslim women, thus daringly reversing the exclusion specifically desired by the legislature.

An activist judge would also legislate to protect and preserve the human rights of ethnic minorities guaranteed by the Constitution. The Indian Supreme Court, for example, has devised (primarily through the medium of P.N. Bhagwati) a unique form of epistolary jurisdiction through which public citizens or groups can activate the Court on account of violation of fundamental rights of ethnic and other minorities in Indian society. Any citizen may now activate the Court by means of a letter which is treated as a writ petition: the traditional law relating to *locus standi* has thus undergone cataclysmic innovation. What is more, the Court has devised an unusual procedure for investigating facts relating to torture, terror, extra-judicial executions, deprivations and denials of rights, and gross abuses of power. It now appoints citizens' commissions of enquiry whose reports are held to establish facts sufficient for the purposes of judicial action (see Baxi, 1983 for a detailed account and analysis). In this process of developing social action litigation, the Court has fundamentally transformed, among other provisions, Article 21 guaranteeing life and personal liberty into a source of inexhaustible new rights and procedures for the victims of governmental lawlessness.

The responsibility for effective execution of legislative mandates expressed through statutes rests clearly upon the executive. If the executive defaults on its legal and constitutional obligations however, courts and judges cannot for too long take a view that violations of rights involved in such defaults are no concern of theirs. If the duly authorised constitutional officers do not appoint judges in time, creating a situation of massive arrears, whatever be the inherited law and wisdom about mandamus, an activist justice may feel justified in issuing directions to them to do their jobs expeditiously. If there are large numbers of undertrial prisoners, not brought to trial for a long time, such a judge might feel more than justified in ordering expeditious trials or their release. If conditions in jails are inhuman and debasing, such a judge may order creation of minimum facilities. If officers under the Contract Labour Act are not doing their duties, or if the relevant Committees under the Bonded Labour or Equal Remuneration Acts are not established, such a judge might order compliance with the statute. India has many laws, including constitutional amendments, which the executive has been authorised to bring into force but which it simply refuses to do. Even the activist justices refused to direct the executive to bring these into force; but their hesitation is a matter of surprise, looking at their otherwise unblemished activist record.

When an activist judge finds that directions given to the executive are not fulfilled, she has three choices:

(i)   to struggle ahead with the effective exercise of contempt powers;
(ii)   to stage a mini-takeover of the concerned department or the institution or
(iii) to accept defeat with grace.

In the Indian experience, alternatives (i) and (iii) have not been as yet resorted to, although governmental intransigence is now manifest over certain matters. Instead, the Supreme Court has been able to stage mini-takeovers, especially of custodial institutions such as jails or remand homes. In the Agra Women's Protective Home case, for example, the Supreme Court has ordered compliance with creation of additional sanitary facilities, supervised medical treatment of inmates, and regularly (over the past two years) supervised discharges from the Home.[4] In the Bihar undertrial cases (see Baxi, 1980), the Supreme Court has monitored thousands of entries in jail records to ensure that no undertrial languishes in courts and, as a result of its labours, arrived at such an understanding of the problem as to direct an annual census of all prisoners to be submitted to the Court. In the Bihar blindings case the Court has supervised medical treatment and rehabilitation programmes, even as the principal hearings on merits are under way. All these furnish outstanding examples of uses of interlocutory jurisdiction; the Court thereby acquires 'creeping jurisdiction' over State institutions hostile to the citizen's basic rights.

Obviously, an activist judge or an activist court soon confronts problems of 'coping'. Daily administrative vigilance or overall policy oversight is simply not possible for any Apex Court in the world. Some activist justices have had, therefore, to fashion substitutes to do these jobs for the Court on a delegation basis. In addition to co-opting the High Courts and District Courts for these functions, the Court through its activist justices has also begun making use of state legal aid boards and other social action groups. The issues of institutional competence are imposing in the extreme when stated at a scholarly level (Horowitz, 1979).

The Indian experience so far shows that the question is not so much one of lack of competence in the Supreme Court but rather of its wider and sustained diffusion throughout the entire judicial system. Indeed, the Indian experience shows that judicial activism can be contagious. The initial reservations, conflicts and tensions, inevitable when some activist justices designed a continental shift in the Court's concerns and profile, have now given place to understanding and even enthusiasm for social action litigation. What was formerly insurrectionary jurisprudence has now become a part of the institutional culture of the Court. Of course, not all justices like the characteristic features marking the birth and growth of judicial activism, especially through social action litigation. Many continue to worry about the future roles of the Court were unrestrained activism to guide most of its actions. For the moment however, the Court has developed far-reaching communication consti-tuencies and has innovated in both juristic and judicial activism.[5] Through all this, it has acquired enormous political legitimation.

An activist judge will also be inclined to use *suo moto* powers when she deems it necessary. The use of *suo moto* powers is not widely prevalent even in India, the home of epistolary jurisdiction, but Justice M.P. Thakkar, now Supreme Court Justice, resorted to this power frequently to achieve justice. He has on one occasion acted on newspaper reports of injustice or atrocities, by taking jurisdiction, with telling effects. Usually, *suo moto* interventions are directed to check a continuing abuse of power by the executive. The most justified case for the exercise of *suo moto* powers exists whenever there is an allegation of atrocity or torture in police custody or jail, because both these institutional processes fall within the direct oversight of the judiciary. Such allegations are prima facie allegations concerning violation of basic human rights; and people are committed to jails only through Court directions. Even when they are not in prison through Court directions, the Court's jurisdiction should extend to them. For example, an activist judge, were she located in Sri Lanka during the recent prison massacres, would not have to summon up too much courage to start *suo moto* enquiries. Such a judge would find jurisdiction over the prison staff and prisoners incarcerated on convic-tion who were allegedly responsible for this brutal violence.

III

An activist judge will thus legislate when she must and will use her executive powers also when she must. An activist judge will do all this in the title of constitutional values, as these grow in interpretative content. Judges who are inclined towards restraint and moderation will not use their powers and continue to maintain that their job is to adjudicate disputes according to something that they call 'the Law'. Such judges must know, or must be told, that their *not* using their powers is indeed a way of actually *using* them. Between judicial restraint and the support of the status quo, there is a very thin line of difference, particularly in third world societies, whose governing elites are still apt to see the state as their private property.

Notes

1. *Standard Vacuum Refining Co. of India Ltd.* v. *Their Workmen* (1960) II *Labour Law J.* 233, S.C.
2. *National Textile Workers Union* v. *Ramkrishnan* (1983) 2 S.C.C. (Supreme Court Cases) 248.
3. See *Bangalore Water Supply Sewerage Board* v. *Rajappa* (1978) 1 *Lab. L. J.* 349.
4. See *Dr. Upendra Baxi* v. *State of U.P.* (1983) 2 S.C.C. 308.
5. For the distinction between *juristic* and *judicial* activism see U. Baxi (ed.), Introduction to *K.K. Mathew on Democracy, Equality and Freedom*, Lucknow, Eastern Book Co., 1978.

References

Baxi, U., *The Crisis of the Indian Legal System*, 1982.
———— 'Developments in Indian Administrative Law' in *Public Law in India*, A.G. Noorani (ed.), p. 132, 1982.
———— 'Taking Suffering Seriously: Social Action Litigation Before the Supreme Court of India', *The Review: International Commission of Jurists*, 1982.
———— *The Indian Supreme Court and Politics*, 1980.
———— 'Some Reflections on the Nature of Constituent Power' in *Indian Constitution: Trends and Issues*, R. Dhavan and A. Jacob (eds.), 1978.
———— 'Undertrials and the Supreme Court: The Supreme Court Under Trial', *Supreme Court Cases* (Journal), p. 35, 1980.
———— 'On How Not to Judge the Judges: Some Reflections on the Judicial Role', mimeo, 1980.

Baxi, U., V. Dhagamwar, R. Kelkar and L. Sarkar, 'An Open Letter to the Chief Justice of India', *Supreme Court Cases* 17 (Journal), 1970.

Bickel, A.M., *The Least Dangerous Branch: The Supreme Court at the Bar of Politics*, 1962.

Dhavan, R., *The Supreme Court Under Strain: The Challenge of Arrears*, 1978.

Dworkin, R., *Taking Rights Seriously*, 1977.

Ely, R., *Democracy and Distrust*, 1982.

Horowitz, D., *Courts and Social Policy*, 1979.

Miller, A.S. and R.F. Howell, 'The Myth of Neutrality in Constitutional Adjudication', 27 *Univ. of Chicago L. Rev.* 661, 1960.

Rushdie, Salman, *Shame*, London, Picador, 1983.

Stone, J., *Social Dimensions of Law and Justice*, 1966.

Weschler, H., 'Towards Neutral Principles of Constitutional Law', 73 *Harv. L. Rev.* 1, 1959.

11 THE JUDICIARY IN PLURAL SOCIETIES
Some Conclusions*

The Suraj Kund Report

The following report was adopted at the Workshop on 'The Role of the Judiciary in Plural Societies' held in Suraj Kund (Haryana), August 13–15, 1983. Judges, lawyers and legal academics from India, Sri Lanka, Malaysia and the Philippines attended the Workshop, which was jointly sponsored by the Committee for Implementing Legal Aid Schemes and the International Centre for Ethnic Studies.

1. In a number of countries in Asia, ethnic* groups are being subjected to exploitation, violence and even annihilation. The State has the responsibility to prevent the occurrence of these incidents and in no case, by action or inaction, to aggravate them.

2. In this climate of exploitation, conflict and violence, judges are not justified in invoking the doctrines of 'self-restraint' and 'passive' interpretation. There are increasing demands on the judiciary for activism and independence as a growing number of citizen groups bring their grievances directly to the Apex Court.

3. The role of the appellate judiciary, especially the Apex Court, is of profound importance in the area of human rights, of which the protection of ethnic minorities is one important aspect. The highest courts, which are the final interpreters and makers of legal doctrine, exercise a unique type of power within the framework of the diverse constitutional systems present in Asia. The judicious and sustained use of this power to further social justice and social transformation is imperative. Judicial abnegation and even judicial self-restraint must give way to a realistic appreciation of the judiciary's important role in preventing and remedying abuse and misuse of power and eliminating injustice and exploitation. In addition, the Apex Courts in Asia

---

* Reports on two International Workshops held in Suraj Kund, India on August 13–15, 1983 and Eldoret, Kenya on February 1 4, 1985. The term 'ethnic' is defined broadly here to mean any group which has a group identity based on linguistic, cultural, religious or other social criteria.

must enforce and implement human rights provisions entrenched in their Constitutions and legal systems.

4. Procedural innovations should also be introduced to assist the judiciary in meeting the challenges of modern times. Experimentation in developing countries and efforts by Apex Courts in Asian societies to liberate themselves from the western system of appellate procedure should be commended, and, where possible, emulated.

5. For example, recent experiments in India may be of interest to other Apex Courts in Asia. Today in India any individual or social action group acting bona fide can invoke the jurisdiction of the Courts by addressing a letter and ensure protection of the constitutional and legal rights of the disadvantaged. Judges are also increasingly acting on their own initiative, especially in cases where blatant violations of human rights are recorded in the media but remain unchallenged due to lack of awareness and organisation. As the judicial role continues to expand, judges in India are also devising unique mechanisms for fact-finding, such as the appointment of independent commissions to research socio-economic data which have bearing on the issues of fundamental rights coming before the Courts. In other countries of Asia, there are also suggestions for the development of independent special funds which could be released by the judiciary for further research in certain areas. Policies and programmes for quasijudicial bodies not confined to the framework of an adversarial system have also been encouraged, especially in fundamental rights cases, where all the parties recognise the need to remedy an injustice, but need informal proceedings for formulating proper and adequate alternatives.

6. The growing importance of the judiciary in cases of fundamental rights must be supplemented by what may be termed a new 'communications style'. The opinions of the Court in this regard should be clear to the layman and should promote an understanding of the issues in all sectors of society. Through clear judicial decision-making and effective dissemination of opinions, people in the more remote areas of the country will not only be made more conscious of their rights but also aware of the forum and the procedure through which they could bring their grievances before the judiciary.

7. No court can long remain ahead of the Bar which serves it. Redress of violations of fundamental rights, especially in areas where structural changes are needed, require members of the Bar to master a large array of facts to support their arguments and to help formulate effective remedies. The Bar should therefore draw on the

resources and talents of the members belonging to other disciplines so as to effectively further the course of social justice. The traditional approach of legal aid to individual litigants is no longer sufficient. Public interest bodies and social action groups should be encouraged by members of the legal profession to promote and encourage social action litigation. Effective redress for the violations of fundamental rights can only take place if there are members of the Bar who are not only ready to organise themselves as guardians of the independence of the judiciary but also prepared to transcend the narrow confines of their legal training with experiments in procedures and doctrines which will further the goal of social justice.

8. In most countries of Asia collective rights are as important as individual rights. The complex problems of the role of the judiciary in plural societies are aggravated by the fact that in many countries of Asia ethnic groups do not have a juridical personality which could challenge court action in the name of the collective. This is particularly important in cases of tribal groupings where land rights are vested in the name of the tribe. In addition, the diversity of strategies being followed by ethnic groups for their political self-assertion prevents a uniform approach to ethnic-related legal issues. The need for an active judiciary which will sensitively and creatively engage in the task of balancing interests of ethnic groups is paramount, as both the executive and the legislature would inevitably reflect the aspirations of the majority community. A policy of judicial self-restraint in regard to ethnic-related issues will result in the minority interests remaining unprotected. Such inaction will only aggravate perceptions of injustice which may eventually lead to violence and wanton destruction of life and property.

9. Judicial approaches to the protection of minorities is integrally connected with the judicial doctrine of equality and equal protection. The elusiveness and the contradictory elements contained within the doctrine of equality have led many to abandon the concept altogether in search of more dynamic notions of participation, self-reliance and redistributive justice. The need to include these factors within the static and misleading concept of equal protection as outlined in many constitutions may be seen as the first step in the reassessment of the Anglo–American doctrine of equal protection in light of Asian realities and Asian expectations.

10. The special problem of women is seen as an important aspect of the responsibility of the judiciary in plural societies. Women often are

the most victimised group in any given country. The sexist bias of the bench and the Bar has historically prevented women from receiving equal justice. Increasing numbers of women's groups have, however, forced some courts in Asia to rethink important issues. Though it was recognised that the Courts have a long way to go in redressing the grievances of women in the economic, social and cultural spheres, new changes of attitude are welcome as an important beginning for judicial activism *vis-à-vis* women's rights. The position of women under systems of customary law, which is often an integral part of ethnic identity, is particularly delicate as Courts have allowed ethnic groups to maintain their traditional system of family relations, which in a large number of cases discriminate against women in the home and in society.

11. There is no doubt that public appreciation of the role of the judiciary in society is no longer conditioned by cosmetic declarations and technical doctrines. Though the judiciary can never prevent a violent revolution, it does have an important role to play in non-violent social transformation. The refusal to accept the task will only serve to delegitimise the judiciary in the eye of the public.

12. Participants in the Workshop agreed to help disseminate the views contained in this report and also to work towards the realisation of the principles and policies outlined in this report in their respective States.

The Eldoret Report

Preamble

The Public Law Institute, Kenya, and the International Centre For Ethnic Studies, being aware of the contradictions and problems posed to the procedures and institutions of the governments of developing countries generally, and those in Africa and Asia in particular, as encompassed by the concept 'pluralism', and realising that the judicial process is an important arena for the resolution of these contradictions and problems, convened a workshop on the theme 'The Role of the Judiciary in Plural Societies'.

The Workshop was held at Eldoret, Kenya, from February 1 to February 4, 1985, and addressed the pertinent issues under three main sub-themes, namely:

(a) The socio-economic and political context of the judiciary.

(b) Contradictions of pluralism.

(c) The legal profession, pluralism and public interest litigation.

Opened by the Honourable Mr. Justice V.V. Patel of the High Court of Kenya, representing the Honourable Mr. Justice A.H. Simpson, Chief Justice of the Republic of Kenya, the Workshop included among its participants eminent judges, among them the Honourable Justice E. Fernando, Chief Justice of the Philippines, the Honourable Justice P. Bhagwati, a judge of the Supreme Court of India, the Honourable Justice R.H. Kisanga, Justice of Appeal, Court of Appeal of Tanzania, the Honourable Justice Mrs. G.H. Welch, Director of the Department of Investigation and Legislation, Ministry of Justice, Mozambique, the Honourable Justice J.R.O. Masime and the Honourable Justice D. Schofield, Judges of the High Court of Kenya, lawyers, legal scholars and social scientists from African and Asian countries. The Workshop assessed the avenues open to the judiciary to provide access to justice to the deprived and vulnerable sections of society and how it can influence social cohesion in plural societies.

Pluralism

1. Plural societies have been defined as those in which diverse groups live side by side, 'combine but do not mix'. In this regard, it was agreed that almost all African and Asian societies are in fact plural societies.

2. Pluralism as a theoretical concept has two aspects. The first involves respect for diverse cultural and ethnic communties which exist in any given society. The second sees pluralism as an aspect of political democracy, in which diverse points of view — political, social and ethnic — are reflected in political decision-making and political action.

3. Pluralism as a form of political ideology and action contains two contradictory aspects. Pluralism may be used to justify dominance and legitimate repression. Linguistic minorities, women and other vulnerable groups may find domination legitimated by the ideology of pluralism. On the other hand, pluralism can assume a liberation dynamic. In this context, it may be important to consider that pluralism in its positive form is an aspect of human rights — an attempt to democratise society and provide a framework for political participation and increasing social justice. In this way, the negative features of pluralism may be contained, especially if they run counter to universal values concerning human rights and human dignity.

4. Pluralism is a concept which aims at social justice at both the national and the sub-national level. This factor becomes important in the post-nationalist period, especially in countries where the nationalist enterprise has failed to live up to expectations and has in fact created new structures of power and ideology which work against social justice. In this context, pluralism provides a framework for the formulation of legal-political instruments which will help democratise post-colonial societies in Asia and Africa. Some of the devices which have been used are: the devolution of power, elimination of sex-based discrimination, litigation under the equal protection clause, defence of cultural, linguistic and religious rights of minorities and other disadvantaged groups, affirmative action, and preferences policies.

Pluralism and the judiciary

5. Of the many institutions of government, it is the judiciary which is centrally placed to protect the democratic rights of citizens and disadvantaged groups. The executive and the legislature are primarily concerned with national development on a macro-scale. They are more prone to constructing majoritarian broad-based policies. It is in fact the judiciary which must ascertain the actual impact of these policies on the lives of individual citizens and social groups in particular situations.

6. There are many devices which the judiciary can use to exploit the contradictions within the state without outright confrontation and to formulate doctrines which effectively protect the rights of citizens and disadvantaged groups. Failure to recognise this duty is therefore to deny citizens the fundamental right to voice their grievances and receive the appropriate remedy.

7. An innovative approach to legal training is required to effectively evolve devices of judicial activism which are relevant in African and Asian societies. Legal training in most of our societies is generally based on the study of the statutes, precedents and legal concepts which are often not relevant to our social context. Traditional legal training makes lawyers and judges extremely uncomfortable with doctrines and concepts which are 'non-legal' in origin. However, other disciplines, especially the social sciences, may provide the judiciary with data and concepts which are relevant to the actual social reality. Concepts such as 'pluralism' attempt to provide the judiciary with legal-political tools for the sensitive implementation

of existing law and for the creative development of new and more relevant doctrine.

Social action litigation and the legal profession

8. Since independence, most African and Asian states have unequivocally articulated, in their legal and constitutional orders, the concepts of freedom, equality and justice for all.

9. The realisation of these judicial constructs, however, has been largely impeded by the pervasive caution displayed by the legal profession and the judiciary. Part of this caution stems from perceptions of the judicial role. The executive and legislature (comprising the political elites) have arrogated to themselves the role of exercising society-wide powers to pursue policies of national development. The role of the judiciary has been perceived as being limited only to adjudication usually involving individual claims, concrete in time and space. In this context, any creative initiative on the part of judges to address society-wide issues is perceived to be an encroachment or usurpation of the functions of the executive and the legislature. Hence the trend towards judicial caution and restraint.

10. The prevailing perception of the judicial role amongst the executive and the legislative and community alike is one of providing justice according to law by interpreting and applying rather than making law. This perception is often shared by the Bar and by judges, leading to the view that mechanical interpretation of the law is both possible and desirable. But, in reality, it is neither, because judging is always an act of will, power and discretion.

11. Judicial activism, far from being a threat to national security or the development of the nation-state, is imperative for the attainment of such objectives. A principal constraint to the principle of judicial activism is the lack of coordination in the responsibilities of the judiciary in aiding the attainment of the goals of national security and societal development.

12. Another major constraint, identified in several African and Asian countries, is the direct and indirect forms of pressures and interference exerted by the executive on the normal performance of the judicial function.

13. Participants in the Workshop reaffirmed the need to safeguard the independence of judges from all forms of interference and to accord full respect for their decisions. Independence of the judiciary is

especially crucial in one-party states for effective articulation and protection of plural interests.

14. Judicial activism can be an important strategy to overcome all forms of oppression, exploitation, impoverishment, unjustifiable on any model of societal development in Africa and Asia. Since the majority of human beings in most African societies are among the impoverished and exploited, there is an urgent need for judicial activism in providing amelioration of such impoverishment and exploitation.

15. There is need to enhance the competence of the judiciary and the Bar in adjudicating matters involving key issues of social justice. Legal education needs to be reformed so as to create competent professionals who are not only legal technocrats but who actively intervene in the problems of the oppressed, impoverished and exploited. In this context, clinical legal aid programmes attached to law schools, active encouragement of students' participation in social action litigation etc., may be some of the innovations in legal education which should be encouraged.

16. For the law and the judiciary to become relevant to the people in their daily lives, the communication of law to the people requires restructuring — especially the restructuring of legal discourse both at the judicial and legislative levels. In addition, social action groups and public interest movements should also evolve programmes for legal literacy so as to enable the poor and the deprived to become conscious of their rights.

17. In some countries popular participation in making laws and in administering justice is the surest means of fostering values of justice and pluralism. In others, social action litigation may become a principal instrumentality, not only for enhanced access to justice for marginal groups but also for long-term renovation of institutional arrangements for social transformation. It is, therefore, imperative that public spirited members of the Bar unite to create movements for such litigation so as to ensure access and justice to the most discriminated groups in society.

18. Judicial activism, encouraged by social action litigation, inspired by constitutional values, may be regarded as a vital human technology for social change in impoverished societies.

INDEX